ENDORSEMENTS

In his book, *The CHOiCE of Leadership*, James Morrison demonstrates his ability to showcase common sense leadership principles that are so uncommon in today's workplace (but are so desperately needed). James' insights coupled with the many examples from leaders from yesterday and today has motivated me to 'choose' to apply these principles.
- Daniel A. Nelson
Regional Trainer, KROGER

Through the centuries before, in like manner, with world conflict of today, the conflicts of war have been about the choice of leadership. After serving in Iraq and now in Afghanistan, as a Senior Advisor for the United States government, the notable cause of conflict is bad leadership. There seems to be a continued and developing chronic ill of leadership. As a consequence of this, the deepest destruction of the world lay in the very essence of our leadership approach.

I have chosen to emphasize this subject because much of my career has been dedicated to the rebuild and stabilization of war torn countries and undeveloped nations. Everyone will hear and be reminded of what can be by reading *The CHOiCE of Leadership*. A few years ago, James was asked to serve his country addressing a critical need in one of the major conflict zones in the world and rose to the responsibility to serve in a moments notice. James lives what he teaches.

This book reflects what is needed in the world. *The CHOiCE of Leadership* is a must read for those seeking to reclaim the one basic element that truly makes a difference - leadership.
- Don Welty
Sr. Deputy Agriculture Advisor, UNITED STATES DEPARTMENT OF AGRICULTURE Former Senior Business Advisor, U.S. STATE DEPARTMENT EMBASSY OF IRAQ

Leadership in today's world of global enterprise, competition, and technology, is the single most important determinate of success or failure of an organization. James Morrison's experience and skills in teaching the principles of leadership, makes this book a must read for leaders and managers at all levels in any organization. *The CHOiCE of Leadership* should not only be read, but studied and applied for success. The principles discussed are unique and offer an "advanced degree" in leadership technology.

- Ronald C. Jones, Ret. Col, United States Army
BS, MHCA, LFACHE (Life Fellow, American College of Healthcare Executives)

Throughout my life, inspiration in business and living has come from great people that I know or that have gone before. My reading has been largely focused on biographies and autobiographies. I have treasured their perspectives and honored their accomplishments. I have tried to incorporate their successes by emulating their behaviors and ideas. In the past, I have been resistent to objective critique or theoretical and conceptual texts. Consistent with my own appetite for real time information, I have found your book enlivened with biographical insights to time tested and principled practices of some of the world's greatest leaders. I really enjoyed your writing style. I felt constantly engaged with simple insights into complex practices. It left me feeling that I could actually use the information towards becoming a more successful business manager and a better person.

- Marcus Southworth
President & CEO, SOUTHWORTH INTERNATIONAL

James Morrison has been a role model for me of a leader who makes a significant contribution not only in his work, but in the community and the world at large. His *Influence Cycle* builds the skills AND character needed for every leader who desires to make a difference.

- Jon Hester
Sr. Consulting Partner, KEN BLANCHARD COMPANIES
Former Director of Learning and Development, NIKE

As the title suggests, James M. Morrison has provided a bridge for understanding and connecting the simple and complex human observations of leadership with the academic knowledge associated with its societal function. By combining historical reference points with current theories and knowledge, Morrison reassures the reader that they have access to proven frameworks and sufficient evidence to execute successful business plans with purposeful leadership effort. As the aspiring leader becomes clear about the metrics necessary to measure their effort and influence within their organization, they can turn to Morrison for clear illustrations and narrative to support their vision.

I highly recommend this book for anyone seeking to better understand the qualities and complexities of effective leadership within the reality of their working environment. The plea for leadership efforts to be honest, self-aware, purposeful, and balanced is refreshing in the current climate of having far too many self-appointed leaders found to be lacking in these critical arenas.

- Dr. McKell S. Withers
Superintendent of a large urban public school district

The CHOiCE of Leadership is a masterful blending of the philosophies of some of the greatest minds, filtered through the core beliefs of Morrison, accented by an optimistic call to action. In a world that becomes more complicated by the instant, Morrison simplifies the why and how of true leadership. This is a must read book for anyone trying to differentiate themselves.

- H Richard Moss
Director of Information Technologies,
NATIONAL BENEFITS SERVICES

The *CHOiCE* of *Leadership*

BRIDGING the Gap Between
Simplicity *and* Complexity

James M. Morrison

Printed in the United States of America

Design by Andrew J. Siddoway
Chief Editor: Andrew J. Siddoway

The Choice of Leadership: Bridging the Gap Between Simplicity and Complexity / James M. Morrison - 1st ed.

ISBN: 978-0-9839434-0-2

10 9 8 7 6 5 4 3 2 1
First Edition

For Trish, Ashlee, Chase, and Lohren. Your commitment and dedication made this project a possibility and made it worth writing.

CONTENTS

Acknowledgements   *xi*
Preface   *xiii*

Leadership   1
Vision   35
Formal and Informal Authority   59
Emotional Intelligence   83
Leadership Moral Decay   103
Self-Awareness   119
Role Modeling   147
Visibility   157
Telling It Like It Is   163
Work Life Balance   173
Decision-Making   181
Organizational Design   189
Execution   215
Removing Barriers   235
Metrics and Numeric   245

Resources   253
Index   273

ACKNOWLEDGEMENTS

Bruce Morrison, my identical twin brother who not only serves as my personal role model, but is an example of all the principles written in this book. His influences allows me to live and learn the concepts.

Brian Wierman for his wisdom and fundamental foundation of leadership. He graciously provided a perspective and valuable insight.

Randy Allen who was patient and persistent and gave tireless efforts, and sustained friendship.

PREFACE

When Roger Maris collected 61 homeruns in 1961, breaking Babe Ruth's single-season record of 60 homeruns set in 1927, his talent projected in a balanced yet heightened way. Despite breaking the 37-year-old record held by Babe Ruth, he is not on the Top 20 All-Time Homerun list. In fact, Maris hit just 275 homeruns in a 12-year career…well behind Eddie Murray, the 20th ranked homerun hitter with 504. What makes Roger Maris' such a great story? In just one year, 1961, he hit 22 percent of his home runs. How was he so successful in 1961? Was it his size and strength? Maybe it was his sure power of driving the ball long distances?

Maris was functioning in a "sweet spot." As the ball connected his bat so many times, the ball itself was instructed and controlled by this great hitter to be moved off the perfect part of the wooden baseball bat 6 1/2 inches from the end of the barrel—the part where the greatest results would come with the perfect amount of effort. There was balance, simplicity, knowledge, skill, elegance, power, and an amazing result. This is a book about these things.

The far side of simplicity is complexity. The biggest opponent of thinking is complexity, for that leads to mystification. It is work done with mechanical advantages, much like a system of pulleys moving a heavy weight. The heavy weight one faces in organizational life is the amazingly difficult nature of leadership. One is burdened to determine how to make sense of leadership, and most important, how to actually use the strong concepts that great writers, leaders, thinkers, and practitioners have built and used over the course of human history.

The answers to most of one's questions about leadership have been addressed. Despite the continued value of breaking new ground with new thought leaders, the problem of great leadership still exists. What one wants is to be working along the bat where the understanding and actions are balanced in a way that acknowledges something one might suspect: the core of what one needs to know as a human has already been exposed. New management theory exists in the margins, not at all a bad thing necessarily, but the core is already built and largely exposed. Despite this, practicing and executing great leadership continues to be elusive. If this was not the case, great thinkers and practitioners the world over, would be agreeing the secret has been identified. Additionally, the countless ethical and financial blunders that plague the economy would only be found in history; instead, they are indeed found everyday and they even create fear of the future.

The key to the problem of understanding and executing leadership fundamentals is approaching leadership in ways that creatively use the wisdom, experience, and learning of others to help one make sense of their own development and challenges. This book should help answer the great questions:

How does a leader go about using the vast bevy of leadership material and knowledge now available?

Where and how does a leader start to implement the principles?

If one knows all of these things about leadership, organization growth, and ethical business decisions, why are there so many organizations that repeatedly fail to deliver successful results beyond shareholder or owner financial return?

One would like to be Google, Gore, Apple, or Hoshi Ryokan (the world's oldest company, a hotel in Japan). One attempts to mimic their operations, thinking, and styles. Individuals are somewhat mystified by their success. Their return on assets is exemplary and their thought leadership is worthy of great praise. The core of what they do are things that have existed for a long time. A comprehensive study of what great companies do seems to appear every five to ten years and is often marketed as a new breakthrough. These discussions are often about 99 percent outstanding reiterations of the core of what makes people and organizations successful with 1 percent new perspective and insight. This is not to be overly critical, this is after all, another business book, with perhaps a similar offering; however, I argue that by framing these leadership lessons with stories and examples from history, one will come to understand and know how the great fundamentals of leadership have been executed successfully.

Individuals will see that one would observe enough core repetition and consistency to suggest that the things that Hoshi Ryokan does are similar to what Apple does. They understand the sweet spot of basic fundamentals such as vision, strategy, leadership, formal and informal authority, self-awareness, and results. Great leaders understood themselves and how to use the tools available throughout history in order to improve.

For one to learn, the key appears to be twofold: understanding the theory (really internalizing it) and making sense of and following through on its implementation. The implementation of great leadership theory and practice is probably the edge for effectiveness and success. Most leadership thought is common knowledge but not common practice. How many of us know well-educated people who cannot seem to get over the hump of realizing their knowledge in practical ways? This is likely an accurate statement: The success of great organizations and leaders is a combination and balance of theoretical understanding and practical implementation. One balances the other and a sweet spot of leadership development, and by extension, organizational function is found.

I recognize that organizations and people are however, not quite this simple. Strategy, for example, is probably best viewed as an iterative cycle that repeats. It merges arguably the mechanistic or design approach, a Kaplan and Norton of Balanced Scorecard frame, with the crafting and emergence of a Mintzberg. I see however, that strategy is constantly worked on by various forces, both internal and external. Making sense of such nebulous topics in business, as "strategy" is often so heavy that it becomes a highly political event and real progress is often not made. Many people and organizations appear to simply shrug their shoulders. The pattern of doing what is necessary to put out fire after fire ensues and the organization suffers alongside its employees. Clearly, it is not acceptable to do this. Too many stakeholders' needs are not addressed if leaders and organizations are not willing to do the work and the heavy lifting despite its relentless challenge.

The "sweet spot" of understanding execution is the key to organizational greatness. I recognize this is not new ground. I wish to pay appropriate homage to the great thought leaders that have shaped personal and organizational development and capture the very best thinking and "bring it home" to the sweet spot of understanding effective leadership.

How will I do this? The general approach is to synthesize the best thinking from history on various topics in personal and organizational development, and ensure that I balance science/rigor with practical and historical application. For example, what is the best thinking on strategy? I discuss Porter, Burns, Kotter, Drucker, and others. I will then illustrate influential leaders from history who exemplify application of this thought. Additionally, I will demonstrate that a reality exists for one to discover and make sense of theory and implementation; there is no new reality that is deeply changing or evolving rather that these times are truly desperate for great leaders.

My goal is to take great thinking, organize it into understandable discussion, and show how it has been used or seen in history or in the current marketplace. By merging the thought leadership with storytelling, historical events, addressing the complexities of business case analysis and case studies, and translating it into an understandable comprehensible process, I propose one will identify and utilize the sweet spot of making the choice to be a great leader.

Chapter 1

Leadership

Who is a leader? What does a leader do? What does a leader look like? How does a leader communicate? In the beginning of history, there were such practitioners as, Lao Tsu, Confucius, Socrates, Plato, Aristotle, and Machiavelli. One is encumbered to learn how the basic fundamentals of leadership have been applied successfully. There are many courses, workshops, books, lectures, and institutions to which leaders can find answers. It is presumed that many can learn the strong concepts and character traits. But what is a leader to learn? Through the point of origin in history to the twenty-first century the range of theory and philosophy has been vast from the soft philosophy of Lao Tsu to the hard attitude of Machiavelli or the middle of simplicity and complexity of Abraham Lincoln. The answers to most of the questions about the nature of leadership have been answered. Leaders are burdened to determine how to make sense of, and most important, how to actually use the strong concepts that great writers, thinkers, and practitioners have built and used over the course of human history.

The great debate of defining leadership tends to be ambiguous along the lines of leadership and management. The context is important to learning and executing on their concepts. An article by Abraham Zaleznik, published in the *Harvard Business Review* in 1977, titled "Managers and Leaders: Are They Different?" Managers and leaders have been locked into the same symbiotic role with each other. But, in variously mobilizing and rewarding forms, managers and leaders are entering into different roles.

John P. Kotter, in the *Harvard Business Review on Leadership*, "What Leaders Really Do" writes, "One of the difficulties of management and leadership is the complexity brought on by the emergence of large business in the twentieth and twenty-first century. Without great management and leadership, organizations will spin out of control and create chaos that threatens existence. Great management and leadership practice and theory stabilizes the enterprise and creates conditions for success."

With the emergence of leadership and to exert practical theory, learners look to such individual's as Lou Gerstner of IBM, Sam Walton of Wal-Mart, Nelson Mandela of South Africa, Jack Welch of GE, or Jesus Christ of Christianity. Some of the oldest questions are: What makes them such profound life changing leaders? Was it their influence and power or their pedigree? Maybe it was the branding of their names? How does one rise from obscurity to leadership influence? The bundles of questions in all their multi-variety must have answers.

In November 1987, *Time* asked in an article, "Who's in Charge?" and they answered their own question, "The nation calls for leadership, and there is no one home."

It beckons the question of the tipping point: How does one rise to such levels of leadership prominence even in the midst of hardship and in many cases poverty? There is no single answer to appeal to those who are asking. To begin to sort out all of the questions and the nature of the responses, the initial effort is in the vast range of history.

Abraham Lincoln was born in a cabin along Nolin Creek, south of Louisville, Kentucky and in a general pattern was no stranger to hardships and disadvantages. He was familiar with death at an early age. He lost his mother at age nine to "milk sickness" and his sister Sarah, who he was very attached, passed away, when he was nineteen. Perhaps in an effort to provide stability his father remarried and yet young Abe was given to long periods of despondency.

Winston Churchill was born a stocky lad with a bursting head of red hair. The young unhappy Winston stuttered with a lisp and did poorly in school. One of his dominant characteristics was an unremitting stubbornness and high-spirited demeanor, which annoyed everyone including his parents. Winston had been slow to develop and was simply another student who entered Harrow Secondary School at age twelve as the lowest student in the lowest academic class.

The receptivity of facts in such historical figures suggests the acquisition of leadership flows out of learned elemental influences with relatively strong achievement and motivation of Knowledge, Skill-Sets, and Attributes to unleash the power of leadership. Yet, leadership is no particular unitary element among the represented theories throughout history.

Nowhere was the rise of leadership more profound and yet more straightforward than one's cause or belief that rises above all other considerations. Jesus Christ was born in a manger in the city of Bethlehem. It was noted that, "Not even a bed to lay his head."

Such leaders rose to the heights of influence to resolve the horrible conflict of civil war and lead in the darkest days of World War II. At junctures of history, it is evident such figures have made leadership a great phenomenon and a discussion among thousands. One of the most important questions in the field of leadership: How can leaders get their followers to do what they want them to do?

The topic of leadership continues to be elusive even to those who are the thought leaders and practitioners on the subject. Many of the concepts can be vague and ambiguous, which further makes it even more problematic. There are no set guidelines and set standards for leaders to follow or mimic.

James MacGregor Burns, in his book titled, *Leadership,* provides his definition of leadership. "Leadership is leaders inducing followers to act for certain goals that represent the values and the motivations—the wants and needs, the aspirations and expectations—of both leaders and followers. And the genius of leadership lies in the manner in which leaders see and act on their own and their follower's values and motivations." Jan Carlzon, President of Scandinavia Airlines further describes the roles of leadership, "The new leaders' tools are a clear, concise vision and consummate communication skills—with soul. There is nothing soft and squishy about it." Carlzon calls the new executive an "enlightened dictator." Leadership by definition implies moral responsibility.

Throughout the history of the United States there are many political role models that possessed exceptional qualities through which they influenced their followers based on the caliber of their value system and leadership theory. Such individuals were George Washington, John Adams, Thomas Jefferson, and Abraham Lincoln. Leaders within any layer of an institution require attention to the natural fundamentals of leadership rather than technique and personality. Influence and development are found with different forms of representation from those of the past, present, and future. Practitioners study the examples of generals, kings, presidents, and events that demonstrate pronounced leadership qualities.

Rudolph Giuliani in his book, *Leadership,* suggests that leadership traits are thing that can be learned. "Leadership does not simply happen," he claims, "It can be taught, learned, developed." What is one to learn?

The manner, in which other theorists define leadership, is in the balance of Greek philosophies on an ideal of Eros and Logos, or feeling and thought, coupled together providing for learning the leadership environment on all levels.

Others argue that it stems solely from a position held within the organization and such a thought reflects the old mind-set that leadership is about position, title, and status. There are many who relied on the social systems of position, title, and status to provide formal authority to get things done and ultimately failing the test of leadership. Conversely, there are great leaders who posses the moral and informal authority who were able to move masses and change governments without the benefit of a position of formal authority.

John W. Gardner, who was Secretary of Health, Education and Welfare under President Lyndon B. Johnson said, "Leaders have a significant role in creating the state of mind that is society. They can serve as symbols of the moral unity of the society. They can express the values that hold the society together. Most important, they can conceive and articulate goals that lift people out of their petty preoccupations, carry them above the conflicts that tear a society apart, and unite them in pursuit of objectives worthy of their best efforts."

Despite the continued value of breaking new ground with new thought leaders, the problem of great leadership still exists. Certainly a full grasp of leadership is understanding the theory and making sense of and following through on its implementation. Leadership is the brand. The brand is a character and competence issue. Welch at GE, Page and Brin at Google, Gates at Microsoft, Jobs at Apple, or Branson at Virgin. Leadership is the foundation of success. Everything depends on it. It is the rock and cornerstone to any foundation of any organization.

Many thought leaders and practitioners the world over have written on leadership theories increasing the likelihood that one can become a leader. During the middle and late twentieth and twenty-first century, Chester Bernard, Peter Senge, Charles Deming, Peter Drucker, and Jim Collins paved the path for leadership. There are many books that address this topic, for example, Jim Collin's, *Good To Great*, James MacGregor Burns', *Leadership*, John P. Kotter's, *The Leadership Factor*, and Warren

Bennis', *On Becoming a Leader*.

The leadership landscape is changing. The first part of the twentieth century, the leadership and management style during the Industrial Age presumably required a greater and authoritative control over subordinates. While the twenty-first century gave rise to the emerging growth of corporate environment and the new age of the knowledge worker requiring a shift in the leadership and management style to be able to effectively lead by being concerned for the welfare of the labor force. Early leadership practitioners such as Follett and Bernard were concerned about general welfare as opposed to the welfare of only a few.

Underlining the conflict between both ends of simplicity and complexity between management and leadership, there are signs that there is a sharp shift from the hierarchical models that assume control and power over their followers to a model based on satisfying needs and wants of potential followers. The eventual test of leadership is the realization of meeting the needs of the followership. There is a global leadership awakening—it is so significant that those with any interest at all have no choice but to pay notice.

In the means of developing leadership capacity, business schools teach fundamental skills specializing in such subjects as the function and utility of business, but not in the areas of quality traits of management and leadership. The clash or incongruence is people tend to believe that business schools will produce managers and leaders out of students who have never served in the roles or the higher ranges of leadership theory supported by higher values and principles to lead.

Between the rival discussion points of the leadership environment, there persist to be various divergent thoughts surrounding the labels of leadership and management. Leadership and management are often used interchangeably in different situations. Largely, past philosophies have been built with strong similarities with a concrete reconciliation of the definition between leadership and management. In reality, leadership versus management has a very different meaning.

According to Henry Mintzberg, "I use the word *management* and *leadership* interchangeably. It has become fashionable after Zaleznik (1977) to distinguish them. Leadership is supposed to be something bigger, more important. I reject this distinction, simply because managers have to lead and leaders have to manage. Management without leadership is sterile; leadership without management is disconnected and encourages hubris."

Arguably, the roles have a unified structure but are vastly different in how they interact with people, motivate, think, and behave. Each has their marked distinctive contribution and function to support the success of the complex system in any organization. Whether the role is a manager or leader both serve critical functions.

In the expanse knowledge and theory throughout history, the usual quota of understanding management is about managing things, processes, budgets, and numeric. In the role of management, is a basic characteristic in the sense that they are someone who was given their authority by nature of their position. The foundation of this kind of control is institutional and formal authority, which makes them the boss, but not necessarily the leader. The manager's role takes many forms and can be dimensional in terms of various responsibilities or an organized set of behaviors identified within the position. Management is a particular control to ensure work gets done, focus on day-to-day tasks, and manage the activities of others. Formal authority gives rise to their ability to manage things and get things done. Being tactical is a positive approach as this is a skill that is needed in business, particularly, in the fast paced environment in which people work. Managers have subordinates and not necessarily followership. They manage and control people by pushing them down the path of production and contribution.

Management is a vital factor and the organization's most common job function. The expectations and requirements make it virtually impossible to satisfy because of the complexity. They are required to know and do a bevy of things—people skills, financial acumen, cost control, product development, customer satisfaction, technology, resource allocation, and division of labor. Is it any wonder that most are failing and organizations are spending time and financial resources to try and figure out management styles?

The pronounced leadership responsibility is leading people. A leader is visionary and strategically focused rather than directing people through tasks; they inspire and motivate people to help them to discover their own abilities to accomplish great things. They drive the workforce to achieve vision and purpose, strategic goals, commitment, and are perpetually alert to the best interests of the organization. Leadership has followership. They motivate employees by satisfying the basic human needs of the labor force. Daniel Goleman writes, "Great leaders move us. They ignite our passions and inspire the best in us."

The distinctions, between the leadership and management roles, need to be curbed to some degree—they are not mutually exclusive. To be a great leader one needs to have learned to be a great manager and follower.

When Jack Welch was preparing his retirement for General Electric, he prepared a succession plan for leadership transition to serve as a guide for the future leader of GE. Those he turned to first were those who were his direct reports the individuals who followed him. They are the one's that took direction and directives from him. Those who were on the short list were Jeff Immelt, James McNerney, and Robert Nardelli. Why were they selected to be the next successor of GE? By being superior at being followers. The skill of being subordinate or a chosen follower served all three leaders very well. Jeff Immelt became CEO of General Electric; James McNerney became CEO at Boeing, and Robert Nardelli CEO of Home Depot.

The transformation of influential leadership is not only found in those individuals who lead large Fortune 500 companies, but also small and mid size companies. They are the one's who are in the elementary schools, community programs, and religious organizations. They are the obscure leaders making a unique contribution igniting the passion and inspiring the best in other people. They are crafting a difference in the lives and organizations they serve.

Obscurity is not a function of weakness rather an aversion for the unnecessary attention and praises from others. The attention and praises are subordinate to the vision and purpose of the leader. Unfortunately, many live in a culture that suggests that, if a leader is not in the public's eye, than they are not qualified for effective leadership. The central role is the motivation to assist those they serve. It is the preferred end-state that serves the leader's personal purpose to pursue end values of peace, joy, and contribution, or they might be goals anchored in other meaningful categories.

Leaders are presented in a number of forms. One does not have to search too far to see the varying styles of leadership. Take, for example, Herb Kelleher who ran Southwest airlines for 39 years; the innovators of technology, Bill Gates of Microsoft, and Steve Jobs of Apple; legends on the football field, Vince Lombardi and Bill Walsh; or the political leadership landscape of Churchill and Reagan. As different as they all are, there is the boundary of doing some of the basics that leadership requires. Abraham Zaleznik, a respected management theorist, from Harvard Business School, suggests that there is a multifaceted layer to leadership.

The traits associated with leaders
The behaviors exhibited
The situation in which they find themselves
The attributions of others in close proximity to the leader

Leaders understand the "sweet spot" of basic indispensable fundamentals such as character traits, vision, strategy, behaviors, formal and informal authority, self-awareness, emotional intelligence, environment, and results. A dynamic quality is humility to give a free rein to learn, progress, and to pursue a course of action, by showing reverence and respect for those things taught in the past, self-assurance for the present, and optimism for the future.

The strategy is to approach leadership in ways that resourcefully use the wisdom, practice, education, and role models of others to help make sense of one's own development and growth. These stable elements in a leadership structure can activate the power to lead. The goal is to understand and practice the leadership core and executing consistently on principles that advocates those things that Bill Gates does is the same that Churchill did. It was said, "One person who really knows how to lead is worth more than a hundred who have merely studied leadership."

When Jan Carlzon was thirty-two, he was hired to run Vingresor, a vacation company for SAS airlines. He was hired straight out of college and became known as the "EGO Boy." In his limited understanding of what leadership was, he started acting and playing the part of superiority because he was now the president. He went about his duty having all the answers and trying to solve everyone's problems. An associate close to him commented that he was promoted not to have all the answers, but to be a supportive presence.

Jan Carlzon acknowledged, "The company was not asking me to make all the decisions on my own, only to create the right atmosphere, the right conditions for others to do their jobs better. I began to understand the difference between a traditional corporate executive, who issues instructions after instructions from the top, and the new corporate leader, who must set the tone and keep the big picture in mind." Setting the conditions for success is the leader's job; no one else can fulfill this need.

Ultimately, the leadership process starts by being in control and having a deep sense of self. The process finally approaches the most concrete choice that leaders stand independent of others and not solely dependent on other's perception to validate who they are. Plato, in the *Republic, book VI*, writes, "Imagine then a fleet or a ship in which there is a captain who is taller and stronger than any of the crew, but he is a little deaf and has a similar infirmity in sight, and his knowledge of navigation is not much better. The sailors are quarreling with one another about steering—everyone is of the opinion that he has a right to steer though he has never learned the art of navigation…" The sailors throng around the captain, begging him to commit the helm to them; when he refuses, they take over the ship and make free with the stores. "…but that the true pilot must pay attention to the year and seasons and sky and stars and winds, and whatever else belongs to his art…that he must and will be the steerer, whether other people like it or not—the possibility of this union of authority with the steerer's art has never seriously entered into their thoughts…"

Leaders are not reliant on others to validate their existence rather they get their sense of value by validating what lies inside and not from external forces. There is an internal strength for what and who they are. The power is within and not at the exploits of others weaknesses and at the necessity to undermine what others do not have.

In the book, *First Things First*, A. Roger and Rebecca Merrill write, "Security is not based on the illusion of comparative thinking—I'm better looking, I have more money, I have a better job, or I work harder than somebody else. Nor do we feel any less secure if we're not as good-looking or have less money or prestige than somebody else."

Leadership is Learned Behaviors

The authority of leadership is transformed in the conduct of human behaviors. It is the predominate element and relevant need followers must see in a leader. Behaviors are either learned or innate and are a result of experiences or genetics—two fundamental approaches of behaviors being "nurtured" versus "natured". One can learn based on what they see and observe such as nurtured behaviors of walking or riding a bike or contrasting the innate natured behavior of chewing.

However, James M. Kouzes and Barry Z. Posner write in their book, *The Leadership Challenge*, "Leadership is not a gene and it is not an inheritance. Rather leadership is an identifiable set of skills and abilities that are available to all of us." The development of leadership is a result of experience and learned behaviors, not a gene or an inheritance rather a set of skills, encoding good leaders are made and not born. Essentially, to the working of every individual is the choice to become a leader. Basically put, the Knowledge, Skill-Sets, and Attributes of an individual are the foundation to develop leadership capacity—it is the basis of their influence. After long and pointed theory, leaders earn the right to have followers based on what they *know, do,* and *be.* They must constantly develop; build it out of every fragment for authority.

Remarkably, the leadership movement is defined as the intersection of Knowledge, Skill-Sets, and Attributes.

Knowledge is things one knows-Competencies
Skill-Sets are things one does-Capabilities
Attributes are things one is-Character

Individuals who actively identify with the framework of Knowledge-Know, Skill-Sets-Do, and Attributes-Be become effective leaders. The unifying atmosphere of the framework is not just about the duty of leadership; it is also the catalyst to act and to relate on the genuine needs, aspirations, and values of would-be followers. In sharp contrast, is a leader who does not mark the understanding of theory and follow through on the mechanics of Knowledge, Skill-Sets, and Attributes will assuredly fail and reflect tension, which cultivates conflict among the staff and purpose of their own leadership capacity.

Authentic authority lies behind a leader's ability to mobilize other people to perform in their job function. At the root of leadership, depends largely on what followers discern when they see and listen to the leader. It is the nature of people to look for the set standards of the leader. They are looking for a role model. They need to see someone who is strong and capable and a leader who has the leadership capacity to lead others.

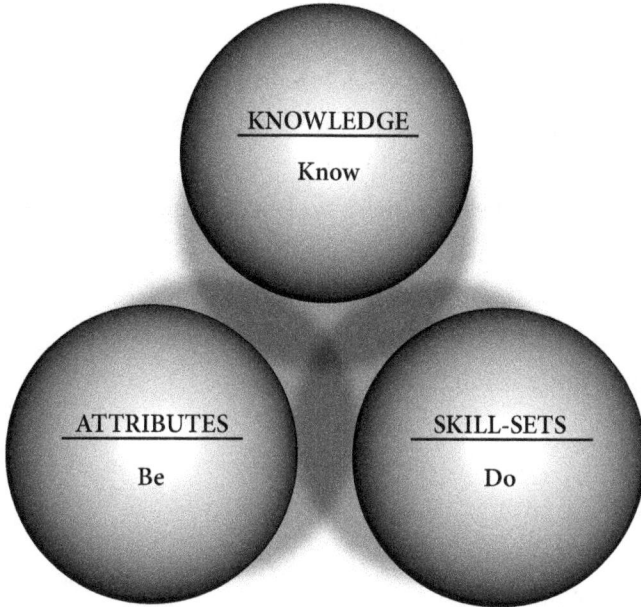

KNOWLEDGE
Know

ATTRIBUTES
Be

SKILL-SETS
Do

Knowledge: Know - Competencies

Taking initiative

Keeping commitments

Taking responsibility

Holding oneself accountable for results

Exerting positive influence on results

Leadership development

Character development

Executing strategy

Focusing on important priorities

Defining tasks to achieve key goals

Prioritizing tasks

Understanding core business concepts

Focusing employee attention on industry and company environment

Tying business concepts to corporate culture

Understanding communication

Defusing high tension situations

Listening effectively

Providing productive input and feedback

Understanding why coworkers act the way they do

Patience in dealing with others

Seeing things differently to appreciate other points of view

Knowing human needs

Skill-Sets: Do - Capabilities

Recognizing the importance of trust

Identifying reactive tendencies

Developing proactive responses to business challenges

Describing positive change

Organizing work into tasks

Assigning priorities to tasks

Ensuring tasks connect with organizational goals

Prioritizing work on a daily basis

Finding work life balance

Writing

Speaking

Using authentic listening

Improving body language

Executing on strategic plans

Mentoring

Working hard

Staying focused

Developing organizational mission, vision, and values

Being a role model

Being truthful

Being self-aware

Following through

Being collaborative

Attributes: Be - Character

Be humble

Be professional

Be loyal

Be of good character

Be responsible

Be selfless

Be honest

Be a light

Be a mentor

Be a motivator

Be mature

Be consistent

Be grateful

Be educated

Be involved

Be positive

Of note, there can be a high degree of overlap between Knowledge, Skill-Sets, and Attributes. Different concepts may apply to different roles and jobs.

Even though a leader has the outwardly discipline of expertise in one of the areas, it would seem insufficient to think that a leader can be proficient in part of the leadership framework and deficient in the other areas and still earn the right to have followers. While the actual extent of development will vary broadly, the manner in which it is expressed depends primarily on the leader's ability to host all the factors of understanding and execution in all three areas.

The struggle requires sitting on a three-legged stool with only one or two legs. It simply does not work, if at all. Though the most energetic and capable leader would seem to represent part of the framework, the intentions, goals, capabilities, and capacity need to be distributed in all three areas. To the extent that a leader is deficient in one of the given areas, there will be major gaps in performance. On the other hand, if a leader is proficient in practice of the intersection of number four, true leadership will be present and employees will consistently follow and perform. Abraham Zaleznik outlines the following four areas and how Knowledge, Skill-Sets, and Attributes build leadership capacity.

1- Only having knowledge and attributes: a leader would perform but does not have the skills

2- Only having knowledge and skill-sets: a leader should perform but does not have the attributes

3- Only having skill-sets and attributes: a leader would have a desire to perform but does not have the knowledge

4- A leader will perform because all capabilities exist

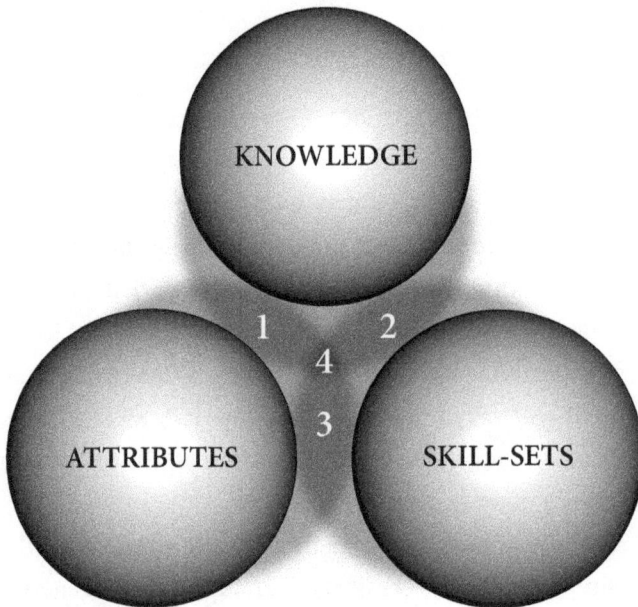

The academic marketplace is responding to the position set forth at the beginning of the preface and this chapter that: leadership is a learned, taught, and developed trait, and is a matter of CHOICE. The potential rallying points become more obvious that the more closely leadership is observed the seemingly poor conditions are worse, requiring expansive and diligent learning and follow-through on implementation.

There are leaders today who are at the point of retirement and ending their careers, and many working their way up the corporate ladder, who advanced to their current positions without having mastered the appropriate Knowledge, Skill-Sets, and Attributes necessary to be effective leaders. Such a concept poses a major gap of unmet needs between the leader and follower. The fundamental tension between leader and follower can be linked to empty shifting expectations of the knowledge age worker. The points of contact are along the lines of trust, self-awareness, contribution, shifting attitudes, and human needs.

The role of a leader is even more complex than in years past because of the nature between the leader and follower relationship. In dialogue of the effects and multiplicity of needs, the core competencies are the hallmark of leadership to rise above the approach of inconsistency and to respect the legitimacy to reconcile the relationship between leader and follower. The conflict is incumbent on the leader to resolve. Some of the leaders today are somewhat stuck in the weeds, and while the very best of them surround themselves with outstanding help, most of them muddle through or fake it.

It is becoming apparent that there are missing pieces in the puzzle of what symbolizes good leadership in today's environment. It is unfortunate that the current atmosphere be in desperate need of strong leaders.

In the hunt for role models, some of the missing pieces of the puzzle are found in such stories of Mahatma Gandhi of India, Martin Luther King of the civil rights movement, and others who rose from obscurity to leadership illumination and power because of their choice and execution of theory and implementation. They relied on such measures of leadership traits to move masses and change governments without the benefit of a position, title, or status rather on the true essence of leadership principles.

Leadership Theory

The essence of leadership theory focuses on the wide-ranging situations that allow a leader to emerge. However, the thorny question of "how" has evaded the essential thesis of the most influential theories ever written. In calling for specific theories, the natural forces of leadership development introduced better-known and more comprehensive hypotheses. While there are many theories expressed from leadership practitioners, the individual perspectives of these better-known theories of Great Event, Character, Behavior, Situational, Contingency, Transactional, and Choice are addressed in the core of the central categories of Character, Great Event, and Choice. The narrow base to shorten the discussion and to bridge the gap between simplicity and complexity is to make it easier and leaner to achieve a firm understanding of leadership rise.

> **Character Theory:** Some personality traits and superior qualities may lead people naturally into leadership roles: personality, strong presence, articulate, etc.

> **Great Event Theory:** A crisis or important event may cause a person to rise to the occasion, which brings out the extraordinary leadership qualities in an ordinary person.

> **Choice Theory:** People can choose to become leaders. People learn leadership skills. It is the most widely accepted theory today and the premise on which this book, *The Choice of Leadership,* is based.

Leadership Theory		
Character	Great Event	Choice

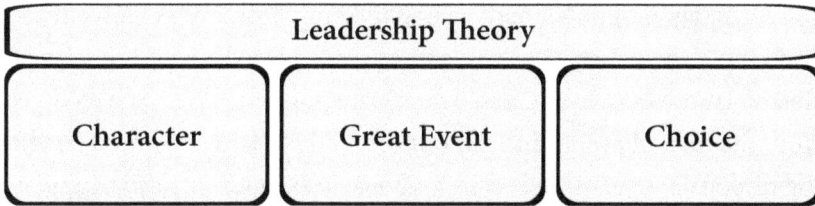

As Shakespeare observed in the *Twelfth Night*, "Some are born great, some achieve greatness, and some have greatness thrust upon them." The theoretical ambiguity that characterizes the old conventional "inheritance" versus the "environment" dramatizes the political ascendant of many kings who have assumed the throne because of birthright and the relationship of military leaders who have risen through the rank and file because of their authority or privilege. These institutional forms of seizing power and wielding authority are a less common practical appeal in today's structure.

The most universal movement toward leadership emergence is a well-grounded link to specific circumstances in a defined moment of time, character traits steeped in pronounced purpose and vision and indeed the series of learning Knowledge, Skill-Sets, and Attributes—they chose to be a leader.

The example of Katharine Graham choosing to assume leadership, in the midst of a tragic story, is evidence of leadership being a choice. In August 3, 1963, Katharine heard a gunshot and quickly learned that her husband had committed suicide. Her husband ran the undistinguished regional newspaper, *The Washington Post*. Immediately the question arose: What would come of the company? Katharine Graham rose to the occasion and immediately informed the board that she would assume responsibility. Katharine stated in her memoirs she had immense levels of insecurities; however, she demonstrated tremendous leadership even in the center of her insecurities. Katharine built a terrific paper and organization. It is ranked as one of the best 50 performing IPOs of the past quarter century and earning the trust of Warren Buffett.

Arguably, despite Katherine Graham's immense levels of insecurities and giving them a shove, she assumed leadership through the foundation of Trait, Great Event, and Transformational theories. She emerged from the turn of events and announced to the board she would be taking responsibility. Blaine Lee, in his book, *The Power Principle*, suggests that leadership is a combination of circumstances, traits, and behaviors. He writes, "What combination of circumstances, traits, and behaviors provides for optimum leadership? And perhaps more timely in this age of choice and opportunity is the critical question—given all the choices that people have today, why would someone choose to follow?"

In the words of Winston Churchill, "To every man there comes in his lifetime that special moment when he is figuratively tapped on the shoulder and offered a chance to do a very special thing, unique to him and fitted to his talents. What a tragedy if that moment finds him unprepared or unqualified for the work which would be his finest hour."

Abraham Lincoln embodied the entirety of all the qualities of leadership to shape a nation. The culmination of traits; behavior, vision, discipline and purpose prepared him for his finest hour of leadership that impacted a nation. Abraham Lincoln formed his leadership capacity through 38 years of experience. It was clear that some kind of political power would emerge that flowed directly from his preparation and development. He made the choice to be a leader 38 years prior to his time of leadership.

Leadership is a choice for each individual during every minute, every hour, every day, and every year. President Lincoln is a perfect example of inducing his followers to attain a specific goal through the combination of leadership theory and by extent the nature of understanding human needs. Abraham Lincoln represented the values, motivation, needs and aspiration of the nation. James MacGregor Burns, says, "The genius of leadership lies in the manner in which leaders see and act on their own and their followers' values and motivations."

The broader and most consistent sweeping success to learn leadership skills are the examples of those who not only influence, but also set high standards and patterns of strong qualities within their own lives. The high noon of leadership history teaches fundamental precepts through hundreds of examples that reflect the wisdom of theoretical underpinning to amass the authority. The instrumental means is to appeal to leaders who continue to be seen as role models in the world leadership orbit exhibiting the core traits of behavior and conduct. However, in close proximity to role models, much of what a leader is must be developed from the raw materials of his or her own life.

In many mistakes and miscalculations, the probability of becoming a leader is distorted and pounded out brought on by everyday insecurities and intractable problems. Perhaps the most decisive shift is the victim mentality that curbs opportunity for any form of leadership. The enormous collapse is to cave into and fall back on determinisms to explain away the lack of ability to become a leader.

Determinisms

Determinisms are presumably the final edge of titanic events and circumstances that determine human behavior that disenables leaders to lead and command authority. The extent of the cataclysm swamps people to believe they can explain away and excuse poor behavior along the lines of determinism theory. The impractical choices advocate people are hopelessly victims of causes and events and are inevitably denied the possibility of free will and choice.

> **Environment Determinism:** Someone or something is acting upon you or doing it to you; your employer, boss, spouse, or something in your environment is acting upon and causes you to act and behave. It is much like Pavlov's dog of being conditioned to respond based on circumstances.

<u>Genetic Determinism:</u> Your birth lineage did it to you. You often hear, "That is how the Morrison's are. My parents did it and their parents did it…It is just in the genes. That is who we are."

<u>Psychic Determinism:</u> This is how you were taught. It is all about the experiences in your childhood and the conditions of your upbringing.

The call for leadership is the keynote address for the current time. The theme of determinisms characterizes the social mentalities and moral conflict that may trend toward victimization. The implication of victimization is much more than personal rather a broader subject that threatens stability in a destructive direction. The address must include comments of the close relationship between free will and choice to overcome social injustice and convert moral issues like understanding, fairness, and forgiveness into themes of conformity.

In many respects, there are leaders who have cultivated societies formed squarely on values, ethics, and the freedom to choose their responses. Surrounded by his will power and vision for freedom, Nelson Mandela never defaulted or demurred from his responsibility. He was not burdened based on environmental determinism or any other determinism. He grew up to be a man of conviction and acted almost single handedly to inspire change, by resisting apartheid movement and refusing to compromise his political position to obtain his freedom. The eventual outcome of his act of reform and leadership landed him to a life of imprisonment from 1964 to 1990, After his discharge, on February 11, 1990, he thrust himself back into his four-decade-old vision and achieved the goals of political freedom and ultimately won the support of the African people and South African Presidency.

Nelson Mandela was not reactive and a product of determinism rather freed by his vision, free will, and choice. In his history, he further explains, "At first, as a student, I wanted freedom only for myself, the transitory freedoms of being able to stay out at night, read what I pleased and go where I chose. Later as a young man in Johannesburg, I yearned for the basic and honorable freedoms of achieving my potential, of earning my keep, of marrying and having a family—the freedom not to be obstructed in a lawful life. But I then slowly saw that not only was I not free, but my brothers and sister were not free…that is when the hunger for my own freedom became the greater hunger for the freedom of my people.

It was this desire for the freedom of my people to live their lives with dignity and self respect that animated my life, that transformed a frightened young man into a bold one, that drove a law-abiding attorney to become a criminal, that turned a family-loving husband into a man without a home…I am no more virtuous or self-sacrificing than the next man, but I found that I could not even enjoy the poor and limited freedoms I was allowed when I knew my people were not free."

Nelson Mandela is a transition leader and a seeker of truth. The search for unity inspired hope and light in the hearts and minds for all of his followers to gain freedom and to live their lives with dignity and self-respect. Much like a lighthouse serving as a light to ships—leaders serve as a beacon of light for the organization; lifting the burden of others and setting the direction and security for all those who follow.

Life lessons are not reserved only for formal education in school; it exists in stories and experiences of others blending them into leadership development. Robert Fulghum shared his experience on the last day of a two-week Greek culture seminar. The teacher Dr. Alexander Papaderos, asks the ritual question at the end of class saying, "Are there any questions?" Quiet quilted the room. These two weeks had generated enough questions for a lifetime, but for now, there was only silence. "No questions?" Papaderos swept the room with his eyes. So, I asked, "Dr. Papaderos, what is the meaning of life?" The usual laughter followed, and people stirred to go. Dr. Papaderos held up his hand and stilled the room and looked at me for a long time, asking with his eyes, if I was serious and seeing from my eyes that I was: "I will answer your question." Taking his wallet out of his hip pocket, he fished into a leather billfold and brought out a very small round mirror, about the size of a quarter. And what he said went like this:

> *When I was a small child, during the war, we were very poor and we lived in a remote village. One day, on the road, I found the broken pieces of a mirror. A German motorcycle had been wrecked in that place. "I tried to find all the pieces and put them together, but it was not possible, so I kept only the largest piece. This one, and, by scratching it on a stone, I made it round. I began to play with it as a toy and became fascinated by the fact that I could reflect light into dark places where the sun would never shine- in deep holes and crevices and dark closets. It became a game for me to get the light into the most inaccessible places I could find. "I kept the little mirror, and, as I went about my growing up, I would take it out and idle moments and continue the challenge of the game. As I became a man, I grew to understand that this was not just a child's game but a metaphor for what I might do with my life. I came to understand that I am not the light or the source of light, but light-truth, understanding, knowledge- is there, and it will shine in many dark places only if I reflect it. "I am a fragment of mirror whose whole design and shape I do not know. Nevertheless, with what I have I can reflect light into the dark places of this world into the black places in the hearts of men- and change some things in some people. Perhaps others may see and do likewise. This is what I am about. This is the meaning of my life.*   **Robert Fulghum**

To what value and purpose is there in sharing a story about light reflected in dark places, crevices and black places in the hearts of men? The heroes of leadership transcend their everyday role and give rise not only to strategy, execution, and financial strength but to sheer consideration on the intangible qualities for leadership effectiveness. This question of value and purpose to provide intangible qualities is far more powerful in the day-to-day pursuit in the common goals and achievement through the needs and motivation of the followership. The differentiation between mediocre and extraordinary leadership is the modification to harmonize the needs of the organization and employees with common goals, values and needs. Leaders, enterprises, and employees are significantly linked together in the total process of achievement and success—they rise and fall together.

Jim Collins, in his book, *Good to Great,* outlined the key factors that enabled companies to move from mediocre to great institutions. Perhaps the most important component of the transition from good-to-great is what he calls *Level 5 Leadership.* He is referencing an intangible quality which leadership hinges on a complex intersection of employee and business needs. Jim Collins defines Level 5 Leadership as the enduring greatness through an essential blend of personal humility and professional will.

Some of life's greatest lessons were taught during the atrocities of World War II. Sir Bertram Home Ramsey was a British admiral during World War II and was skilled in amphibious warfare. He was appointed as Naval Force Commander for the invasion of Europe. He shares his perspective of personal humility and professional will to operate more effectively. Before retiring to bed, Admiral Ramsay made a final entry in his handwritten diary: "Monday, June 5, 1944. Thus has been made the vital & crucial decision to stage the great enterprise which shall, I hope, be the immediate means of bringing about the downfall of Germany's fighting power & Nazi oppression & an early cessation of hostilities. I am not under any delusion as to the risks involved in this most difficult of all operations…Success will be in the balance. We must trust in our invisible assets to tip the balance in our favor. We shall require all the help that God can give us & I cannot believe that this will not be forthcoming."

Admiral Ramsay's personal "will", reliance, and humility transcended his own ability into a higher power, which undoubtedly broadened his options to end the atrocities in Europe. The moral and practical criteria of the leader are measured in the values carried out in the commitment to the followership. Outside the immediate responsibility of physiological needs: safety, food, and air, are the supreme long-term needs, those which sustain the motivation of the human spirit: fairness, responsibility, honor, and honesty.

The apparent difficulty of leadership differs in the duality of leader and manager. The attitudes of leadership need to reflect the needs of the followers where as the attitudes of management focuses on the tasks. I have spent the past 20 years teaching and coaching executives in every sphere about the emergence of soft-skill development as a distinguishing factor from ordinary to extraordinary leadership. The network of the soft-skills is discernible in the effective leader. Those who embrace soft-skill development are directly interconnected with the very nature of producing successful results. They take full advantage of their responsibility for the continued existence of the follower. The ultimate test of great leaders, in contrast with poor leaders who are lost in the maze of self-absorption and not reflecting the true needs of others, is the ability to liberate the levels of significant contributions.

Tying the ends of hard-skill and soft-skill development to structure the effective leadership knot advocates the model of Knowledge, Skill-Sets, and Attributes. The model needs to be built into the capabilities of every leader. One of the most notable leaders in American history, President Abraham Lincoln the 16th president of the United States was always recognized as confidant, yet a humble countryman of unusual resolve and humor; he left Springville, Illinois to Washington D.C. saying, "I now leave with a task before me greater than that, which rested upon Washington. Without the assistance of that Divine Being who attended him, I cannot succeed. With that assistance I cannot fail."

The sharper form of leadership is in the instrumental attributes of humility, listening, understanding, and fairness, which are only a few of the basic needs of humanity. There is nothing soft or deficient about these concepts. Those who underestimated and took no notice of Abraham Lincoln's leadership strength because of his high emotional intelligence were greatly erroneous. The powerful forces of humility, forgiveness, and all other attributes carried citizens down the path for the broader purpose and transformed an entire nation. While many have yet to learn eminent forces behind leadership, Abraham Lincoln was the thrust.

History has revealed one of the major weights to crush hatred and distrust among neighbors. Abraham Lincoln profoundly said, "What I deal with is too vast for malicious dealing." He welcomed the South back with open arms and, in his second inaugural address, he asked his fellow countrymen to do the same. In the closing remarks of the address, which has been called his "Sermon on the Mount," Lincoln expressed in most eloquent terms the depths of his conviction:

> *With malice toward none; with charity for all; with firmness in*
> *the right as God gives us to see the right, let us strive on to finish*
> *the work we are in, to bind up the nation's wounds, to care for*
> *him who shall have borne the battle and for his widow and his*
> *orphan, to do all which may achieve and cherish a just and*
> *lasting peace among ourselves, and with all nations.*
> **Lincoln's Second Inaugural Address, March 4, 1865**

Survival for leaders leading in the Knowledge Age environment is wielding the tools of not only hard-skills of strategy, execution, and decision-making, but also in the perfect precision balance of the soft-skills. It is the shift from the encrusted routine of the management mentality of the Industrial Age managing processes to the leadership approach of the motivational base of the Knowledge Age worker.

In all the vast halls of the leadership portraits, the support bracket is the followership and movement of purpose. The issue is presiding over as a caretaker of the entire enterprise. Jim Collins makes an insightful point, "Great leaders never wanted to become larger-than-life heroes. They never aspired to be put on a pedestal or become unreachable icons. They were seemingly ordinary people quietly producing extra ordinary results."

Great leaders channel their egotistical needs away from themselves for the best interest of those they serve. The extension of the leadership arm is not to encumber those they lead, forcing their efforts and day-to-day work to feed the leader's egocentric personality. Rather they are independent as to whom they are and stand-alone from the need of public praise and recognition. Honor comes from the private arena of respect one has for the leader which highlights the true character to rise above selfishness. They are quietly going about their duty to produce significant results for the cause they serve.

In 1992, I was asked to welcome George and Barbara Bush and the press secretary, Merlin Fitzwater to Salt Lake City, Utah. Upon their arrival, I was invited in the presidential suite with the President and First Lady. The notable Presidential sphere gave way to a traditional experience of human interaction. Barbara sat down in a chair next to me while the President placed his suitcase on the bed. During the 15-minute customary conversation, the President unpacked his suitcase. In a simple application of inquiring, President Bush turns to the First Lady and asked, "Did you pack my pajamas?" This is part of the real person that lies behind the leader.

The authenticity of a leader is grounded when both the personal and professional life is fairly balanced. Leaders do not orchestrate themselves in one or the other rather the emergence of leadership qualities is congruent with the whole person. The most powerful leader of the Free World is discussing his pajamas without sacrificing the integrity and fundamental principles of the role and office in which he serves. I excused myself and bought the President a pair of royal blue maroon piping pajamas. I learned that ordinary people are doing extraordinary things.

The realistic resolve to many social and world issues is at the influence of ordinary people. As a side note, Barbara Bush expressed the most central level of leadership within the family organization and the walls of every home across the world. "Whatever era, whatever the times, one thing will never change: Fathers and mothers, if you have children, they must come first. You must read to your children and you must hug your children and you must love your children. Your success as a family, our success as a society, depends not on what happens in the White House, but on what happens inside your homes."

At the very least, leaders must capture the qualities of the expressed values and foundational principles and furthermore become, to a much larger degree, performers to execute on the nature of explicit purpose in which they represent. The movement of leadership is not built on duplicity, manipulation, exploitation, and false representation rather the vital aspects of momentum through the direct environment of followership.

Certainly, the finer points of leadership are grasping the interrelationship between leader and follower. It is becoming apparent that the leadership role and the follower role are closely coming together. The margin is narrowing. It is no longer the "great person in charge." It is more along the lines of teamwork and providing direction. In an article in *BusinessWeek,* "…senior executives seem to be battling for the congeniality prize. Humility, authenticity, and responsive leadership are new buzzwords at the top. Many chief executives talk about being 'servant leaders' and team players. They care openly about everything from employees to Mother Earth. In short, they're more likable."

Underlying conflict between the ends of leaders and followers is the lack of positive attitudes in individual leaders, which has delivered hammer like blows to those they serve. The mind-set of "servant leader" is now taking center stage. The verification suggests great leadership and followership depends on the relationship—one cannot have the one without the other.

In an outcry to remove the one who was in charge, the voices were heard. "A couple of years ago the unthinkable happened. Riccardo Muti, who for nearly two decades was the feared, but widely revered conductor of the orchestra at Milan's legendary opera house, La Scala, was pushed from his perch. He was obliged to resign by La Scala's eight hundred musicians, singers, carpenters, and janitors, who, finally furious with his high-handed ways, demanded that he "Resign! Resign!" Muti's departure signaled the end of an era. Times have changed in the world of music, as they have changed everywhere else. For example, the new conductor for the New York Philharmonic, Alan Gilbert, is very different from his predecessors. He is young and he is by all accounts affable and approachable, with not a hint of the fearsome maestro about him. In sum, the imperial CEO is no more, and neither is the imperial conductor."

People of today are speaking out just as it was in the period of reform. The Declaration of Independence "We hold these truth to be self-evident, that all men are created equal, that they are endowed by their Creator with certain unalienable rights, that among these are Life, Liberty, and the Pursuit of Happiness." The Knowledge Age worker is shouting. They want to be lead by a different style of leadership.

The reverberation of the echo in the 21st century raises the consciousness for emergence in a new leader. The most common thread to tie organizational success with followership is through the basic needs of both. Synovus Financial Corporation is one of the *Fortune* magazine's 100 best companies to work for in America. They have been consistent in achieving number one over a sustained period of time by meeting the needs of the employees.

Chairman, James Blanchard shares his beliefs as to their success: "There's a common thread that runs through those very few organizations who are just busting out on top all the time. They're meeting and exceeding their goals. They're realizing their visions and aspirations. They're always over and above their expectations… And yet this group of robust, energized, enthusiastic, continually successful organizations, they seem to have a secret. And frankly, we have studied it, we try and find that formula that says, 'We'll be one of these in this very small, select group that seems to achieve perpetual success.' The secret, the clue, the common thread is simply how you treat folks. It's how you treat your fellow man, and how you treat your team members and how you treat your customers, your regulators, your general public, your audiences, your communities. How you value the worth of an individual, how you bring the human factor into real importance and not just a statement you make in your annual report."

Unfortunately, the consciousness has not been aroused to the extent where it has fully impacted the fabric of corporate life. People continue to be scripted and taught that leadership is the hard nose mentality exercising their authority to get things accomplished. What might have been the management technique during the Industrial Age where workers were assigned to do one function and nothing more than moving a widget, necessitated management and an authoritative voice to ensure the tasks were complete and production was on schedule. The role of a manager in the Industrial Age did not require soft-skills to be an effective leader. Stephen R. Covey says, "The main assets and primary drivers of the economic prosperity in the Industrial Age were machines and capital—things. People were necessary but replaceable. You could control and churn through manual workers with little consequence-supply exceeded demand. You just got more able bodies that would comply with strict procedures."

Today, the environment is completely different. People live in a Knowledge Age were they have options and education. The nature of the work is different and so is the workforce—it requires more of the mind, heart and intellect. Employees perform differently; the jobs and work are no longer manufacturers working on the assembly lines of the 20th century. The tendencies a century ago were to manage laborers as expendable things. Today, the employee should be the greatest asset.

The elephantine slowness of information during the Industrial Age suppressed the available options for the manual laborer. The worker was completely dependent on their jobs. It was not, after all, the era of opportunity. The single greatest revolutionary application is the speed and access to information at light speed. This is precisely the measure; people are bright, smart, and capable ultimately the intellectual resource providing available options. The new human intellectual resource requires a whole new set of skills for the leader to effectively lead in the new world economy of the Knowledge Age worker.

Drucker contrasts the Industrial Age manual labor-type employee with the Knowledge Age thinker. He said, "The most important and indeed the truly unique contribution of management in the 20th century was a fifty-fold increase in the production of the manual worker in manufacturing. The most important contribution management needs to make in the 21st century is similarly to increase the productivity of knowledge work and the knowledge worker. The most valuable assets of the 20th-century company were production equipment. The most valuable asset of a 21st-century institution, whether business or non-business, will be its knowledge workers and their productivity."

In Stuart Crainer's book, *The Management Century*, states, "The information age places a premium on intellectual work. There is a growing realization that recruiting, retaining, and nurturing talented people is crucial to competitiveness."

The key and the greatest working capital of any workforce is the knowledge base of employees. What was once a labor intensive and material intensive work environment is now knowledge intensive. The world economy competes on knowledge to drive innovation of new products and other knowledge driven ideas. The leader's ability to effectively lead is a strong capable mind, but it demands much more, it requires the qualities to honor the human spirit. The Knowledge Age worker needs a shrewd leader's eye to unleash the esprit de corps of the human spirit. That is real leadership!

The leaders of today must choose to be great. It requires a whole new mind-set, a new way of thinking about the wisdom, experience, and learning from others to help them make sense of their own development. The leadership pulley is to leverage Knowledge, Skill-Sets, and Attributes that support the leadership capacity.

With the immense rapid movement into the 21st century, Peter Drucker in his book, *Managing Knowledge Means Managing Oneself*, expresses the importance of moving in a direction of personal accountability "In a few hundred years, when the history of our time is written from a long-term perspective, it is likely that the most important event those historians will see is not technology, not the Internet, not e-commerce. It is an unprecedented change in the human conditions. For the first time-literally-substantial and rapidly growing numbers of people have choice. For the first time, they will have to manage themselves. And society is totally unprepared for it."

Individuals will see that one would observe enough core repetition and consistency to suggest that the things that Hoshi Ryokan does are similar to what Apple does. The towering question is not only how does a leader transform rather the broader landscape of a more enduring meaning that will impact the world over in individual and organizational life. Perhaps this is the most profound uprising and overriding purpose for leadership development. The interplay of leadership transformation will be found in the following pages of this book, *The Choice of Leadership*, and provides the resources of how to use the tools available throughout history to improve.

The success of great organizations and leaders is a combination and balance of theoretical understanding and practical implementation. One balances the other and a sweet spot of leadership development and by extension, organizational function is found.

Chapter 2

Vision

More often than not, the topic of vision is discussed in many circles. Whether it is heard from an exuberant high-spirited coach, a passionate executive in the corporate boardroom, a newly elected president defining his or her presidency, or a soul searching individual in the deepest part of their heart or mind; vision continues to burn within because it provides a sense of being and a sense of direction. Individuals have accomplished great achievements because vision awakened the "will power" to see the possibilities and their inherent capacity to do great things.

There are many observers in the vast principles and structures of leadership, but the bursting point in such concepts of vision gives way to the energy and the passion to drive one and to pull others. Such concepts are very much a product of, and remain always, a part of the bridge between simplicity and complexity in the leadership structure of which they heavily influence others. As long as employees perceive their leaders as visionary figures, there will be a higher level to bind people together and kindle the imagination and work ethic. Vision reflects the needs and attitudes of the followers and organizations and in simplest form provides the power and motivation over the long haul for sustained superior performance. As the great English poet William Blake, of the late 16th century once said, "What is now proved was once only imagination." Vision translates into a based reality of meaningful contribution to guide effort. Throughout the ages, people have been tying their contributions and accomplishments to purpose and existence.

Vision is a widely used word, but unfortunately most do not understand the definition. There are many labels and definitions: mission, values, purpose, and strategic goals, which make it even more problematic to capture the force behind the concept. Amidst all the definition ambiguity, the social and economic answer of vision is a set of priorities that defines the conditions of a future state. The paramount question is arguably the relevance and credibility to those who are asked to buy into the vision.

In calling for such a need as the power of vision, I would invite senior leaders to echo their thoughts only to hear silence. Leaders need to be well voiced in vision and linked firmly to the understanding of the importance. How does a company attempt greatness without vision? Without vision, where does an individual, a company, or government find the capacity and strength to trounce life's challenges to make a significant contribution? The importance of the theory provides strength and passion to accomplish the ultimate vision. In the book, *The Leaders Voice*, Boyd Clarke and Ron Crossland positions the centrality of vision:

Vision is a love affair with an idea.
Vision is not something created by a committee.
Vision is not something generated by analysis.
Vision is not the by product of a ...consultant report.
Vision is about ...wild, passionate, intemperate...Love.

The development of vision is to determine how to make sense of, and most importantly, how to actually use it to move an individual or organization down the path of success. A biblical proverb advises, "Where there is no vision, the people perish." Many organizations have some form of vision statement to only satisfy a page in the annual report, is displayed in the reception lobby and changes nothing. Michael Useem, from the Wharton School of Business at the University of Pennsylvania has stated, "Leadership is at its best when the vision is strategic, the voice persuasive, the results tangible." The concepts of strategic, persuasive, and tangible are critical elements to coordinate a collected effort for everyone to link to the vision.

The battle of Agincourt of 1415 models the vision of King Henry V's warriors to stretch beyond the traditional limits against a numerically superior French army. Prior to the battle, Henry V led his English troops across France to recapture Calais and other cities to win back holds in France that once belonged to England. It is noted as one of the greatest battles of all time.

Henry's troops were weakened and fell ill to the plaque of dysentery— the footmen were dwindling due to their environment. With the morale and all hope lost in the attempt to seize their property, the English lines were lost. As they looked upon the overwhelming forces of heavily armored and highly skilled French Knights, their vision of victory was trumped by thoughts of certain defeat. The inevitable consequence of death was on the horizon. King Henry V, rising to the new dawn of opportunity spoke words of encouragement and displayed remarkable leadership capabilities with hope to rally his troops to victory. King Henry V's speech set the thousands of defeated hearts and minds into one direction, one purpose, and one vision—the vision of *Victory*.

Although Shakespeare penned the speech "St. Crispin's Day" nearly two hundred years after the battle of Agincourt in 1415, it remains one of the finest interpretations of what leadership and vision represent.

Battle of Agincourt
Saint Crispin's Day
25 October 1415

English	French
Men-at-Arms: 1,500 (0 mounted)	**Men-at-Arms:** 10,000 (1,200 mounted)
Archers: 7,000	**Archers:** 26,000
Total: 8,500 men	*Total:* 36,000 men
Casualties: 450	*Casualties:* 10,000
VICTORY	DEFEAT

We would not die in that man's company
That fears his fellowship to dies with us.
This day is call'd the feast of Crispian.
He that outlives this day, and comes safe home,
Will stand a tip-toe when this day is nam'd,
And rouse him at the name of Crispian.

He that shall live this day, and see old age,
Will yearly on the vigil feast his neighbours,
And say 'To-morrow is Saint Crispian.'
Then will he strip his sleeve and show his scars,
And say 'These wounds I had on Crispian's day.'
Old men forget; yet all shall be forgot,
But he'll remember, with advantages,
What feats he did that day. Then shall our names,
Familiar in his mouth as household words-
Harry the King, Bedford the Exeter,
Warwick and Talbot, Salisbury and Gloucester-
Be in their flowing cups freshly rememb'red.
This story shall the good man teach his son;
And Crispin Crispian shall ne'er go by,
From this day to the ending of the world,
But we in it shall be remembered-

We few, we happy few, we band of brothers;
For he to-day that sheds his blood with me
Shall be my brother; be he ne'er so vile,
This day shall gentle his condition;
And gentlemen in England now-a-bed
Shall think themselves accurs'd they were not here,
And hold their manhoods cheap whiles any speaks
That fought with us upon Saint Crispin's day.

The tip of the spear is simply vision. It pierces the hearts and minds of people to motivate and aspire contribution. Although the speech is a work of fiction, it tapped the talent and evoked the spirit with which Henry V inspired passion and discipline to accomplish the improbable. The vision lead a band of brothers outnumbered 4 to 1, to an overwhelming victory. Although great vision can lead individuals and organizations to produce unbelievable results—there is the reconciliation to bridge the gap between realistic and idealistic. The vision must be realistic, with a defined path to execute on the objective and idealistic to broaden the efforts of everyone. Warren Bennis, the founding chairman of The Leadership Institute at the University of Southern California said, "Leaders must encourage their organizations to dance to forms of music yet to be heard."

The complexity of vision is the organizational boundaries of infrastructure to support purpose and execution. The central question to be asked: Is the organization aligned with a clearly defined strategy, processes such as decision-making, structure of reporting, compensation, information systems, and more importantly capable employees to carry out the vision? (*The concept of organizational alignment will be addressed in greater detail in the Organizational Design chapter of this book.*)

All of the Organizational Designs and other forces to develop and execute vision have a propensity to degenerate into a certain mystic. Some of the brightest people are not able to make sense of vision or the possibility of even accomplishing the task. Creating and detecting a vision can be difficult and is a mental lifting exercise performed not only by the artistic and creative minds, but also by broadband strategic thinkers and leaders.

In the book, Harvard Business Essentials: *Your Mentor and Guide to Doing Business Effectively* captures, "As you shape your organization's or unit's vision, remember that an effective vision touches people's inner aspiration. Its language can be translated into realistic strategy. Its fulfillment may be challenging, but achievable. It also has these characteristics: it serves the interests of the company's most important stakeholders and it clearly defines the benefits to them. The vision must be easy to explain and understand; it must also be focused and straightforward. Even if implementing the vision is a complicated process, explaining it should not be."

The role of the leader becomes critical in drafting, communicating and executing the vision. A compelling vision speaks to the inner soul of all stakeholders, which inspires action and commitment. Most often they are succinct and easily translated into measurable tasks—inspiring passion that can construct a significant difference.

Throughout time, individuals gave their lives for their vision and subordinated life to the purpose and cause, thereby confirming their personal vision represented their life. In the late 1420's, emerged a visionary figure who became known as Joan of Arc. In the book, *Leadership*, James Burns, "The birth of Joan of Arc in a poor peasant home, her insistence on confronting military men who had little time for peasants, and much less for an eighteen-year-old farm girl, her summons to the Dauphin to act like a king, her courage in battle, her martyrdom, and subsequent rehabilitation and (much later) canonization—all this stuff out of which heroes are fashioned." At the age of nineteen, she was given a chance to gain her freedom by denouncing her purpose. In the play of *Joan of Lorraine*, Maxwell Anderson wrote describing her purpose:

> *I know this now. Every man gives his life for what he believes.*
> *Every women gives her life for what she believes. Sometimes*
> *people believe in little or nothing, and so they give their lives to*
> *little or nothing. One life is all we have, and we live it as we be-*
> *lieve in living it and then it's gone. But to surrender who you are*
> *and to live without belief is more terrible than dying-*
> *Even more terrible than dying young.*

Noel M. Tichy, an American management consultant and former director of global development at General Electric in his book, *The Leadership Engine*, said, "Leadership is about leading others. It's about taking people from where they are now to where they need to be. The best way to get people to venture into unknown terrain is to make it desirable by taking them there in their imagination." Executing vision can be emotional work on behalf of those being asked to agree. There are many questions that have to be answered in order to give freely full support and buy in. People will invariably ask such questions of: What is in it for me?

What are the options? What will be required to fulfill the vision? How great is the sacrifice? What will change? Those who have the responsibility to draft, communicate and execute vision need to satisfy the questions with solid answers.

What will require hours, days, and months to craft a guiding vision; there is an expectation that everyone else in the organization should accept the vision instantaneously. The vision will be poured in the oceans of people where it will become diluted, having no meaning or acceptance without time to absorb. Those who are required to accept have not yet had the time to develop an internal co-mission of their personal life and purpose to support the vision at large.

The extraordinary vision in some of the most noteworthy leaders and achievers, such as Nelson Mandela, Steve Jobs, Sam Walton, and Lee Iacocca, made things come about by allowing individuals and organizations to see the realm of possibilities. It is much more than a dream; it is the future state and an ambitious view of the purpose. A pipe dream is when people hear a weak competitor promote that they will be number one. Stating they will be number one is not the future state of the organization. It is a panacea of understanding and leadership deficiency.

Poor visionary leaders do not recognize the business environment or the Organizational Design to appropriately align the various elements of strategy, processes, systems, and structures. These elements connect and serve the interest of all employees, leaders, customers, and other stakeholders. Without a vision, leaders are left for a direction that does not exist. The power of the leader to motivate and inspire themselves and the organization allows the vision and goals to generate long-term energy. Vision with a clear direction is the best index to employee's contribution.

Reflecting back on a fictitious play, one can learn a very important principle. In Alice's Adventures in Wonderland, Alice asks the cat,

"Would you tell me please which way I ought to go from here?"

"That depends a good deal on where you want to get to," said the Cat.

"I don't much care where..." said Alice.

"Then it doesn't matter which way you go," said the Cat.

On May 25, 1961, John F. Kennedy announced, before a special joint session of Congress, the dramatic and ambitious direction of sending an American safely to the moon before the end of the decade. His purpose was to catch up and overtake the Soviet Union in the "space race." This was on the heels of Russia sending cosmonaut Yuri Gagarin who became the first human in space on April 12th 1961. NASA's program of human flight was guided by John F. Kennedy's vision. His goals were achieved on July 20, 1969, when Neil Armstrong uttered the extraordinary words, "One small step for man and one giant leap for mankind."

Of interest, the ultimate goal of putting a man on the moon was successfully accomplished six years after the death of the creator's vision. The thirty-fifth President of the United States, John F. Kennedy, was assassinated on Friday, November 22, 1963, in Dallas, Texas at 12:30 p.m.

John F. Kennedy's brief presidency reflects the staying power of vision and the importance of communicating the message to build a common purpose and set standards of excellence. The purpose unified the masses of people to execute on the most important goals and distinctive contribution of the organization. Vision can be so powerful that even opponents and naysayers cannot thwart the strength of the motivational effect of the few—exponential energy and motivation unleashes the esprit de corps.

John F. Kennedy's vision generated the commitment for the nation to share in the importance of the ideals of the United States. In his inaugural address on January 20, 1961, he said, "Let every nation know, whether it wishes us well or ill, that we shall pay any price, bear any burden, meet any hardship, support any friend, oppose any foe, in order to assure the survival and the success of liberty."

Like lightening flashes in the night, the vision illuminated ambitious and noble commitment, which created synergy among all those involved. What seemed only plausible or even impossible became reality. An inspiring vision has made it commonplace for man's exploration in outer space. Space shuttles are launched so regularly into space that it hardly makes the news. The expressed vision to Congress on May 25, 1961, not only satisfied the man on the moon, but also shattered the impossibilities of satellite transmission of billions of pieces of information. John F. Kennedy's vision paved the path for exponential growth in many industries including communications through cell phones, internet, and space exploration with space stations and galaxy discovery. It has utterly changed how people live.

There are countless organizational stories that teach the power of vision and what the organization can become. Vision takes on a life form that involves everyone who is associated. It resonates with the majority of members in the organization and assists them to feel important and a part of something much bigger than themselves. Vision ultimately stretches the organizational capabilities to provide a distinct contribution and to attain lofty goals. Whether one is creating revitalization, a manufacturing site, or a new product, one needs to have vision. It is, after all, the vision that allows the work to have importance and significant meaning. It is the creative force that generates the energy of the organization to move forward.

At great junctures throughout corporate America, is the evidence of the power of vision. Sam Walton is the greatest merchant of the twentieth-century. His legacy grew from a single five-and-dime store in Newport, Arkansas, into a retail behemoth that earned $405 billion in net sales in 2010. Sam Walton's vision of being a merchant started in 1945 when he invested $5,000 of his own money and $20,000 of his father-in-law's, to buy his first discount store.

Before Sam Walton's death in 1992, he had a revenue goal to grow annual sales from less than $30 billion to $125 billion by the year 2000. Under the leadership of David Glass, Wal-Mart not only exceeded the $125 billion, but also surpassed the goal by producing $165 billion. Sam Walton's leadership was by no means a solo performance on the corporate stage rather a collected effort of everyone bound together in a common vision of enhanced life. He was surrounded by remarkable followers to guide the communication and execution of his created vision.

Consider the classic case of a young disciplined visionary thought leader of modern time, which created a rising new industry. On April 1, 1976, the Apple computer was born. Two high school drop outs, Steven Wozniak and Steve Jobs, set out to build a computer. After tremendous innovation, Steve Jobs left Apple only to rejoin the floundering company in 1997—Apple was all but dead. The vision of Steve Jobs produced such innovation as the iPod, iTunes, and iTouch. The Boston Consulting Group and *BusinessWeek* ranked Apple as the most innovative company in the world. Steve increased Apple's market value by $150 billion and delivered a 3,188 percent industry-adjusted return. Steve Jobs' vision was strategic, persuasive and tangible in order to coordinate a collected effort to execute. Those two individuals revolutionized the industry and built an enormously successful story.

Contrasting the stories of a leader who creates their own industry and those who are currently operating in established industries both rely on vision to carry the purpose and mission forward. Benjamin Zander, the conductor of the Boston Philharmonic shared a story about vision and the art of possibilities. He wrote, "A shoe factory sends two marketing scouts to a region in Africa to study the prospects for expanding business. One sent back a telegram saying,

"Situation hopeless, No one wears shoes"
The other scout writes back triumphantly,
"Glorious business opportunity... They have no shoes"

Within the process of shaping vision, is the formidable opportunity to do a special thing and unique to the organization to unleash the human potential to accomplish what must ostensibly appear to be impossible. Vision yields phenomenal results and revolutionizes conditions of living. While the concept is indispensable, the practice is seldom understood.

The practical advantage of vision creation is the consideration of the time horizon, in which the past meets the present. To be truly visionary, one must understand the past personally or organizationally and then think about the future. The ways history serves within the points of vision can best be seen in times gone by, to position prognosticators to see twice as far into the future—the key to unlock the future is the past.

Individuals and organizations that want to move from an iceberg like speed to an avalanche momentum need to ask such questions: What is the organizational vision? What is the ultimate purpose? If one knows, it should add greater force of meaning and importance to the work. How about other employees? If they do not know the vision, they are encumbered to figure out how their work contributes to the vision or goals of the organization. That is very problematic and translates to wasted effort and eroded profits.

Outside the scope of addressing organizational vision, there are personal stories that exemplify the strength and power of personal vision and purpose. Sir Edmond Hillary grew up in Auckland, New Zealand where he became highly interested in mountain climbing. Although professionally he was a trained beekeeper, he became one of the worlds greatest mountain climbers. After climbing the Alps and Himalayas where he climbed 11 different peaks of over 20,000 feet, it was time to confront the world's highest mountain, Mt. Everest. Everest lies between Tibet and Nepal and reaches over five miles above sea level. Between 1920 and 1952, seven major expeditions had failed to reach the summit. On one occasion, Mountaineer George Leigh-Mallory had perished in his failed attempt. Sir Hillary on his attempt in May 1953, said, "We did not know if it was humanly possible to reach the top of Mt. Everest." His vision, of being the first human along with his Nepalese guide, stretched their own capacity and understanding of what was possible. At 11:30, on the morning of May 29, 1953, Edmond Hillary and Tensing Norgay reached the summit 29,028 feet above sea level, the highest point on earth.

When everything seems vulnerable and ominous, even at the hands of the most extenuating circumstances and challenges, it is vision that keeps the human and organizational spirit alive to bear the adversities. Vision needs to reside within the fabric of every individual. It is what provides the strength to overcome the most unseemingly possibilities. In other respects, people are so accustom to the mundane work that they need meaning to the nature of work for greater contribution. Drew Gilpin Faust, a historian and the president of Harvard University said, "Human beings need meaning, understanding and perspective, as well as a job. It buys the spirit and intellect of people allowing them to overcome any obstacle that stands in their way. It galvanizes everyone who is involved." Peter Drucker, one of the great leadership thinkers of the 20ᵗʰ century has suggested, "The chief object of leadership is the creation of a human community held together by the work bond for a common purpose."

Especially these days, in today's world economic conditions of a volatile financial climate, it is mission critical that leaders send a clear and concise message to sustain the employees. Employees need to understand the organizational dimensions and purpose. The message needs to be expressed in several ways so everyone understands without being encumbered to figure what is being communicated.

They need to see and hear the strong leader accepting responsibility and communicating the vision time after time. They should not only hear the vision rather they must understand how to translate the vision into action. They need to understand that the leader knows what he or she is doing. They need to believe in something when everything else seems to be crashing down around them. The towering achievement of leadership is about the way in which various messages are communicated to reach down to the hard ground truths and current brutal realities, to deal with the present, while balancing the needs for the future without crippling the people.

Revisiting the puzzle pieces of leadership and management, the piece of leadership is about leading people and not managing them as things, which is why leaders need to communicate passion, support, values, assurance, and confidence. When leaders do not deal with the human side of leadership, it can only be unmercifully damaging to everyone around them. Rudolph W. Giuliani, in his book, *Leadership* said, "It's up to the leader to instill confidence, to believe in his/her judgment, and in his people even when they no longer believe in themselves. Sometimes, the optimism of a leader is grounded in something only he knows—the situation isn't as dire as people think for reasons that will eventually become clear. But sometimes the leader has to be optimistic simply because if he or she isn't nobody else will be. And you've got to at least to try to fight back, no matter how daunting the odds."

There are countless opportunities for a leader to inspire, support, reassure, and restore confidence. Mayor Giuliani captures the profound essence of the responsibility, "Suppose Churchill had walked out from 10 Downing Street during the battle of Britain and said, 'There is really not much we can do about this.' There must have been times when he doubted. Germany had occupied virtually all of Europe. America was not responding, at least not in a way he wished, and Roosevelt seemed unable to bring his people around to enter the war. The British were there, alone, bombarded by a Luftwaffe whose capability had not even been tested. Suddenly, the impregnable island empire was being invaded from the air—something that had never happened to England. Its cities and its civilian population were being bombed on a daily basis." People who surmount life's most difficult trials are those who understand the purpose of their suffering.

Perhaps the most remarkable aspect of this event was the leader, who directly confronted the reality and in the midst of communicated vision to draw people out of insecurities, fears, and despairs and enlisted them to remember their purpose. He would walk the streets doing what he could to calm people with his presence and courage to keep hope alive.

The diagnosis of leadership strength, to support those who follow, is in the prescription of walking around the offices being visible to the organization inspiring confidence and hope within the people. Hope is the ability to provide strength and optimism related to the circumstances in life. It is not so much about the circumstance and situation rather one's attitude to deal with the current environment. Viktor Frankl's book, *Man's Search for Meaning*, shares of his survival like so many German and East European Jews who were thrown into concentration and extermination camps said, "The last human freedoms—to choose one's attitude in any given set of circumstances, to choose one's own way."

A leader who knows and acts on their full purpose rather than the dictates of the environment will have more substance and meaning in their own life. They become more significant, while opening immense opportunities for the present and future when they are living their purpose. The analogy of two seas illustrates the purpose of living. The Dead Sea is dead because it only receives, but the Sea of Galilee is alive and vibrant because it receives and gives. Leaders must remember that one must not only receive, but also continuously give, which reinforces the purpose of life. When leaders are more concerned with those they serve, there will naturally be less time worrying about themselves, creating greater influence with those they support.

Unfortunately, many individuals choose their attitudes based on their circumstances and situations—the social climate rather than choosing their attitudes based on values. One who behaves from a profound sense of purpose can remain consistent regardless of the external environment of how others interact with them, social culture, and circumstances. Victor Frankl, in all of his wisdom said, "Between stimulus and response there is a space. In that space is our power to choose our response. In our responses lie our growth and our freedom." Even in the most difficult times and challenges, one can choose how they will respond. What enables one to move forward down the path of life is a deep purpose and sense of contribution. By any reasonable criteria, leaders must lead in accordance with the vision and purpose of the organization. George Bernard Shaw, an early 20th century Irish playwright and co-founder of the London School of Economics wrote the following poem.

A Splendid Torch

This is the true joy in life… being used for a purpose recognized by yourself as a mighty one…being a force of nature instead of a feverish, selfish little clod of ailments and grievances complaining that the world will not devote itself to making you happy. I am of the opinion that my life belongs to the whole community and as long as I live it is my privilege to do for it whatever I can. I want to be thoroughly used up when I die, for the harder I work the more I live. I rejoice in life for its own sake. Life is no "brief candle" for me. It is a sort of splendid torch, which I have got to hold up for the moment, and I want to make it burn as brightly as possible before handing it on to future generations.

The heart of the theory of purpose is firmly linked to vision. One of the most influential character traits and one that will ultimately lead to effectiveness is being a force of nature instead of complaining that the world will not devote itself to making you happy. The true joy of life is not being a victim of the environment or a set of circumstances rather being used for a purpose of meaningful contribution. The potential for leadership is found in the difficult circumstances to serve and provide hope. One of the potent leadership instruments is being visible to inspire confidence and hope, which only builds the centrality of leadership. People are watching and noticing what the leader is doing. At the highest stage of visibility—the leader must provide strength and support to subordinates and followers who have lost their confidence and determination to continue forward. The important task cannot be washed over and around the boundaries of responsibility of being present; walking and talking with those they serve which is the best test of fiber in a true leader.

The consequence of doing the small and simple task flows the great and significant consequences of moving an entire organization. Spencer W. Kimball once said, "If we are not careful, we can be injured by the frostbite of frustration; we can be frozen in place by the chill of unmet expectations. To avoid this, we must just as we would with arctic cold-ness—keep moving, keep serving, and keep reaching out so that our own immobility does not become our chief danger."

The emergence and explosion of vision has provoked practitioners the world over to consider the moral force by adjusting to stories that embody the power of vision. Most may have heard of the name Gertrude Ederle, the first women to swim across the English Channel. Prior to her successful swim on August 6, 1926, only five men in history had been able to accomplish the English Channel swim. During her twelfth hour at sea, Gertrude became so bothered by the unfavorable winds that someone on board the tugboat called to her, "Gertie, you must come out!" Gertrude, exhausted but dedicated lifted her head from the choppy waters and replied, "What for?!" adding "I am going right through with it this time."

In the midst of the destitution and the futile prospect of finishing the 24-mile channel, she walked up the beach at Dover, England, after 14 hours 39 minutes breaking the previous record of 16 hours, 33 minutes held by Enrique Tiraboschi. Not only did Gertrude achieve her purpose, she shattered the record by 1 hour and 54 minutes. It was her vision that gave her the capacity and strength to continue. It was her vision that sustained her against all odds in accomplishing her goal.

Unfortunately, unlike Sir Edmond Hillary and Gertrude Ederle, people lose sight of the vision and purpose and succumb to potential obscurity. When individuals ignore the farsighted muscle of vision, they lose the will power and deep reservoirs of strength to bear the largest part of the adversity.

The story of Florence Chadwick illustrates how sharply one is affected when individuals lose sight of vision. Florence Chadwick had previously swam the English Channel and held the record for being the first women to swim both directions of the English Channel. She embarked on a journey to swim the 26 miles from Catalina Island to the California coastline. As she entered the coast, a heavy fog settled in and the waters became increasingly cold and irregular. Her mother encouraged her when she had only a few more miles to go. Finally, just a few hundred yards from completing the swim, she asked to be pulled aboard the boat. She felt defeated and heartbroken when she realized how close she really was to reaching her goal. The central learning in this failed attempt was when she told a reporter, "I am not making excuses for myself, but if I could have seen the land, I think I would have made it."

She determined to try again and just one year later, under the same conditions of thick fog, she made it. Why? Because she could clearly see her vision through her mind's eye. She kept the vision with every single stroke drawing upon the reservoir of her life's purpose. What more can be said broadly of meaningful vision? It is passionate, discipline, dedication, hope, and strategic. A strategic vision allows the possibilities to be accomplished by binding all those together with a deep sense of purpose and direction.

The concept of Sears & Roebuck emerged from the vision of a young entrepreneur by the name of Richard Warren Sears. In 1886, Richard was working as a station agent for the Minnesota and St. Louis railroads. As sales literature crossed his path, the 23-year-old read and became familiar with the pricing structure of products being sold across the country.

Given the right conditions, Sears and Roebuck built an empire on merchandising product through a mail order catalog that contained 532 pages. A harmony, between the need and value, formed one of the most trusted enterprises in the twentieth-century and became the seventh largest corporation. Between 1927 and 1928, Sears expanded operation from 27 stores to 192 stores nationwide. Ultimately, the company had over 400 stores and became the retail contender of the 1940's through the 1970's.

The retailer's success rested on the vision to support people's wants and needs. Transportation and shopping malls were scarce and the mail order catalog offered a distinctive alternative. Even with the most potent vision, an institution can be out of step with current market realities. The once original vision that created success no longer provides long-term stability, thereby threatening a collapse. Organizations who accomplish their original vision or purpose might revolve to new goals and milestone or altogether draft a new vision. The commitment, aspiration, and focus of the goals might give way to a new market condition or reality requiring re-engineering. The validity of the vision will depend largely on the external environment based on market conditions.

In light of the widespread importance for vision, it requires a closer inspection of the mechanics; the importance of what is communicated, and uniformly as important, to clearly communicate every detail of the vision. It must be presented, in such a way, that everyone can accept personal responsibility and translate the vision to his or her job function within the organization. At the end of the day, all visions must translate into hard work. The formidable task is to assist others to see the vision. It was once said, "New infantryman to commanding officer; 'Sir where is my foxhole?' The officer's quick reply, "You are standing on it; just throw the dirt out!"

In the broader discussion of, and one of the most fundamental tenets to great leadership, is simply vision. The premise of responsibility is to shape the message followed closely by the communication and execution of the meaning to potentially unite in the pursuit of accomplishing the goals. In today's complex and changing environment, it becomes even more critical that all employees understand the vision of what the organization is trying to accomplish. The world has become more competitive and volatile; faster technology change, greater international competition, and smaller market share. By extension, the organizations that are best positioned with an expressed compelling vision will have the competitive edge to compete in the global economy.

One example, "Hewlett, Packard, Merck, Johnson, and Watson didn't sit down and ask, 'What business values would maximize our wealth?' or 'What philosophy would look nice printed on glossy paper?' or 'What beliefs would please the financial community?' No! They articulated what was inside them-what was in their gut, what was bone deep. It was as natural to them as breathing." It's not what they believed as much as how they believed it and how consistently their organization lived it.

Visionary leaders can shape not only personal and organizational layers but also entire nations. In the hundreds of acts of leaders communicating vision, none other than the "I Have a Dream" speech imposed heights of inspiration, passion, and motivation. Martin Luther King, a pastor of a Baptist church in Montgomery, Alabama and one of the principle leaders of the United States civil rights movements made national notoriety, when he helped mobilize the black boycott of the Montgomery bus system in 1955. He organized the boycott, after Rosa Parks refused to give up her seat on the bus to a white man. The 382-day boycott led the bus company to change its regulations and the Supreme Court declared such segregation unconstitutional. In August 1963, Martin Luther King led an enormous civil rights march in Washington, D.C. and delivered his famous vision, the I Have a Dream speech predicting a day when the promise of freedom and equality for all would become a reality in America.

The dream pierced the hearts and minds of the American culture touching people's inner aspirations. The message resonated with most who heard it. On that given day, the masses became something much larger than themselves ultimately stretching the American social fabric. On July 2, President Lyndon B. Johnson had no choice but to sign into law the Civil Rights Act of 1964.

From the uttered vision of a once obscure pastor, the will power to overcome the discriminatory practice of employment and the culmination of segregation in theaters, restaurants, public transportations, swimming pools, and libraries were banned. As freighting as it was with a narrow opportunity, with measured improvement toward political reform and social change, life's challenges were defeated because of the conventional wisdom of an individual, enterprise or government based on purpose. Vision is more than just words; such events are shaped by the conspicuous public figure of the leader who is found in the corridors, offices, and public areas in which they lead. Albert Schweitzer, a recipient of the Nobel Peace Prize in 1952 wrote, "In everyone's life, at some time, our inner fire goes out. It is then burst into flame by an encounter with another human being. We should all be thankful for those people who rekindle the inner spirit."

Reaching back through corporate history, James Burke of Johnson & Johnson made a decision to pull the poison-laced Tylenol product off the shelves because it was the morally right thing to do. One of his greatest leadership moments was in the corporate boardroom with the 20 executives. He held his executives accountable to the mission and vision of the company credo that was penned by R.W. Johnson: "We hold these truths to be self-evident" of which one of the higher duties was "mothers and all others who use our product." James was concerned that the company employees viewed the credo or vision as an antiquated document no longer having relevance or importance. Subsequent meetings were held throughout the world to restore the importance of the mission and vision as a living document. The credo was of a scale of significance. It allowed for the decision to be made to protect all who used Johnson and Johnson products by pulling it from store shelves. The $100 million of lost earnings were subordinate to the overall mission. Vision is the basis of all decision-making. It is the moral compass of how people behave to move forward with success.

In all the analysis and general theory, leaders must include an enormous variety and range of communication to keep the vision flowing. Unlike other resources, a shared vision actually increases in value as it is shared to benefit everyone in the organization. In the fundamental nature, it creates the awareness of why people are in business and keeps the organizational eye focused on what's most important. Communicating the vision is one of the most important elements of leadership. The wrong message can be very problematic.

The example of British Antarctic explore Sir Ernest Shackleton (1874-1922) placed this advertisement in London newspapers in 1900 in preparation for the National Antarctic Expedition, which subsequently failed to reach the South Pole. *Men wanted for hazardous journey. Small wages, bitter cold, long months of complete darkness, constant danger, and safe return doubtful, honor and recognition in case of success.*

It is not enough to assume a written vision will produce anything of value. Vision requires follow-through and tenacity. Presumably, the real work is to strike a balance between the message and possibilities of vision. Subsequent to an inspirational and emotional connection, people need to have a sense of direction and understanding to achieve the vision. The process of communication is not a simple or smooth one, nor can it be done only once. Communicating organizational vision a few times at company meetings and posting a few nicely framed copies will have little to no merit or significant value.

Based on my experience, usually only fifty percent of the group is "Listening" to what is being said, of the fifty percent listening, only fifty percent "Care" about what is being said, and of the fifty percent who care, only fifty percent "Translate" the vision to real work, and of those who can translate only fifty percent take "Action". The main concept requires

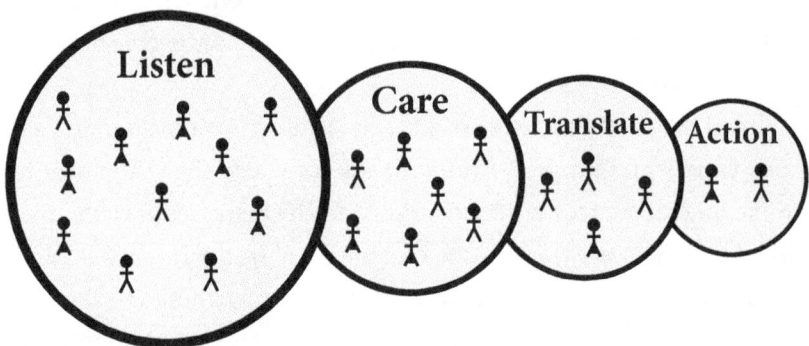

leaders to find a broadening and deepening base of people from which they can motivate. In real meaning, one has captured less than 10 percent of the organizational core workforce. One has to wonder and ask, "What are the other 90 percent of the workforce doing?"

The ability to communicate is an extremely important skill for a leader-second only to such character traits of honesty and integrity. Skillful leaders take advantage of the numerous opportunities to communicate vision and build a culture around correspondence. Jack Welch said, "Setting the mission is top management's responsibility. A mission cannot be delegated to anyone except the people ultimately held accountable for it." Moreover, Jack taught that he harped on his vision and mission constantly at every meeting large and small. Every decision or initiative was linked to the mission and vision. The Sioux proverb says, "If you do not know where you are going, any path will take you there." It is the leader's job to communicate vision; no one else can fulfill this need.

Closely allied to this view of potential and indispensability of vision is the conscious effort to communicate. Phil Knight's, CEO and Founder of Nike, story is legendary. I learned and gained an appreciation of the great Nike culture and permanent tradition, by spending eight years consulting and being taught in the way in which those who activated and channeled the vision. When most people think of Nike, they think of the superstar athletes Bo Jackson, Michael Jordan, Pete Sampras, and many others. Their campus is filled with retired jerseys, shoes, and rackets that tell personal history of the honored competitors. Nike has created a legacy through the common threads of a shared vision. Senior executives have rightly emphasized their ability by spending great amounts of time serving as "corporate storytellers."

Leadership swings on the doors of a conscious and calculated effort to develop and implement hinges of a clear and concise vision into a structure for performance. Without free movement of purpose, all other leadership capabilities close.

Chapter 3

Formal and Informal Authority

In academic discussions, there is a broad understanding about the various forms of power. Underlying the understanding between the ends of power and the choice is an evermore serious question: What is the most appropriate form of power? The traditional measure of one's power is reflected in the inter-personal relationships of the leader/boss and the follower/subordinate. The article, *The Bases of Social Power* describes different kinds of "social power" in the extent to which leaders use forms of control including reward power (the capacity to reward), coercive power (the capacity to punish), legitimate power (consequence of title or position), and expert power (consequence of knowledge).

Recently, there are new lines drawn between two forms

of power "hard power" and "soft power." Joseph Nye, Professor of International Relations at the Kennedy School of Government at Harvard University suggests, "Power is the ability to influence the behavior of others to get the outcomes one wants." Furthermore, Joseph positions various ways to affect behavior; "you can coerce others with threats," or you can "induce them with payment," or the other option is to "attract and co-opt them to want what you want."

At the opposite ends of the leadership spectrum are the corporate bullies, totalitarians, autocrats, and dictators and on the other end are those who integrate and homogenize the human needs of followers and subordinates yet balance the needs and purpose of the enterprise. The sources of power can be as mysterious as the inspiration to an artist or writer.

On the face of leadership, are some tales of bad bosses. The bad boss phenomenon is told in many past and present leaders. Exactly who are these leaders who justify their poor behavior based on their position of "hard power?" Manhattan hotelier Leona Helmsley who was known as the Queen of Mean bullied the hotel staff and often berated the staff and regularly handed out pink slips to anxious workers. She was once quoted as saying, "Only the little people pay taxes." The story of John L. Allbritton, chairman of Riggs Bank was well-known for yelling at executives and firing them over the phone. Or, the story of Bernard J. Ebbers who was on the stand in his own defense pushed fault to the MCI employees for the multibillion-dollar fraud scheme professing he was unaware of the inappropriate dealings.

Underlying this disparity between "hard" and "soft" power, a leader establishes greater influence based on "soft" power. Blaine Lee, the author of, *The Power Principle: Influence with Honor,* positions influential power, "This category suggests that the person you believe is powerful is someone others believe in, someone they honor, someone they respect." This is influential power, the power with people and not over people. Pittacus, who challenged the Athenians general to a single combat in hopes of sparing bloodshed on both sides said, "The measure of a man is what he does with power."

The American story of Nathan Hale, a schoolteacher turned revolutionary officer who valued above all the liberty and preservation of the natural and imprescriptible rights of man. He was caught returning to his regiment with captured information about British troop movements and arrested for treason in the early days of the Revolution. Many such events are shaped by inconspicuous figures rather than by the public figures. Many leaders, as mentioned, are ill suited for leadership and influence because they lack the absolute dedication to the cause that they represent in order to endure exile, captivity, and even death. Nathan Hale's commitment ended in martyrdom.

"He was only twenty-one—rich and promising life lay before him. 'Have you no regrets?' they reportedly asked him, mocking, and demeaning his patriotic fervor. 'Yes, he replied.' 'I regret I have but one life to lose for my country!' He lost his life, but it was given in pursuit of freedom for his children and grandchildren, ancestors or ours. Two generations later, a grandnephew, Edward Everett Hale, who was similarly challenged by the same pious, judgmental functionaries, answered the question this way, demonstrating the legacy that was in his blood: 'I am only one, but I am one; I cannot do everything, but I can do something; what I can do I ought to do, and what I ought to do by the grace of God I shall do.'"

Fundamentally, people need to turn to the first principle of leadership; leadership is a choice rather than a position, title, or status. One can have influential power as a prime power to influence others, which is traced to one's character and competence and a broader enduring respect to governing principles. Such a foundation bring into being some of the profound remarkable leadership stories in history. The theoretical underpinning of leadership is supported on followership.

Colonel Clause Schenk Graf Von Stauffenberg, who at first willingly supported the ideas and philosophies of Hitler, soon grew aware of and understood the need to eliminate Hitler. In his attempt to remove Hitler, it became challenging because of his lack of access to be close to him. In

July 1944, Clause Stauffenberg received a promotion which allowed greater proximity to Hitler. His attempt to remove him was no longer dependent on others, but he could do it himself—he would plant the bomb in his own briefcase.

Kershaw describes the scene: "Hitler had been bent over the heavy oaken table, propped up on his elbow, chin in hand, studying air reconnaissance positions on a map, when the bomb went off—with a flash of blue and yellow flame and an ear-splitting explosion. Windows and doors blew out. Clouds of thick smoke billowed up…Parts of the wrecked hut were a flamed. For a time there was pandemonium." As a result of the attempt, eleven were badly injured and several soon died. Hitler himself had "the luck of the devil." He survived the assassination effort with no more than a few surface wounds. Less than twenty-four hours after the bomb exploded, Stauffenberg and his supporters were placed under arrest and were instantly shot to death.

The Clause Stauffenberg story brings to bear on the atmosphere of power. The influential leader transcends their own needs in place of values and purpose. The whole idea of power is deeply complex when one considers all of the varying forms of power. The extent to how effective a leader is at motivating people to perform and take action depends on the extent to which power is used. In discussing the effects of power, the best form of power is someone others believe in, someone they honor, and someone they respect. This is influential power, the power with people and not over people.

The concepts of power have fertilized the discussions on leadership. Its very uncertainty has allowed individuals to use the different forms in a variety of situations and a range of disciplines. The extent of actual application remains a debate. Of the numerous stories thorough history, the most striking stories are those who on the rise of leadership wielded influential power such in the case of Mahatma Gandhi, Nelson Mandela, Jesus Christ, and Martin Luther King.

In the most practical sense, power is derived from either a formal or informal basis. Formal power is often associated with a social structure providing a legitimate and perceived value of authority. Power is given to individuals in the form of position, title, and status. Social power provides important organized and stable environments from family to corporate configurations. This form of power is very intoxicating and one might associate this power with complete control. Those who possess authority might feel invincible, superior, or strong, and without it, vulnerable, insecure, or weak. It is the principal foundation of any organization. It allows for governments, enterprises, and institutions to operate effectively. Formal power can inspire people to achieve incredible accomplishments or be the destruction of many. Like nuclear power, it can power cities providing light to citizens or be the atomic bomb devastating entire nations. The central identity of informal power is the unique capacity to influence human beings towards a set of needs without the distinction or orientation of social power.

Formal Authority - the source of power to get things done through position, title, and status; authority that is given by someone else.

Formal authority is the gauge to control environments and getting things accomplished. In spite of position, title or status, it merely makes one the boss to facilitate work, manage tasks, and own the decision-making process. The linkage consists of direct reports applied to a hierarchy structure that provides greater authority as individuals move higher in the chain of command. Formal authority resides at the top.

Informal Authority - is a position of credibility, character, and influence, authority that has been developed through self.

Simply put, informal authority is someone who has no formal authority; position, title or status over people but has wielding influence to

lead informally without structure. Informal authority rests essentially in the people who are willing to follow based on those they trust.
The conclusion of leadership is the leader-follower relationship, which
draws on the principles outlined in this book.

Through traditional representatives such as Stauffenberg, and others
like him, emerges the profound importance for the lessons in power and
the sharp lines drawn between formal and informal authority. Rarely,
people can draw the lines promoting the idea that every individual has
a choice to become a leader through one's purpose and capacity. It is not
so much about social and hierarchy structure rather it is the moral authority and aptitude behind the individual.

Mahatma Gandhi provides a great example of informal authority that
inspires leadership. I reference him many times throughout this book.
Perhaps he is the finest role model of a principled leader. Richard Attenborough made a movie about his life in 1982. One of the scenes in the
movie captures the essence of leading with honor. It also illustrates what
John Erskine, an English professor meant when he said, "In the simplest
terms, a leader is one who knows where he wants to go, gets up, and goes."

"In the movie, Gandhi is attending a meeting. The prime minister and various other dignitaries sit with him to discuss affairs of state.
All of a sudden, unannounced and without invitation, a runner bursts
into the room. He is bloody, dirty, out of breath. He exclaims that fighting has broken out in one of the provinces that people are dying in the
streets and something must be done. He stands, breathing hard, await-
ing an official response.

The individual responses of the officials at the meeting provide an
intriguing study in leadership. Gandhi says nothing, but quietly pushes
back his chair and slips on his sandals. In contrast, the prime minister
responds loudly, pounding his fist and informing everyone that he pre-
dicted this and that troops must be sent to the provinces. Someone from
the military replies that there are not enough personnel to have troops

in every province. Someone from the treasury adds that the government could never afford that number of troops anyway. The whole idea seems, to him, impractical.

Meanwhile Gandhi moves toward the man who has brought the terrible news and begins asking questions: What is happening in the province? How long has the fighting been going on?

The prime minister makes another declaration. Someone else responds defensively, reactively. In the background Gandhi and the messenger move toward the still-open door. When the prime minister realizes that Gandhi is about to leave, he jumps to his feet, informing Gandhi that the meeting is not over. 'Where are you going?' he asks. 'I am going to the province,' Gandhi replies.

Gandhi travels the distance to the province and learns more along the way. Civil war has erupted in his own land. His beloved people— Hindu and Muslim—are fighting, killing one another. When he arrives, it is worse than he has been told. The fighting escalated. Blood is literally flowing in the streets. Women, children, and entire families are being slaughtered. His great heart nearly breaks. He has invested so much in these people in an attempt to help them see things differently, to value their differences instead of being threatened by them. Yet despite his efforts, things are falling apart. Gandhi surveys the scene and determines that he will not eat until the fighting has stopped. He stays in the province and begins to fast.

The word begins to spread in the province that Gandhi, the great soul who is their teacher, their leader, their friend, has arrived and has embarked on a fast. The fighting rages on. Gandhi stays in the province. He goes a day without food. Then two days, three days, four days pass. The fifth, sixth, seventh, and eighth days come and go. On the ninth day, somewhere in the province a surprising incident occurs. Somebody, weapon in hand, makes a decision. Knowing his beloved leader is dying, he makes a personal decision not to fight, and throws down his weapon.

On the tenth day, someone else makes a similar decision. A ground swell of resistance mounts among those who are sick of the bloodshed, sick of the fighting. Finally, thirteen days after Gandhi arrived in the province, someone comes to him with some grape juice and bread and asks if he will eat, because the fighting has finally stopped.

Years later, someone approached Gandhi, wanting to know how they could develop the kind of power that had enabled him to influence literally millions of his own countrymen. The reply: 'I claim to be no more than an average man with less than average ability. I am not visionary. I claim to be a practical idealist. Nor can I claim any special merit for what I have been able to achieve with laborious research. I have not the shadow of a doubt that any man or woman can achieve what I have, if he or she would make the same effort and cultivate the same hope and faith.'"

Mahatmas Gandhi liberated 300 million people from repression in India. He held no position, title, or status. He had no formal authority. He held no political office. Consequently, Gandhi's informal authority eventually became stronger than the British government's formal authoritative power in India. He challenged the British controlled country and brought them to government reform. His influence and power was driven from his core character, which is rooted in attributes "BE," and the environment to change the political fabric of India.

Leaders who behave according to their core character and purpose, grounded in principles of human conduct, imbue their followers in bringing about a significant influence because of what takes place to those who choose to follow. This moral authority is transformed into power to accomplish significant change, which otherwise was originally inconceivable as a range of possibility. In the analysis and the range of leadership theory, the conclusion is not defined only by certain attributes, competencies, and qualities such as mental and physical strength or discernable patterns of conduct, but also by the environment and circumstances surrounding the opportunity.

Many of the storied role models have been widely noted as traditionally average people who accepted extraordinary challenges to make a difference in society. Historically, they have been the rule and not the exception. The key measures of their ability to lead are carried out through the combination of traits, circumstances, and skills to influence followers or subordinates who are motivated to conform based on their respect of credibility and legitimacy in the leader, which is the ultimate test of authority and to the accumulation of considerable influence. In sharper form, they rose to the occasion and acted upon the opportunity rather than being lost in the maze of perceived insecurities and deficiencies of formal authority. They broadly carried the demands that were placed upon them in accordance with the needs of the followers. In the most pronounced outwardly appearance, what they did determined who they became.

Beyond the theoretical description of authority, Mother Teresa who spent her entire life dedicated to the cause of alleviating the suffering of the poor considered herself as "a pencil in the hand of God. He has not called me to be successful; but to be faithful."

The doors of influence hinge on central characteristics that form an individual. The most basic swing is the character and competence of the individual, which opens the rights for leadership authority. These rights, moreover, often operate in a context of moral principles.

Among the news items of an earlier date was the report of a burglary. The details included incidents, of which are unusual in the literature of crime. The safety-vault of a wholesale house dealing in jewelry and gems was the object of the attack. From the care and skill with which the two robbers had laid their plans, it was evident that they were adept in their disreputable business.

They contrived to conceal themselves within the building and were locked in when the heavily barred doors were closed for the night. They knew that the great vault of steel and masonry was of the best construction and of the kind guaranteed as burglar-proof; they knew also that it contained treasures of enormous value; and they relied for success on their patience, persistence, and craft, which had been developed through many previous, though lesser, exploits in safe-breaking. Their equipment was complete, comprising of drills, saws, and other tools, tempered to penetrate even the hardened steel of the massive door, through which alone entrance to the vault could be affected. Armed guards were stationed in the corridors of the establishment, and the approaches to the strong room were diligently watched.

Through the long night the thieves labored, drilling and sawing around the lock, whose complicated mechanism could not be manipulated even by one familiar with the combination, before the hour for which the time-control had been set. They calculated that by persistent work they would have time during the night to break open the safe and secure the valuables they could carry; then they would trust to luck, daring, or force to make their escape. They would not hesitate to kill if they were opposed. Though the difficulties of the undertaking were greater than expected, the skilled criminals succeeded with tools and explosives in reaching the interior of the lock; then they threw back the bolts and forced open the weighty doors.

What was it that they saw? Drawers filled with gems, trays of diamonds, rubies, and pearls? Such and more they had confidently expected to find and to secure; but instead they encountered an inner safe, with a door heavier and more resistant than the first; fitted with a mechanical lock of more intricate construction than that as which they had worked so strenuously. The metal of the second door was of such superior quality as to splinter their finely tempered tools; try as they would could not so much as scratch it. Their misdirected energy was wasted; frustrated were all their infamous plans.

Character affords no more significance and foundational case of the power of influence than persons who draw much of their strength from the espoused values system of their inner core. In the end, it is the character issue far more than the forces of one's reputation that brought leaders to the front. This is precisely the measure behind the authority. The value in such a story of the vault links one's reputation to the outer door of the treasured-vault and character to the inner portal. Character is the expression of what one has become.

The trend toward broader character development has been noted in the choices one chooses based on principles of human conduct: integrity, fairness, discipline, honesty, accountability, civility, strong work ethic, and other such traits. The decisions people make and the way they behave is what ultimately shapes character. People have incomprehensible latitude in the manner in which they spend time in their thoughts. What one thinks of on a continual basis will influence actions. The actions of their appetites and impulses give measure to their character. People externally radiate what they are internally. The radiation widens the boundaries and influences every person that comes within contact. Character is the most influential possession one can own. It is more important than any asset, knowledge, skill or accomplishment. It provides for leadership strength and it expands the perimeter to influence thousands to follow.

David O. MacKay, said, "Day by day, hour by hour, man builds the character that will determine his place and standing among his associates throughout the ages…more important than riches, more enduring than fame, more precious than happiness is the possession of a noble character. Truly it has been said that grand aim of man's creation is the development of a grand character, and a grand character is by its very nature the product of a probationary discipline."

Some of the many conceptual considerations of character apply to the environment when it is most difficult to stand tall and do what is right, even in the midst of difficult decision-making. Character turns on the central value system in setting in motion the resources of those core values. Few stories have better exemplified the strength and courage of character than the stories of World War II. The classic views of German rescuers, who at the perils of their own lives, did what they thought was the principled thing to do to save Jewish lives.

In the book, *The Hand of Compassion: Portraits of Moral Choice During the Holocaust,* Kristen Renwick Monroe toiled with the ideas of discovering the answers that differentiated the rescuers from the rest.

"What drove these particular individuals?" "What caused them to engage in their moral acts?"

Monroe answered such questions through the stories of the rescuers to explain their motivation. A common thread—perhaps the only common thread are the resources through the beliefs, values, and attitudes that provide strength to do the right thing even in the environment of such heavy consequences.

In the face of behaving appropriately, Margot subordinated directly or indirectly her self interest to the refinement of purpose. Her father was in charge of the General Motors operation in Europe. Her prominence allowed her to be highly educated and to speak many languages. She lived abroad through out Europe, England, Switzerland, and left for Czechoslovakia just before the war. Margot gave voice to saving the lives of the Jewish people.

While living in Holland, she saved many lives. In her quest, she was sent to prison for her efforts. When Monroe interviewed Margot, She asked her, "How did you decide whom to help then?" Margot replied, "Well, I didn't decide. There's no decision…You either help or you don't."

Later on Monroe asked, "So how did you get into the Resistance?" Margot replied, "I don't know how I came. Somebody asked me to help because I knew all these languages and so forth. It's not like you have a particular job with the resistance. You don't get a job. You just do what you think is right. Somebody comes and says, 'Can you hide me?' I know of a women who came and said, 'Oh, God, I'm scared.' I said, 'Come on the couch.' I made a bed for her. Things like that. You help."

The extent of authentic character, as I have defined it, is promoting values in environments when it is most difficult to stand tall and do what is right. Barbara Kellerman, in the book, *Followership*, wrote, "Bystanders observe but do not participate. They make a deliberate decision to stand aside, to disengage from their leaders and from whatever is the group dynamic. This withdrawal is in effect, a declaration of neutrality, which amounts to tacit support for whoever and whatever constitutes status quo."

Character is most profound when the collective effort is present. I have taught the concept of neutrality through a principle of what I label "Conscious Dichotomy."

Anything less than a conscious effort to "A" is a subconscious effort to "B". The subconscious effort to "B" is a declaration of non-support.

Nowhere was the rise of conscious effort more dramatic than those who sacrificed their lives for moral principle. If Margot's decisions were not to assist in the protection of the Jewish people, her non-effort would be in support of Nazi Germany. George Eliot, a mid-19th century poet and lecturer wrote, "What do we live for, if it is not to make life less difficult for each other?" Margot's declaration of, "you just do what you think is right" is a conscious support against the heinous crimes against humanity. Great leaders are not merely bystanders—they act on moral principle.

At great junctures of history, it was a matter of a choice to be a leader such as the achievements of all others whose stories are never told. The emergence of leadership starts by making the decision to become a leader and aligning life's purpose built on core values. The process is not a transactional one rather the intersection development of character and competence that enable leaders to influence change. In fact, many such giants were a product of, and remained true to the direction, in which they not only represented their own life but also influenced others. Richard Evans, past president of Rotary International, asked the hard question: "In what direction are you headed? If you don't change direction, you'll end up where you are going...For life moves in one direction only—and each day we are faced with the actual set of circumstances, not with what might have been, not with what we might have done, but with what is, and with where we are now—and from this point, we must proceed; not from where we were, not from where we wish we were—but from where we are."

In retrospect, one can draw parallels of direction from lofty figures who tower over such landscapes as Admiral Peary, who was trying to reach the North Pole. He found his position and drove his team of dogs northward in hopes of reaching his goal only to discover later that he was many more miles south, from his intended destination, and farther than he was at the start. He shortly realized that he was on a giant ice flow that was drifting southward. So it is with many in an attempt to develop a strong character anxiously engaged with vast effort, failing to develop because of not being in the direction of absolute truth.

It was said of Rome, at her pinnacle, that men did not love Rome because she was great, but Rome was great because men loved her. Character will be developed through the respect and love in the convergence and implementation of true and correct principles lived on a daily basis. People augment character as they ascend the dysfunctional mores and social patterns of today, which are the subject of perhaps hundreds of articles and story lines.

Day-by-day, hour-by-hour, one builds the character that will determine their place and standing in their ability to earn the right to have followers. The world knows a great deal about leadership however, at the foundation of many and extended written materials, many are encumbered to determine how to make sense of leader/follower relationships.

The equilibrium rests in the leaders ability to live up to core values and meet the needs of the followership. In the grand scale of leadership, the balance of conditions is in the reshaping and realigning of the follower's value system to purpose and sharpened set of goals, desires, and expectations of the leader. Leaders rise and have direct appeal with those who follow. In stark contrast, true leaders have followers and not subordinates. There is a vast difference; followers are following based on their own volition and subordinates are based on obligation.

Followers are every bit as important as the leader. Robert Kelley's book, *The Power of Fellowship,* takes on a new idea of legitimacy from the leader followership identification relationship. The concept is centered on the genuine concern for, "what it feels like to be a follower." Kelley's attention is in the exemplary follower. They are the one's who perform with "intelligence, independence, courage, and a strong sense of ethics."

In the quest to discover the perfect follower, Kelly turns to Hermann Hess, who in *Journey to the East* depicts a group on a journey. The central character is a person by the name of Leo. He is viewed as the great servant by the rest of the group. He performs the most menial tasks. He does the cooking and the cleaning and manages all of the other tasks based on his role and job function. In spite of his responsibilities, Leo goes about his duty with complete support. Unexpectedly, he disappears and the tasks that were once well cared for are now left unattended, which impacts the rest. "The group, it turns out, cannot continue on its own without their servant and supposed follower, Leo. The journey is abandoned."

One might interpret the story as Leo being the real leader. But Kelly saw it entirely different. He saw Leo not as the leader but as an "exemplary follower, the kind of person that no leader or group can succeed without."

In review of the importance of followership, one might ask, who is more important, the people who perform the tasks of production; provide the customer service, or the bosses who manage them?

Ira Chaleff's book, *The Courageous Follower,* captures the ability to bring followers and leadership "into parity." Great followers support and carry out the responsibility. They "contribute to leadership development." Great leaders support and create conditions of success for their followers.

Followership is of equal importance to that of leadership. Organizations must not only spend resources in the development of leadership, but also followership skills. The very best followers are anything but expendable rather mission critical. They are anxiously engaged in promoting the mission, vision, and values of the organization and serving the best interest of all the stakeholders' needs. Coupled together, they form a relationship. One cannot have the one without the other.

Clearly, the first and most important strategic position leaders must take is to align the relationships between leader and follower. The very nature of the discussion of leadership and followership suggest a movement towards the relation of the two. Leadership requires a relationship of two or more people, one leader and one follower, or one follower and one leader.

George Orwell published a story about a British police officer stationed in Burma, when the British were the formal authoritative power. "Responsible for maintaining law and order, the officer was held in contempt by the Burmans for whom he was officially responsible, which further fueled his belief that 'imperialism was an evil thing.' Inexperienced and still ignorant of the ways of the world, he detested his job, the more so because the town where he was situated seethed under British rule.

One day the young officer, who was Orwell, received a call. A few miles away an elephant that was normally tame had briefly gone wild (as elephants apparently are disposed to do), ravaging the bazaar and killing one man. The expectation was that Orwell would come immediately, take charge, and somehow repair the situation.

As soon as Orwell appeared on the scene, a mass of Burmans gathered, roused by the prospect that he, now toting a rifle under his arm, would provide entertainment by killing the elephant. But, Orwell was not inclined to shoot. Moreover, by the time he, along with rapidly growing crowd, had located the elephant, it had returned to its normally peaceful state, 'tearing up bunches of grass, beating them against his knees to clean them, and stuffing them into his mouth.'

Orwell writes that as soon as he saw the elephant, he 'knew with perfect certainty' that he ought not to kill it. Not only was it a serious matter to kill a working elephant, but also Orwell makes clear that he did not have the stomach to shoot an animal now appearing 'no more dangerous than a cow.' His plan was to make certain that the elephant was once again calm, and then to go home.

But the crowd right behind and in hot pursuit had grown—now it was some two thousand strong. 'All happy and excited over this bit of fun,' they were convinced that the elephant should and would be shot, and that it was Orwell who should and would be the shooter. In this instant, it seemed to Orwell the situation had changed. Now there was no choice:

he had to kill the elephant. Although the one in the position of authority, the one in possession of the large rifle, Orwell felt powerless, completely unable to stop, 'two thousand wills, pressing me forward, irresistibly.'"

This idea takes on a form of legitimacy from complex issues of formal and informal authority. The person with the formal authority and the influence to enforce the rules of law was unable to do what he wanted to do. On the other hand, those who were without the formal authority received their wishes by having Orwell shoot the elephant. Overtime, the voices of the informal authority bent the will of the superior authoritative voice.

Nowhere is this kind of influence displayed more profoundly than examples of leaders who represent their own needs and interests and not of those they lead. The story of the former leader of World Bank, Paul Wolfowitz, illustrates the power of the informal authorities voice to bend the power of the formal authority. Prior to his call to serve, as President of World Bank, Paul served as Deputy Secretary of Defense under the leadership of Donald Rumsfeld. A conversation was made public that he was giving a promotion and a pay increase to a prior employee, who was a woman with whom he was having a personal relationship. The subordinates, men, and women throughout the entire organization demand that he resign. The *Financial Times* called the situation a "staff rebellion."

The World Bank Group Staff Association issued a statement for Wolfowitz to resign which read: "The president must acknowledge that his conduct has compromised the integrity and effectiveness of the World Bank Group and has destroyed the staff's trust in his leadership. He must act honorably and resign." They requested to the board that they take "clear and decisive actions to resolve this crisis," which was damaging the bank's "credibility and authority to engage" and furthermore "declared that the controversy over his conduct was undermining their work." Weeks after the story broke, those who were subordinates and followers forced Wolfowitz's resignation.

The widespread recognition of power does not only reside in leadership but also in the followership, which transcends time, culture, ethnicity, and all group entities. In many areas of the relationship between leaders and followers, the answers have not yet come and only are the questions beginning to be asked. The subject of formal and informal authority continues to encumber thought leaders and practitioners of today.

Some of the names branded on the pages of history are those individuals who brought actual change through the forum of informal authority. Blaine Lee, in the book, *The Power Principle*, shares Mahatma Gandhi's story. "In an attempt to stop Gandhi and his crusade from freedom; the British government imprisoned the Indian leader. Their move backfired, however, as Gandhi was perceived as a martyr his cause continued to grow. They cracked down in India, implementing and enforcing stricter laws against the native people, yet support for Gandhi's mission remained unhindered. Finally the British government invited him to come to England to attend the Round Table Conference, and perhaps to speak before the House of Commons, the lower house of Parliament.

When Gandhi arrived at the great hall where the historic meeting was to take place, a swarm of curious reporters, eager to catch a glimpse of the famous leader, gathered, poised to encounter the man. What they saw surprised them. They assumed he would be charismatic, striking, and powerful, but instead he appeared small and weak. He was dressed in the simple robes of his people. The press wondered aloud as to the source of this power. He held no political office, had no great wealth. Perhaps he was a magician with words. They waited to hear what he had to say.

Gandhi came up to the front of the hall and approached a bare podium. He stood behind it and began his remarks to the members of the Parliament. He spoke out of the abundance of his great heart, describing the plight of the Indian people. He explained the evils of British rule and the need for home rule in India. It was to this cause he had dedicated his life. He made a soft-spoken yet bold call for England to leave India."

He went on to speak for over two hours outlining his vision of a free nation. He did not dwell on the oppressive nature imposed by the British government. He did not focus on the atrocities, pain, and humiliation inflicted on the Indian people rather he spoke of the opportunities of what could be.

At the conclusion of his remarks, a conversion took place in the hall of the meeting. The very people who imprisoned him and enacted laws to control him stood to their feet and gave him a standing ovation. "Who was this man," they inquired.

To answer such a question, Eknath Easwaran, in his book *Gandhi The Man*, describes Gandhi; "There was nothing unusual about the boy Mohandas Karamchand Gandhi, except perhaps that he was very, very, shy. He had no unusual talents, and went through school as a somewhat less than average student: self-conscious and serious, deeply devoted to his parents, and only vaguely aware on anything outside the quiet sea-side town of his birth."

Gandhi writes, "I used to be very shy and avoided all company. My books and my lessons were my sole companion. To be at school at the stroke of the hour and to run back home as soon as the school closed—that was my daily habit. I literally ran back, because I could not bear to talk to anybody. I was even afraid lest anyone should poke fun at me."

Sterling W. Sill, in his book, *Leadership*, extends congruency to the foundational precepts concerning the nature of principles: "Imagine what it would mean in the world if all of the present-day leaders of nations had that kind of integrity. What if we could depend on their word in any situation? What if trust and confidence were the foundation of every relationship? In trustworthiness, Gandhi excelled. Everyone understood he was absolutely honest, that he could be trusted, that his motives were right. When Gandhi said something, everyone knew exactly what he meant. Millions trusted Gandhi; millions learned from him, multitudes counted themselves as his followers. Strangely enough, only a few ever attempted to do as he did. Gandhi's greatness lay in doing what everybody could but does not do."

Robert K. Greenleaf, the previous director of management research at AT&T, has embraced the thought that people will generously follow leaders who have proven themselves as trusted servants. He said, "A new moral principle is emerging which holds that the only authority deserving one's allegiance is that which freely and knowingly granted by the led to the leader in response to, and in proportion to, the clearly evident servant stature of the leader. Those who choose to follow this principle will not casually accept the authority of existing institutions. Rather they will freely respond only to individuals who are chosen as leaders because they are proven and trusted as servants. To the extent that this principle prevails in the future, the only truly viable institutions will be those that are predominantly servant-led."

Amidst all the leadership theory ambiguity the ultimate question rises up to the front, who is eligible for leadership? The foundational cornerstone of such a concept is the choice of leadership. The broader and decisive question is found in the leadership framework of what a leader needs to "Know" (Knowledge), "Do" (Skill-Sets), and "Be" (Attributes) to influence with honor. (See leadership chapter)

What Mahatma Gandhi had was far more influential than a supreme intellectual mind or political prowess rather he had an absolute resolve for the truth that carried his followers in front of all the challenges. He simply washed over and around the narrow boundaries of leadership power and acted on pure conviction and honor. Gandhi said,

I am not a visionary. I claim to be a practical idealist.
I have not the shadow of a doubt than any man or
woman can achieve what I have, if he or she would
make the same effort and cultivate the same hope and faith.

The servant leader relationship sets off in people's minds and hearts an authentic necessity to follow someone who addresses the needs and hopes of the followership. What can be said broadly of leadership? It remains to only ask what is the purpose, if it is not for the support of others? As long as this is the case, the decisive success is trust. In wake of such stormy or tranquil circumstantial weather, people need to follow an enduring leader in whom they trust.

One of the most devastating attacks on United States soil was the terrorist attack on the World Trade Center. The Mayor of New York City was none other than Rudolph Giuliani. His popularity was unfavorable and prior to the attack on September 11, 2001 a poll was taken which reflected only a "32 percent" acceptance rating.

Tying back the book's pages of leadership the great event theory was made obvious. Shortly after the attack on the iconic World Trade Center, Mayor Giuliani became a hero. He performed commendably in the most difficult situations. Nine days after the attack an editorial in the *New York Times* read: "He moves about the stricken city like a god. People want to be in his presence. They want to touch him. They want to praise him. The governor defers to him. The president seems somehow inadequate beside him. He is not only respected, but revered. And not only revered, but loved."

There is an outpouring of need for followers to have a leader they can turn to for support and comfort. The true leader, in the midst of chaos, is to create stability for all those they have responsibility. Who better to calm one's fears than the reassurance of their leader.

One of the most interesting stories of trust is that of Alexander the Great, King of Macedon and King Darius III of Persia. King Darius had offered 1000 talents to anyone who would kill Alexander. Alexander fell very ill, with pneumonia, and was lying on his deathbed. All the physicians presupposed that in the event that Alexander could not be cured that they would be held accountable for his death of poisoning and accepting Darius's bribe. But there was one who accepted to treat Alexander with medicine. Philip a long time friend from childhood was willing to help. As historian H. A. Guerber writes:

"When the fever was at its worst, [Philip] said he hoped to save the king by means of a strong medicine which he was going to prepare.

Just after Philip went out to brew this potion, Alexander received a letter, which warned him to beware of his physician, as the man had been bribed by the Persian king, Darius III, to poison him.

After reading the letter, Alexander slipped it under his pillow, and calmly waited for the return of his doctor. When Philip brought the cup containing the promised remedy, Alexander took it in one hand, and gave him the letter with the other: Then, while Philip was reading it, he drank every drop of the medicine.

When the physician saw the accusation, he turned deadly pale, and looked up at his master, who smilingly handed back the empty cup. Alexander's great trust in his doctor was fully justified; for the medicine cured him, and he was soon able to go on..."

This classical view has yielded the power for trust to be present. Leadership effectiveness turns on the ability to be trusted which activates all other skills—it breeds followership to commit to the one in charge. True followers respond naturally to trust. Alexander extended trust, which inspired trust in his follower built on consistent behavior in a way that exemplifies the values and ideals that are shared by both parties. Trust is only extended to those who are deserving of trust.

The more the character is developed; the power to build and influence critical mass will be exponential and the influence cycle continues. This process is by no means mechanical rather the essence of the power is in meeting the needs and motivation of the followers. One must build an impenetrable foundation of Knowledge, Skill-Sets, and Attributes in order to establish self-influence. Subsequent to the capability of strong character and self-influence, the bandwidth of influence expands as it reaches into the gradient levels of followership.

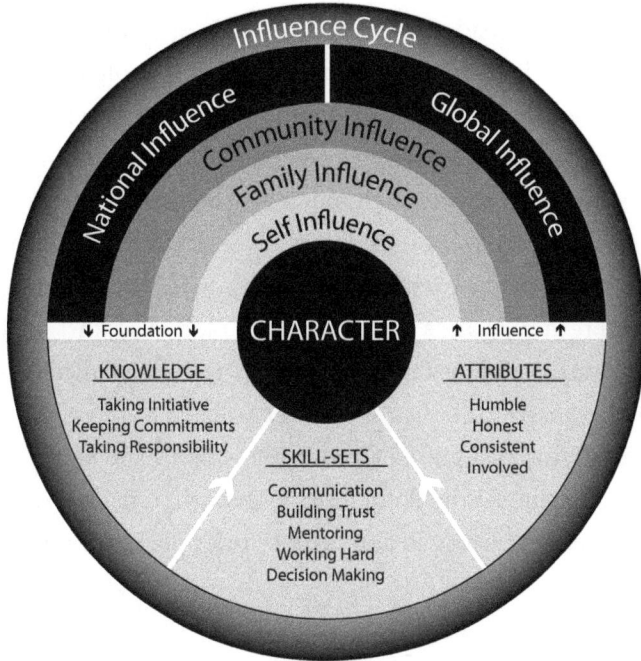

The question customarily is how does one become a trusted servant? Robert K. Greenleaf wrote, "You have a dream you show others the way. You have a sustaining spirit, you listen, and you empathize. You believe that the typical person-immature, stumbling, inept, lazy is capable of great dedication and heroism if he is wisely led." In comparison to a number of formidable powers of Roman and Egyptian emperors and pharaohs leading with no connection to the needs of those they led.

The extent of actual social change in the cases of Mahatma Gandhi, Martin Luther King, Nelson Mandela, and Jesus Christ was most profound because of the relationship of leader and follower. They did not suffer the fraud of leadership rather influenced based on their deep conviction to serve those they led. The relationship of manager and subordinate is much like the contrast of the roles master and slave. A different relationship exists between leader and follower, by in large making the leader as the servant, because it is about the people and not task orientation.

One of the ties to history is the story of Abraham Lincoln who embodied the servant leader role. In a plea to hear more about the man Lincoln, a tribal chief in Russia's Caucasus region wrote to Leo Tolstoy: "...you have not told us a syllable about the greatest general and greatest ruler of the world. We want to know something about him. He was a hero. He spoke with a voice of thunder, he laughed like the sunrise and his deeds were strong as the rock and as sweet as the fragrance of roses... He was so great that he even forgave the crimes of his greatest enemies and shook brotherly hands with those who plotted against his life. His name was Lincoln and the country in which he lived is called America... Tell us of that man."

The most powerful pulse of leadership is that leadership is a choice. Furthermore, leaders throughout history operated from an essential positive purpose either by formal authority or informal authority.

Chapter 4

Emotional Intelligence

For many decades, there has been an overwhelming emphasis placed on ascertaining certain aspects of intelligence. Intelligence creates a predictive model to project a significant degree of professional and personal success. In short, the system is built to address success. A score is derived from the standardized tests placing the subject into a mathematical curve. The customary throngs of tests will measure logical reasoning, problem solving, spatial learning, verbal, and written skills, and a myriad of other intelligent quotient (IQ) measures.

With the design of the IQ system, how is it remotely possible that someone with such high intelligence do something so illogical and irrational as to throw adult tantrums? The answer to such a thorny question is a lack of emotional intelligence. It is however, a vital function that requires diligent effort, careful planning, and effective use of quality tools. It is important to develop a constant mind-set in each leader that emotional intelligence is essential.

There is nothing more important, there is nothing more significant, there is nothing more ennobling, there is nothing more critical in all the learning of leadership development than controlling one's emotions. Emotional immaturity is a growing, vile and destructive behavior. It reaches out in ways that destroys those who participate in such actions.

Daniel Goleman, in his book, *Emotional Intelligence,* says, "IQ offers little to explain the different destinies of people with roughly equal promises, schooling, and opportunity. When ninety-five Harvard students from the classes of the 1940's—a time when people with a wider spread of IQ were Ivy League schools than is presently the case—were followed into middle age, the men with the highest test scores in college were not particularly successful compared to their lower-scoring peers in terms of salary, productivity, or status in their field. Nor did they have the greatest life satisfaction, nor the most happiness with friendships, family, and romantic relationships."

Emotional Intelligence (EQ) is outside the margins of intellect. One can be very intelligent and be emotionally immature. In the book, *Emotional Intelligence 2.0,* "There is no known connection between IQ and EQ; you simply can't predict EQ based on how smart someone is."

Unfortunately, and sadly enough, people see dysfunctional lives in some of the brightest and most capable people scoring high on the IQ curve. High IQ does not prevent dysfunction and many lives are destroyed and relationships ruined because of poor social skills, abrasiveness, and ill-mannered behavior. Intelligent quotient tests serve a purpose in predicting educational projections however; they are very insufficient and have limitations in measuring one of the greatest gifts in human development of emotional maturity.

Despite the importance of emotional intelligence, most people are not skilled let alone have ever heard about the concept of how to deal with private and public emotions. Individuals are hired into a workforce with many skill-sets of writing, problem solving, analytics, and other valuable skills, but not the ability to manage emotions.

In the landscape of the almost barren theory of emotional intelligence, Travis Bradberry and Jean Greaves additionally write, "Emotional Intelligence (EQ) is your ability to recognize and understand emotions in yourself and others and your ability to use this awareness to manage your behavior and relationships." As the idea matures, emotional control must be stronger than the physical appetites to behave based on impulse driven by pure emotion.

"There's an old Chinese proverb that says, 'Give a man a pole, and he'll catch a fish a week. Tell him what bait to use, and he'll catch a fish a day. Show him how and where to fish, and he'll have fish to eat for a lifetime.' The flip side to the proverb is that the man or woman without a pole, without bait, and without knowledge of the how and the where runs a serious risk of famine. Similarly, emotionally ignorant people with little understanding of how and where emotions affect their lives will have an exceedingly difficult time reeling in success."

"On the other hand, those who use the right tools and strategies for harnessing their emotions put themselves in a position to prosper. That same truth applies to individuals, organizations, and even entire countries." For many reasons, not the least of which, leadership fails because the focus is placed on intellect as opposed to emotional feelings. The mature leader pays attention to both the Intelligent Quotient and Emotional Quotient. The key is to understand how to use both horizontally in all areas of life and vertically to intersect them for the greatest opportunity to influence others. Aristotle said, "Anyone can become angry—that is easy. But to be angry with the right person, to the right degree, at the right time, for the right purpose, and in the right way—this is not easy."

In all human interaction, even in the most tangential relationships, emotional maturity becomes a hologram of life. Emotional expression is a critical characteristic of self. Every relationship demonstrates how proficient persons are to communicate, commit, follow-through, and listen. The relationship is the supreme test to reflect the level of emotional maturity, or lack thereof. The flow of emotional specifics is to communicate, behave, react, and feel in the appropriate degrees that stream naturally from the point of emotions; behaviors are outwardly signs of emotional maturity. Think about the effect a pebble has on water, when it is tossed into the pond. The very nature of emotions are representative of the tossed pebble to create a ripple effect not only on those they interact rather a cascading influence on all those who are observers of the emotional behavior.

Too many people are given the opportunity to observe from the lectern of life to see others misbehaving. I have come across corporate boardrooms with some of the world's brightest people who are well educated from some of the most notable universities. In spite of their prestigious education, the very nature of IQ was their greatest barrier to create and maintain effective and productive relationships. They were either void of emotion, much like a robot, or emotionally immature, as a child behaving erratically based on impulse. Such individuals are stuck in the weeds by being self-centered and preoccupied with their own thoughts, ideas, and feelings, which obstruct the necessary skills and abilities to work well with others.

Salovey and Mayers tie emotional assessment to the course of action, "The ability to monitor one's own and other's feelings to discriminate among them, and to use this information to guide one's thinking and action." The important capability is to perceive emotions to know how to personally adjust what to say and what to do.

The cluster of leadership skills comprises of emotional awareness and control, which will be immediately apparent in the most visible and consequential aspect of leadership. Leadership capacity and the ability to influence others are directly related to awareness and control over emotions; the leadership picture hangs on such principles. The structure of influence increases to the degree the boundaries of emotional immaturity narrows. When individuals do not understand the appropriate edges, emotions will surface at the most inopportune time highlighting the deficiencies of character, which will only continue to harm those around them. Not until people take note of the importance to control emotions further damaging actions will take place.

The wisdom of "actions speak louder than words" continues the discipline to behave appropriately. The fact of the matter is what people do is a much stronger message as opposed to what they say. People can attempt to explain away poor behavior but regardless of what the explanation is the actual behavior is the current reality. Stephen R. Covey said, "You can't talk yourself out of a problem you've behaved yourself into."

The embarrassment of poor emotions will invariably create a desire to attempt a cover-up of the poor behaviors. What does an individual do and say when there is a moment of emotional immaturity? Invariably, people would hear the old sayings:

"I wasn't acting like myself"
"I don't know what happened"
"I don't know what came over me"
"The devil made me do it"
"I just went crazy"
"You caught me in a weak moment"
"I just couldn't help myself"

The nature of both the array of improvement and commitment to have a better display of behavior by making promises and compliance will further erode the ability to be trusted unless the behavior reflects the improvement and commitment.

The inescapable principle of "Will Power" plays a consequential role in converting self-indulgence into self-control. It is an endowment and a human trait unlike animals that behave based on instincts and set patterns of behavior. In many situations, animals have predisposition to perform and behave a certain way. On the other hand, human beings learn to direct behavior based on experience and knowing right from wrong. The conversion of the endowment is a strong and concrete sense to know how to direct and act for oneself—the ability to reshape and redirect emotions.

Underlying one of the powerful principles is absolute truths—truth that is never changing and remaining constant. Truth transcends culture, time, environment, and circumstance regardless of one's point of view toward right or wrong. The sharp contrasting view points of what is right or wrong operates regardless of what people think is appropriate or inappropriate. Consequences emerge from behavior that are predictable in nature. The simple observation is a cause and effect relationship between behavior and consequence.

Appropriate emotional choices present better outcomes as opposed to inappropriate choices that present worse outcome that are less subjective. Most people have a receptivity to know immediately when emotions are appropriate or inappropriate for the given circumstance and situation; for example, when an adult lashes out in anger towards a seemingly innocent interruption from a young child.

Adults displaying childish and infantile behavior suggests that somehow they are more special and further deserving to act out, which only highlights they have not grown up and incapable resulting in misery and suffering of other people. The most central revealing aspect is how people cope with their problems. In his book, *7 Habits of Highly Effective People*, Stephen Covey says, "Reactive people build their emotional lives around the behavior of others, empowering the weakness of other people to control them. Reactive people are driven by feelings, by circumstances, by conditions, by their environment. Proactive people are driven by values—carefully thought about, selected and internalized values."

The fingertip sensitivity to such thorny behavior is the barbed barrier of denial or lack of awareness—not wanting to own up to the realities of one's actions. People will attempt to justify their actions based on a false perception that it has not hindered their ability to move forward in their careers and it is in the best interest for everyone involved. Ira Chaleff, in the book, *The Courageous Follower,* writes, "Often, however, the leader has been successful because of a less extreme and functional version of this behavior or because of another trait used in tandem with the destructive behavior."

Perhaps the full measure of achievement is recognizing the consequences of poor behavior and how it is destroying and tearing apart relationships, which might be the cause that represents one's life. The unaware leader and immature emotional person have a remitting focus to stay aware and learn their sense of inadequacy that influences all aspects of his or her life. The hallmark ambition is to be self-aware in accurately perceiving feelings and emotions of others and to control emotional needs to actively choose appropriately what to say and do. The eternal quest is personal development which is found within and not without. In the article, *Clustering Competence in Emotional Intelligence* says, "Emotional competencies are not innate talents; rather, they are learned capabilities that must be worked on and can be developed to achieve outstanding performance."

Commonly and ultimately, communication channels highlight emotional intelligence. The key principles of powerful communication are words, sounds or how one says the words—intonation, and most certainly body language. To the realities of the structures of communication, suitable strong and subtle forms convey a greater air of legitimacy to influence people at virtually every level and height of society. The clear and present objective is to communicate clearly and unambiguously and equally respectfully. However, the risk in the structure is the potential lost and muddled message because of emotion, which leads to tremendous confusion and mixed messages. Poor communication is the springboard for anger, resentment, nastiness, and aggressiveness.

The sheer sense of effective communication are the marked characteristics of *Courage* and *Consideration* which is the ability to approach an individual with one's needs, yet balance the conversation to include the needs of others.

The expression of "Courage" represents the head, which is the ability to be honest and confidently communicate one's viewpoint. The strength of courage is found in the convictions of right and wrong despite the pressure and culture that does not support courage to share the truth. The book, *The Courageous Follower,* outlines that most courageous acts go unnoticed. But when the expression of courage is valued the consequences are significant. "…a United States Army field commander who refused to follow his superior's repeated orders to fire back because he believed the position was occupied by other elements of his own army. He was right, and by refusing to comply, he saved his fellow soldiers' lives from "friendly fire." The second act was by the army officers reviewing the incident. They recognized the commander's refusal to obey orders as an act of courage, not insubordination, and rewarded it with a medal."

I want to make perfectly clear the consequences of demonstrating courage are risky and dangerous: subordinates who challenge the superior authority in any way should expect heavy repercussions. I am also not suggesting that leaders are intolerant of feedback and a new perspective. Rather I wish to highlight those who ultimately hold the formal authority traditionally hold the power to punish when one tries to force.

The burning frustration is the inability to be courageous to share the ground truth of realities in fear of damaging the relationship. From a position of a parent child relationship, nurturing and loving parents will share the truth to a child in spite of the stresses and pressure because of the devoted feeling towards the child.

On the other side of the scale of courage, is "Consideration" representing the heart, which is the ability to respect the feelings of others and their viewpoint. The potent need for consideration is people cannot expect to defraud others of their feelings and expect to have influence with them. By not honoring emotions and perceiving the emotions of others, only falsifies the relationship and they will question the intent. Individuals must act and feel with consideration—they must treat others as they expect others to treat them. The calibrated behaviors are those measured in honor and decency in all human interaction. A lack of application destroys the very essence of life; relationships and families are shattered, organizations ruined and societies destroyed. The difficulty lay not simply in understanding the behaviors rather aligning life to the full purpose and standard of existence. Great leaders need to stand on principles of moral identity, set standards, and absolute truth. Leaders with the greatest influence are those who defer their own feelings and needs for those of the other persons.

The towering view for effective communication is a balance between *Courage* and *Consideration* in order to maintain a centerpoint of emotion for both parties. If the communicator is high on "Courage" and low on "Consideration," they appear to be arrogant and bullying. Conversely, if one is high on "Consideration" and low on "Courage," they appear to be weak, insecure, and a pushover.

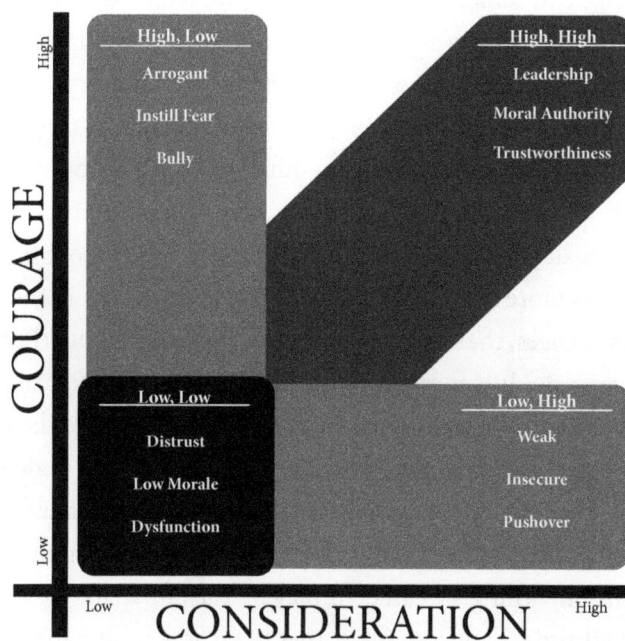

High emotional intelligence draws a line between high Courage and Consideration, which leads to leadership, moral authority, and trustworthiness. In spite of the importance and critical nature of communication, most will tend to violate the principle leading people to fight back and struggle creating dysfunctional relationships. Regrettably, the natural and easiest course of action, the course dictated by pure emotion, is most often the preference.

Appropriate behavior necessitates contemplation and deliberate thought to act with character and meticulous discipline. The appropriate and suitable approach requires emotional maturity and self-control to be aware of the current time and place and how to act with correctness. In theory, emotional intelligence describes the capacity, or a self-perceived ability; to identify, assess, and manage the emotion of others and of oneself.

Viktor Frankl, a Jewish prisoner held in a concentration camp during WWII, discovered that human beings have a choice in their attitudes. He described this as the last freedom. "We who lived in concentration camps can remember the men who walked throughout the huts comforting others, giving away their last pieces of bread. They may have been few in number, but they offer sufficient proof that everything can be taken away from man but one thing: the last of the human freedoms—to choose one's attitude in any given circumstances...to choose one's way."

Charles R. Swindoll, an American writer and clergyman writes, "I realize the impact of attitude on life. Attitude, to me, is more important than facts. It is more important than the past, the education, the money, than circumstances, than failure, than successes, than what other people think or say or do. It is more important than appearance, giftedness or skill. It will make or break a company... a church... a home. The remarkable thing is we have a choice everyday regarding the attitude we will embrace for that day. We cannot change our past... We cannot change the fact that people will act in a certain way. We cannot change the inevitable. The only thing we can do is play on the one string we have, and that is our attitude. I am convinced that life is 10% what happens to me and 90% of how I react to it. And so it is with you… we are in charge of our attitudes."

Given the premise of attitude, it was once said, "That emotionally mature people do not wrap their emotional life around the weakness of others." Strong emotionally mature individuals stand independent of the environment and circumstance—they do not empower others to dictate how they act and behave. It is impractical and absurd to give control and power to others, especially those they do not even know or just met in passing. Other people's dysfunction does not need to be adopted and nurtured feeding one's own emotional context. Life is fashioned out of the ability to act for and not to be acted upon. Despite endless discussions, the clearly drawn set of guiding principles generally end up being ignored, expressing dysfunctional behavior in the fabric of life, whether they are the bosses of Fortune 100 companies or parents in a household; society is virtually defined by reactive and emotional deficiency.

There are countless examples that set the environmental tone because of arbitrary incidents such as being cut off while driving. These and many other events disrupt the logical patterns of behavior. Unfortunately, in the alternatives lay a choice of offense, hurt, and a victim mentality, which alter the emotional context of people's lives. The impulse of irrational choices draws from the worst of human nature rather than the best it has to offer.

The inability to subdue impulsive behavior inflames adult tantrums, long periods of pouting, and rapid mood swings, which detach a leader from the capacity to effectively lead. It is unacceptable and erodes everything that comes in contact with the emotional whirlwind. Leaders are something more: an individual adept in emotional intelligence distinguishes the emotional needs of others that transcend immediate personal needs.

Perhaps the most remarkable characteristic of emotional intelligence is the developing character, which is driven from feelings, thoughts, words, and actions. Leaders must believe in the absolute truth of character, which is deeply rooted, in the espoused core of the individual. The vital idea is human responses flow from the most inner parts of the core value system of thinking, values, and beliefs.

Most character traits of human development are those things that are intangible and most often not immediately valued in leadership. Influential leaders are deeply engaged in kindness, respect, understanding, forgiveness, and the ability to care and mentor. The main influence of trust comes from puzzling out these key pieces of attributes.

In the book, *Mentoring,* Chungliang A. Huang and Jerry Lynch write, "The Shu Ching indicates that the length of a dynasty's governance is in exact proportion to the amount of love, compassion, and kindness showed by its rulers. The ancient story about the legendary kingdom of Shambhala serves as a model of peace and prosperity. The citizens were well taken care of by kind rulers, and in return they were kind, obedient and giving to their rulers. They gave kindness and received the same in return. Confucius speaks of kindness as welcoming and protecting others; it commends what is good in them and forgives their ignorance. When people's dogs are lost, they go out and look for them, yet the people who have lost their hearts do not."

To further develop the theory, A. Huang and Jerry Lynch write, "Loving kindness towards others will create a spirit of unparalleled reciprocity. Followers will become leaders, leaders will become willing followers, jointly overcoming hardship and honoring sacrifice toward mutual goals. With loving kindness, you will win hearts. Through compassion, you will gain loyalty and cooperation."

Not surprisingly, when followership honors the leader, there will be trust and respect for the one they choose to follow. They will willingly and wholeheartedly commit to the common goal and are inspired for the common strength of the team—the strength is larger than the sum of all the individuals. Ray Kroc, who built McDonalds said, "All of us is better than any of us."

Daniel Goleman, in his book, *Working with Emotional Intelligence,* writes the manner in which the leader seems to achieve a balance of influence among people, "For star performance in all jobs, in every field, emotional competence is twice as important as purely cognitive abilities. For success at the highest levels, in leadership positions, emotional competence accounts for virtually the entire advantage…Given the emotional competencies make up two-thirds or more of the ingredients of a standout performance, the data suggests that finding people who have these abilities, or nurturing them in existing employees, adds tremendous value to an organization's bottom line. How much? In simple jobs like machine operators or clerks, those in the top 1 percent with emotional competency were three times more productive by value. For jobs of medium complexity, like sales clerks, or mechanics, a single top emotional competent person was twelve times more productive by value." In the story, "*The Little Prince and the Fox*", the fox shares with the prince the secret, "And now here is my secret, a very simple secret: It is only with the heart that one can see rightly; what is essential is invisible to the eye."

One of my life's most visible and consequential lessons was taught in the context of a baseball diamond, coaching a little league baseball team of 10 and 11-year-old boys. In preparation for the game, I assumed the catchers position and proceeded to warm up the starting pitcher. The rest of the team was on the side of the field loosening up their arms. On many occasions, a stray ball would fly by my head and in a broader landscape of coaching, but with no enduring learning, one boy continued to throw errant balls. Before I knew what was happening next, the ball hit me behind my right ear and knocked me out. What emerged out of the poorly thrown ball was a central lesson on emotional maturity and self-awareness.

After I lay unconscious for many minutes, I saw a group of boys who readily surrender and encircled me with their hands on their knees calling out, "Are you okay Coach Morrison? Are you okay?" The decisive and consistent reaction was to get to my knees and punish the defenseless boy who was directed countless of times to move further away. Here in the moments of weakness my emotions were about to be torn from my values. In a stupor, I visualized myself chasing the young boy, in front of all the spectators straddling him in the saddle of his chest punishing him. The impending separation of emotions from values would have been the biggest mistake; the disharmony would have been converted into the ultimate punishment and the most severe consequence. For a fleeting moment, I remembered my governing values, and regardless of the environment and circumstances, I would behave according to my value system and experience.

The potential storm to assail me in the wrong direction was calmed by the purpose of my value system. In search for a solution to this event, I slowly rose to my feet, placed my arm around the boy, and gradually walked away from the group. I said, "Nathan… you have a strong-arm would you like to pitch an inning in the game?" With tears in his eyes, he hung his head and apologized for not listening. The equilibrium of leadership not only allowed for emotional support, but also instructing on principles of accountability, obedience, and discipline for the balance of leadership.

What happened next pierced me to the core and cemented my understanding of emotional intelligence and self-awareness. No sooner had I arrived home from the game, I answered the phone to the weeping of a parent. He said, "Coach Morrison, this is Nathan's father. Thank you for saving my boy's life tonight. You see, he has no friends and feels that he does not belong. Because of the deep-seeded hurt, he has tried to commit suicide on several occasions. Had you embarrassed him he would have taken his life tonight." He graciously thanked me for my leadership. I was humbled and deeply thankful that, in a moment of potential weakness, I exhibited emotional maturity. In the potential clash between values and responses, the appropriate choice was made based on the purposefulness of life. For many years, Nathan would seek me out earning me the right to lead simply based on an emotional response.

Emotional maturity is about controlling the instinctive tendency to react rather than letting raw emotions prevail. Perhaps one of the unparalleled principles is discipline. The ability to learn from one's and others' experiences differentiating the response and emotion based on time and circumstance. Discipline will enhance the capacity to act appropriately with all types of relationships and difficult situations without being encumbered to figure out proper interaction because the set standard is to act based on principle of human conduct. The task of thinking through the potential responses has been previously determined because of a changeless core set on values.

Some of the most gifted and talented leaders are those who accept responsibility over their own deficiencies. The strength seems to lie in the cause of their life instead of the ambiguity of being something they are not. There are obvious gaps in many people between attitude and discipline, but they cannot expect others to close the gap for them. They cannot blame or fault others for making them unhappy, angry, or miserable. The decisive balance in the condition of mental health is choosing happiness, excitement, and joy. The advice is to carry his or her own weather with him or her. Bishop Fulton said, "Each of us makes his own weather, determines the color of the skies in the emotional universe which he inhabits."

Clearly the most monumental decision of any leader is the choice to be emotionally mature. The rival set of immaturity incurs heavy costs and consequences in terms of employee collaboration, innovation of new products, corporate growth, and execution of strategy. There is a perpetual fleecing of corporate capital because of emotions being expressed without control.

People allow feelings, offenses, and hurt to take center stage in place of those things, which matter most. The broader implication is found in the destroyed relationships, families, marriages, ideas, opportunities, and corporations. The reactive approach is to become offended, when someone merely brushes against him or her because they wear their feelings on their sleeves and are emotionally dependent on others. The conscious effort to respond must be aligned to the purpose of life so they can respond by being responsible. The management philosopher, Peter Koestenbaum said, "The visionary leader thinks big, thinks new, thinks ahead—and most important, is in touch with the deep structure of human conscious and creative potential." The deep human conscience is the crucial aspect in the leadership system.

Travis Bradberry & Jean Greaves in their book, *Emotional Intelligence 2.0,* focus on emotional intelligence as a wide array of competencies and skills that drive leadership performance.

<u>**Self-Awareness**</u> — the ability to read one's emotions and recognize their impact while using gut feelings to guide decisions.

<u>**Self-Management**</u> — involves controlling one's emotions and impulses and adapting to changing circumstances.

<u>**Social Awareness**</u> — the ability to sense, understand, and react to others' emotions while comprehending social networks.

<u>**Relationship Management**</u>— the ability to inspire, influence, and develop others while managing conflict.

I have found that individuals vary in processing emotional information. The ability to process emotions dictates their emotional responses. The responses are manifested in certain behaviors which encompass 4 types of emotional categories. The higher the level of emotional intelligence, the higher the level of maximum performance and contribution.

<u>**Recognize Emotions**</u> — the ability to distinguish all the various emotions expressed in body language, intonation, and word choice. Identifying the emotional environment will help facilitate awareness to respond appropriately.

<u>**Connect Emotions**</u> — the ability to support the wide-ranging emo-

tional needs of one's own emotions and emotions of others through appropriate behavior and language that fit the situation.

Control Emotions — the ability to balance all emotions positive or negative for effective problem solving and creating solutions.

Apply Emotions — the ability to determine the timing and human interaction to inspire and motivate through appropriate emotional application.

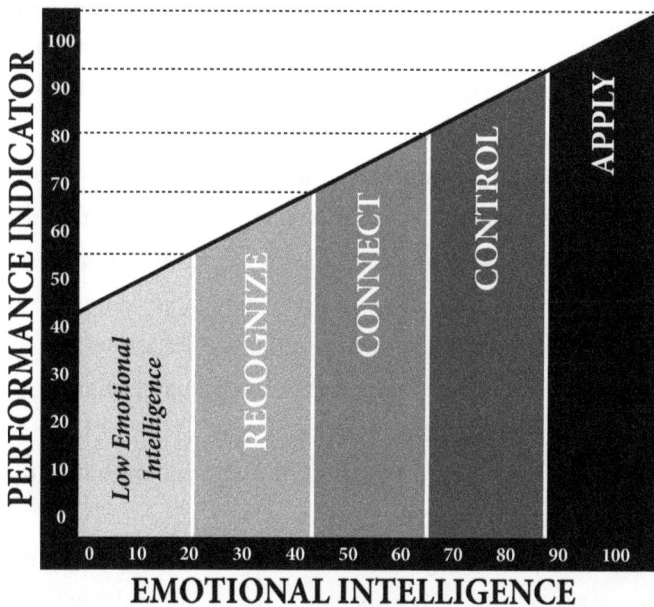

In situations where subordinates, managers, and leaders are deficient in their emotional intelligence, others are burdened to determine the timing of human interaction. Prior to interaction, there is a need to get a pulse as to the mood and emotional state of the other individual. They ask other co-workers the more certain question: "Have you seen him/her this morning?" "What kind of mood are they in?" In each case, one has to plan the timing of their interaction based on mood and attitude forcing the daily structure around the emotional whirlwind of the other person.

Emotional immaturity delivers hammer like blows to any organization and is highly problematic. Invariably, people work around others, perpetually slowing down work, affecting the organizational goals and strategy, which directly, and negatively, impacts the company, such as thought, innovation, and speed for product going to market. It erodes profits and has an extensive list of other damaging and negative results. The extent of the hard stuff balanced exactly with the soft stuff allowed the country to move forward. Instead of demanding vengeance thereby threaten the entire country against the South, Lincoln asked for "malice toward none" and "charity for all." Just as it was for the president of the United States, in such a tenuous time and with the country hanging in the balance, there is a direct correlation between soft skill development and organizational success.

On the whole, organizations maintain conducive work environments when leaders foster a culture on the varied principles of emotional intelligence. While intelligent quotient is clearly considered necessary in a complex, competitive, and fast paced world, it alone is not the answer to what makes life and organizations productive. Relationships need to be cultivating, full of nurture, balanced with compassion and empathy so people do not live in isolation and loneliness. Without high emotional intelligence and strong self-awareness, one can feel overwhelmingly isolated in a room full of people.

The emotional intelligence skill-sets of a leader are different than those of a manager. There is a spectrum, or gradient, by which each roll operates; however, the core principles of emotional intelligence are much stronger in a true leader and not as pronounced in a manager although there is a level of consistency in both. As discussed, in the Leadership chapter, leadership and management are two separate functions. Leadership is about leading people. They inspire and motivate people to help them discover their own ability to accomplish great things. They drive the workforce to achieve vision, strategy, and commitment by continuously being attentive to the basic human needs of the labor force. Management is about managing things, processes, and budgets. The manager makes sure work gets accomplished through the daily tasks of employees. The following chart takes a deeper dive into the discipline of emotional intelligence between a leader and manager.

Discipline	LEADER	MANAGER
Essence	Change	Stability
Focus	Leading People	Managing Work
Create	Followers	Subordinates
Horizon	Long-Term	Short-Term
Seeks	Vision	Objectives
Approach	Sets Direction	Plans Detail
Decision	Facilitates	Makes
Authority	With People	Over People
Appeal to	Heart	Head
Energy	Passion	Control
Culture	Shapes	Enforces
Dynamic	Proactive	Reactive
Persuasion	Sell	Tell
Style	Transformational	Transactional
Motivation	Excitement	Money
Wants	Achievement	Results
Risk	Takes	Minimizes
Conflict	Resolves	Avoids
Direction	New Roads	Existing Roads
Truth	Seeks	Applies
Concern	What is Right	Being Right
Credit	Gives	Takes
Blame	Takes	Distributes

Despite the importance of the physical needs of food, water, and air to sustain the physical body, people have psychological emotional needs of understanding, purpose, and contribution. What physical air is to the body, psychological air is to the human soul.

Chapter 5

Leadership Moral Decay

The social and corporate fabric has exponentially changed in recent years. The vast and most seemingly infinite number of corporate scandals have become commonplace in news broadcasts, newspapers, and discussions at many levels. It has now become the water cooler discussion. More often than not, the moral decay of leadership is making headlines. Corporate and enterprise America is incrementally and systematically working outside the margin of ethics. The once unseeded leadership mentality is now under siege with unconscionable dysfunctional behavior that is eroding by degrees.

Some of history's entangled stories and daily news reports are filled with perpetual stories of poor behavior, arrogance, ego brought to justice, and of strong capable individuals who simply knew better ruined by destructive behavior. The divisive and immobilizing impact of moral decay may be more of a conflict for leadership. Such stories will never be disentangled from CEOs being kicked out of their offices, wealthy money managers on Wall Street being indicted, radio talk show hosts and political officers resigning because of a loose tongue of prejudices in conversation and Hollywood icons going to jail and over dosing on drugs into elements of moral conduct. The once formal authority, in the elected offices, darlings of Wall Street and Hollywood elites were too blind, by their success, and flawed way of thinking to pay any attention to the warning signs and advice until the consequences had to be paid. Most of the world's leaders, however powerful they may appear, must act within the boundaries of ethics.

In discussing the effects of moral decay, the potential destructive behavioral forces can and will tear through the social fabric of homes, communities, corporations, and virtually every other layer of society where people live. The extent to which people have such competing forces within themselves between choosing right and wrong will naturally sow poor decisions. The function of leadership appears to be even more complex when considering all of the moral responsibilities.

The most influential and consequential type of leader is the individual who protects those they lead. The fundamental appeal is possibly the moral imperative in a leader. There are as many vast descriptions and interpretations of leadership as there are practitioners and thought leaders who try to characterize the mechanics of leadership. Barbara Kellerman, in her book, *Followership,* said, "For example, some define leaders by rank: leaders are people in position of authority. Others consider that the word has a moral imperative: leaders engage their followers in influencing relationships. And still others define leaders as the few who get the many to do what they want and intend, by any means necessary." In the world opinion, these definitions have possible merit, but none is more tangible than the kind of leader with moral imperative.

One might consider such individuals as good leaders, although misguided, brutal, and oppressive, Stalin, Hitler, and many others of late established far-reaching influence. However, the ways in which they accomplished their goals can best be seen in those situations that have had horrific consequences.

The collectivities of thought and architecture combined with all the wisdom, theories, principles, and hypothesis of leadership, will spin out of control and erode without integrity and trust—integrity and trust are the basis that holds organizations together. Tom Peters reported, in his research that the best, most aggressive, and successful organizations were the one's that stressed integrity and trust.

Is there any wonder why most people are becoming cynical about CEOs and leadership in general? There seems to be a void of any current leadership heroes. Those who were once revered as role models that emulated and patterned great leadership styles, are becoming something of the past. There is a looming grayness and judgment that all leadership is in moral decay.

The common thread and perhaps the only common thread is selfishness, which led to the downfall of many corporate leaders such as Boeing CEO Harry Stonecipher, Fannie Mae CEO Franklin Raines, and Pfizer CEO Hank McKinnell. In an article in *Business Week,* "The Boss on the Sidelines" shares the story of AIG's CEO, Maurice R. "Hank" Greenberg. While the imperious chairman and CEO of American International Group Inc. was holed up aboard his yacht on the Florida coast, his company's independent directors were packed into a conference room in their lawyer's Manhattan office.

The board members faced an urgent crisis: a growing accounting scandal that seemed to lead straight to the CEO. As directors debated whether to cut Greenberg loose, the 79-year-old titan lashed out at them by telephone. "This board is being run by a bunch of lawyers who can't spell the word 'insurance,'" he shouted. It was the kind of intimidation that had helped Greenberg consolidate unprecedented power in his four decades at the helm of the insurer. But this time, the bullying didn't work. Within a day, Greenberg, once the most powerful man in the industry, was out as CEO. Two weeks later, as the scandal widened, he was also forced to resign the chairmanship. Is it any surprise CEO turnover is in overdrive?

The sharp distinction between unethical and ethical leaders has completely uprooted the entire system, causing disruption to the current structure. The problem faced by ethically motivated leaders in today's corporate society is multiplied and compounded by growing distrust of the one in charge. Leaders are burdened to demonstrate trust and moral conduct in a transparent way to dispel any hint of suspicion.

Contrary to the unparalleled stories of moral decay, there continues to be occasional stories of leadership greatness, which provide hope for all followers and future leaders. Bill Allen's story of Boeing continues the rays of optimism. Bill appeared in front of the House Committee to address charges that military manufacturers were inflating profits and pilfering government funds. He stood in front of the committee with no lawyer at his side giving him neither counsel, nor any script for his speech. At the conclusion of his explanation, it was apparent that there was no deceit of gouging government funds for profits rather the funds were for research and development. The committee stood in standing ovation applauding the moral conduct of Bill Allen.

Unfortunately, in the wide battlefront to maintain a position of ethics, two thousand and two was an unprecedented year for corporate scandals; Enron, Tyco, and Global Crossing. The failed companies centered on corporate governance, outright greed, manipulation, accounting abuses, and a crowd of other ethics violations. Part of the reshaping of arsenal is the reward system. Warren Bennis, *On Becoming a Leader,* wrote, "Long before Enron became synonymous with corporate corruption, scholarly studies linked a lack of professional ethics to a business climate that not only condones greed, but rewards it."

The critical problems were centered on the accounting practices Enron implemented to hide their losses to the extent in which they were so abused that Enron was bound to fail. Lives were destroyed, retirement accounts lost, and dreams ruined due to poor moral conduct. As a result, businesses are faced with new accounting practices and restrictions. There are now corporate expenditures that do not produce any financial merit, they simply safeguard against illegal accounting practices. It is the fleecing of corporate America.

One of the dominant views of unethical leaders is the false justification in which they hide behind the mask of their cause for the presumable best interest of everyone involved—they construe poor behavior as being good. In the book, *The Courageous Follower*, speaks about the self-centered approach, "Leaders may come to consider their own welfare so critical to the success of the organization that they justify anything they do for themselves, regardless of its appropriateness, on the grounds that it enables them to better serve the organization." The role of the immoral leader turns largely on the approach that they are the victims and it is a question of circumstance or a condition beyond their control. By such perception, leaders act for self-interest with which they use the defense mechanism of rationalization to explain away unacceptable behavior.

1- Believing that the activity is not "really" illegal or immoral
2- That it is in the individual's or the corporation's best interest
3- It will never be found out
4- It helps the company and the company will condone it

According to this view, a leader is bound hand and foot to moral destruction. This mind-set pattern circulates to and perpetuates dysfunctional behavior supported by a flawed and misguided value system. Essential to the paralysis is the mental manipulation to rationalize the justification in order to alleviate the sting of sharp misalignment between values and behaviors.

"I am not hurting anyone else"
"It makes me feel better"

"I deserve to be rewarded and it will help others"

Take for example the story of Robin Hood, England's most famous outlaw, who robbed from the rich to give to the poor. The tendency towards justification is always the same with slight disparity. It is an old-age issue and the great question of human behavior and judgment. How does a traditionally honest and capable human being become so insensitive, misguided, and confused? The distortion of reality and selfish motives to feeds one's ego, or attitudes of today contributes to illegal behavior, which ultimately fosters patterns of destruction. If by virtue, one is not willing to live by truth and principles, they will be led by their appetites and be greatly occupied by the self-serving things of the day.

Amitai Etzioni, professor of sociology at George Washington University, concluded that, in a ten-year period, roughly two-thirds of Americans, in the 500 largest corporations, have been involved, in a varying degree, of some form of illegal behavior.

More than 40 years ago, information reached the Manville Corporation, then Johns Manville, medical department and through it the companies top executives. The information implicated asbestos inhalation as a cause of asbestosis, a debilitating lung disease, and mesothelioma, a fatal lung disease. Manville managers suppressed the research. Moreover, as a matter of policy, they apparently decided to conceal the information from affected employees. Furthermore, the company's medical staff collaborated in the cover-up.

Money may have been the motive. The prosecuting lawyer questioned the corporate policy of concealing the chest X-ray results from employees. In testimony, he asked, "Do you mean to tell me you would let them work until they dropped dead?" The reply was, "Yes, we save a lot of money that way."

Winston Churchill observed, "When one has reached the summit of power and surmounted so many obstacles, there is danger of becoming convinced that one can do anything one likes, and that any strong personal view is necessarily acceptable to the nation and can be enforced upon one's subordinates."

In the certain certitudes of power, when men gain a little authority, most tend to abuse the power for self-interests. If any person needs any further persuasion as to how vital the virtue of moral correctness is, they do not have to look too far to see the drenched destruction of damaged lives and the frayed fabric of society.

The end value of power is a wonderful tool. The concept of power is central to the discussion of leadership. Arguably, it could be used for good or evil and is the foundation of management, governments, communities, enterprises, and religion. It is highly intoxicating and enticing and has a mystic of seduction. The resource is used to accomplish spectacular things, advance civilization, and to better mankind. Unfortunately, people abuse the power at the peril and destruction for their own self-gratification.

The heavy discussion in the political arena is the use of nuclear power. Nuclear power is incredibly important and serves a tremendous purpose. It can power and provide light to millions of people or it can be used to destroy or kill millions. Pittacus considered as one of the Seven Sages of Greek practical wisdom and statesmen shared his thoughts over 2500 years ago, "The measure of a man is what he does with power."

In 1952, George Merck II declared on the cover of *Time Magazine* a rule for his company; "Medicine is for people, not for profits." This comment was centered on the distribution of streptomycin to Japanese children following World War II. He simply believed that the purpose of a corporation is to do something useful and to do it well. He further believed that people's interests were first and profits were second. He said, "And if we have remembered that, the profits have never failed to appear. The better we remembered, the larger they have been."

Unfortunately, the reverse mind-set has started to plaque the minds of many leaders of today. They have lost the most important economic and social purposes of institutions. The moral compass has swung from people to profits. There is an unhealthy fixation with Wall Street. Merck understood it well. They served people first and profits second.

The George Merck II story requires a broader understanding of the inter-relationship between a corporation's economic and social responsibility. The most consequential aspect and objective of a company's contribution to any society and community are first to make money and produce jobs for the economy. The advancement of social development comes through economic strength by investing capital, trading of goods and services, and making profits. The key is to have mutual values in the operational practices and social aspect, not only to promote economic strength, but for social development. When government enacts certain laws and rules hindering production, the social fabric will degenerate into impoverished conditions which only leads to lower wages, less work, and fewer jobs. The economic strength of an enterprise is the support system and foundation for social stability.

Michael E. Porter, the leading authority on competitive strategy, competition, and economic development writes in his book, *On Competition*, "Corporations are not responsible for all the world's problems, nor do they have the resources to solve them all. Each company can identify the particular set of societal problems that it is best equipped to help resolve and from which it can gain the greatest competitive benefit. Addressing social issues by creating shared value will lead to self-sustaining solutions that do not depend on private or government subsidies. When a well-run business applies its vast resources, expertise, and management talent to problems that it understands and in which it has a stake, it can have a greater impact on social good than any other institution or philanthropic organization."

Leadership, especially in the balance of economic and social responsibility makes decisions in a context that influence the best interests in the scale of both responsibilities. The extent of decision-making is in the conceptualized structure of values sharply defined and deeply etched in the core of the leader. The ability to act and do what is right is based on the principles of a moral and ethical system aligned to one's life, which is conscience and values to dictate the decision-making process. Moral leaders reflect on the circumstances and situations that form thoughts on how to act. Broadly construed as the practical reasoning, of moral responsibility, and the ethical beliefs of "should", "right', "wrong", "good", and "bad." One behaves based on how one thinks and the espoused values of their life.

The question remains: What are the exact behaviors of ethical conduct? The issue of ethics might appear to be complex. However, it is quite simple. Within each individual, there is a consciousness of moral conduct knowing between right and wrong. Beyond the social pressures dictating correctness, there lies an even greater compass at the core of human beings, a human endowment that provides awareness of the principle *Opposition in All Things*—right and wrong. This immutable law governs every aspect ranging from science to human behavior. For example, the opposition of day and night, fast and slow, good and bad, and humility and arrogance. A leader's chosen responses and behaviors create either internal liberty or captivity. There is not an option in usurping the law of opposition; therefore, actions lead to the support of moral decay or to the sustaining power of ethical progression.

The concept of opposition in all things fertilizes the essential endowment of life to choose based on the absolute law of free agency. Every person has the freedom to choose his or her own course of action—one is "free to choose" and "free to act" for oneself resulting in a consequence.

The most successful leaders are those who respond to a code of conduct within the periphery of what is right and inherently good in order for effective leadership and moral correctness to take root. C.S. Lewis in his book, *Mere Christianity,* wrote, "A man who gives into temptation after five minutes simply does not know what it would have been like an hour later. That is why bad people, in a sense, know very little about badness. They have lived a sheltered life by always giving in."

When a leader does not give into temptation, and refrains from choosing a rocky road, trust is built. The travel toward the end of the road of trustworthiness is paved with character and competence.

Stephen M. R. Covey in his book, *The Speed of Trust*, said, "Trust is a function of two things, character and competence. Character includes your integrity, your motive, and your intent with people. Competency includes your capability, your skills, your results, your track record. And both are vital."

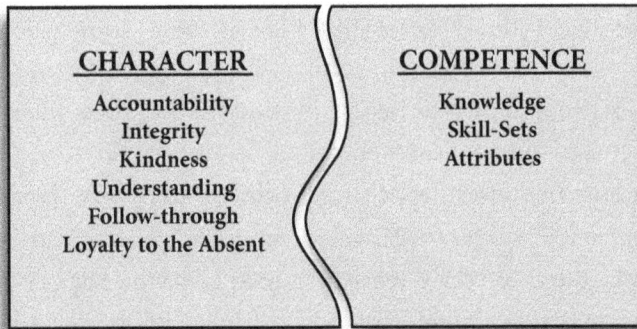

CHARACTER	COMPETENCE
Accountability	Knowledge
Integrity	Skill-Sets
Kindness	Attributes
Understanding	
Follow-through	
Loyalty to the Absent	

The footing for all leaders is grounded in such leadership topics of character and competence. Leaders are being required to develop a character to guide their leadership authority. John Sloan Dickey, an American diplomat, scholar, who also served as president of Dartmouth college for 25 years said, "The end of education is to see men made whole, both in competence and in conscience. For to create the power of competence without creating a corresponding direction to guide the use of that power, is bad education. Furthermore, competence will finally disintegrate apart from conscience."

Some years ago, I was in a terrible accident. I was snowmobiling and flew off a ridge at 70 MPH. The injuries were not only extensive but life threatening. In the full diagnosis, I severed my small intestine in three places and the large intestine in two locations. Furthermore, I broke open my stomach, bladder, and appendix. The following day, in intensive care, an artery ruptured requiring additional surgeries. Due to the nature of the injuries and life-threatening situation, the most competent surgeon was called even though there were other surgeons on duty. Subsequent to rehabilitation, I was informed that if the appropriate doctor had not performed the operations, I stood no chance of living.

On the other side of a balanced leader is character. How many have read in the news about the character issues being problematic in spite of strong competence, which leads to a leader's termination? Some years ago, a prospective football coach was being touted as the best available coach to take a premier position at Notre Dame. Unfortunately, the acceptance of the new position was short lived. It was discovered he plagiarized his resume leading to an immediate dismissal from the contract. Mahatma Gandhi said, "The moment there is suspicion about a person's motive, everything he does becomes tainted." Character is constant—it operates 24/7 and never sleeps. Competence is situational based on the required knowledge and specific skill-sets to perform a task with success.

The very nature of poor choices narrows the character and then ultimately corrodes—inherently good people lose their senses of what is right and what is wrong by degrees. Much like a pilot who needs to constantly check their instruments during flight, leaders need to have a moral and ethical barometer to check codes of conduct. In large part, the ethical barometer is the gauge to reflect awareness of weaknesses and strengths to avoid the pitfalls where there is a tendency to give into temptation.

Some of the important questions confronting leaders are the questions of purpose. The greatest force behind any life is purpose, which provides the power to enhance the resistance of selling out to dysfunctional and immoral conduct. Behaviors trend along the lines of purpose and extend to the point they touch the most inner part of the soul. The theory of moral conduct and purpose bring to bear on their centrality the most important human effort to operate from a position of good. Society's decay is festering and accelerating at a phenomenal rate, unlike any other time in history, whether it was in the era of the Egyptian, Roman, or Renaissance, whatever the time, one thing will never change the importance of moral and ethical fiber in the leader.

With the increasing spotlight brightly focused on leadership, the moral issue of a leader gives rise to the importance of character and competence. It is the switch that provides the power of trustworthiness and allows trust to operate for effective relationships.

Consider the example of Herb Kelleher, chairman and former CEO of Southwest walking down the hall one day; Gary Barron—then executive vice president of the $700 million maintenance division for all Southwest—presented a three-page summary memo to Kelleher outlining a proposal for a massive reorganization. On the spot, Kelleher read the memo. He asked one question, to which Baron responded that he shared the concern and was dealing with it. Kelleher then replied, "Then it's fine by me. Go ahead." The whole interaction took about four minutes. The high level of trust that existed allowed a massive reorganization to be approved in a matter of minutes.

In search of other examples of trust and the consequences, the example of Warren Buffett—CEO of Berkshire Hathaway who completed a major acquisition of McLane Distribution (a $1.45 billion purchase) from Wal-Mart. As public companies, both Berkshire Hathaway and Wal-Mart are subject to all kinds of market and regulatory scrutiny. Typically a merger of this size would take several months to finalize all the extensive details and cost millions of dollars to pay for the supporting cast of accountants, auditors, and attorneys to verify and validate all aspects. But in this instance, because both parties operated with high trust, the deal was made with one two-hour meeting and a handshake. In less than a month, it was completed.

Such competent and talented leaders are taking note of the importance of leadership. The most practical advantages are found in the soft-skills of development, which are identified, in historical and current examples. While at Apple, John Sculley talked about the new leadership model to effectively lead in a global environment based on the foundation of people, values, and skills. "If you look at the post-World War II era, when we were at the center of the world's economy during the Industrial Age, the emphasis was on self-sufficiency in every sort of enterprise—in education, business, or government. Organizations were hierarchical. That model is no longer appropriate. The new model is global in scale, in an interdependent network. So the new leader faces new tests, such as how does he lead people who don't report to him—people in other companies, in Japan or Europe, even competitors. How do you lead in this idea intensive, interdependent network environment? It requires a wholly different set of skills, based on ideas, people, and values."

Given the moral erosion of leadership and the establishment of such basic fundamental truths of consciousness in moral conduct between right and wrong—there is a remaining question: Is there any way to change the course of the ethical and moral slide facing the world? The conclusion has been drawn based on a deep resolve to live life centered on ethical principles, truth, and the cause of one's life. Furthermore, it starts with each individual having a character planted in the landscape and the responsibility to garden the appropriate chosen behaviors.

Shakespeare wrote, "To thine own self be true, and it must follow, as the night, the day, thou canst not be false to any man." Starting with self is the creative force behind the required approach to influence others. As Gandhi said, "You must be the change you wish to see in the world." The key to the large is the small. If a leader wants to have any influence in the team concept, he or she must start with himself or herself first. The cascading ripple affect will then influence something larger such as the corporate division. The magnitude and the strength of such a rippling concept of self and the personal agent of change is exponential. An Anglican Bishop shares his thoughts written over 900 years ago:

When I was young and free and my imagination had no limits, I dreamed of changing the world. As I grew older and wiser, I realized the world would not change and I decided to shorten my sights somewhat and change only my country. But it too seemed

immovable. As I entered my twilight years, in one last desperate
attempt, I sought to change only my family, those closest to me;
But alas they would have none of it.

And now here I lie in my death bed and realize, perhaps for the
first time, that if only I had changed myself first, then by exam-
ple I may have influenced my family, with their encouragement
and support I may have bettered my country, and who knows,
I may have changed the world.
Anglican Bishop - Circa 1100 AD - Crypts of Westminster Abbey

Out of the countless concepts found within the pages of this book, the maximum value is the individual and core to create change at a larger level. The key to the 99 is the one. It only takes one individual to influence the masses as seen throughout history with Jesus Christ, Nelson Mandela, Mahatma Ghandi, Martin Luther King, and other such notable influencers of good. Eknath Easwaran, a follower of Gandhi, shared the following incident: "Gandhi spent every moment of his adult life living the cause of Indian freedom. It was congruent, spontaneous, and it had a sustained effect on the British people because Gandhi identified so completely with his message. Once, while Gandhi's train was pulling slowly out of the station, a reporter ran up to him and asked him breathlessly for a message to take back to his people. Gandhi's reply was a hurried line scrawled on a scrap of paper: 'My life is my message.'"

This message did not require the vast stage of world politics, but could be put into practice here and now, in midst of daily life. Gandhi was not only a political and spiritual leader—he was a great teacher. He did not have to plan speeches, or stage events, because everything he did embodied what he believed. His true character flowed from his value system.

A mentor of mine, Blaine Lee, *The Power Principle*, once said, "The principles you live by will create the world you live in; if you change the principles you live by, you will change your world." Leaders have a moral responsibility to take care of their employees and not lead them into the muddy waters of destruction where they might never come back. Leadership is about leading, guiding, and mentoring the greatest asset of the organization—the employees. All great leaders operate within the boundaries of moral and ethical conduct preserving the moral core of the people, which is simply humane.

Chapter 6

Self-Awareness

In one's profound central life, one can use the gift of self-awareness to control their life and the nature to conduct themselves in set patterns of behavior. Rene Descartes, in the *Discourse on Method* wrote in 1637, "I think, therefore I am."

The highest framing of leadership, in a narrow sense, is the mere existence of self-awareness. Although it is probably one of the least discussed leadership competencies, it is the root with an assured degree for operative influence. The extensive discipline is to bring to bear the real person. The story by Frank Koch in *Proceedings*, a Naval Institute magazine proves the rise and fall unless there is an analysis of self.

Two battleships assigned to the training squadron had been at sea on maneuvers in heavy weather for several days. I was serving on the lead battleship and was on watch on the bridge as night fell. The visibility was poor with patchy fog, so the captain remained on the bridge keeping an eye on all activities. Shortly after dark, the lookout on the wing of the bridge reported,

"Light, bearing on the starboard bow."

"Is it steady or moving astern?" the captain called out.

Lookout replied, "Steady, captain," which meant we were on a dangerous collision course with that ship.

The captain then called to the signalman, "Signal that ship: We are on a collision course, advise you change course 20 degrees."

Back came a signal, "Advisable for you to change course 20 degrees."

The captain said, "Send, I'm a captain, change course 20 degrees."

"I'm a seaman second class," came the reply. "You had better change course 20 degrees."

By that time, the captain was furious. He spat out, "Send, I'm a battleship. Change course 20 degrees."

Back came the flashing light, "I'm a lighthouse."

We changed course.

The analysis of self-awareness lends itself to a moment of truth to grasp an intuitive understanding of one's core and identity. The parts of the self-awareness model are to explain and know the central thoughts, feelings, talents, strengths, and weaknesses, and furthermore the attitudes, beliefs, and conscious and unconscious paradigms that drive human behavior. The decisive move for both the leader and follower is to know and recognize how to direct life and govern in order to act and behave appropriately. The supreme quality of self-awareness is to not only understand personal emotional needs but also how to support and provide the needs of others. The self-perceived ability is to have power over individual emotions and perceive those of others.

A brilliantly self-aware leader is not merely skilled in the influences of behavior, of how to act and behave, but also is far more attuned with how people influence individuals to behave. There are natural trigger points, pet peeves that invariably rub or push others the wrong way. Possibly the co-worker who tries relentlessly to be the center of attention, by dominating the conversation and speaking louder than the rest of the group to be the focal point of everyone else. The supporting forces are knowing what situations and conditions that create immediate reaction through inappropriate body language, intonation, and the words others might use to respond. An unparalleled identification, with or responding to the real needs, will allow people to remain poised and to take control, which would otherwise expose inability to manage around the emotional deficiencies of others.

Encapsulated in the self-awareness structure is the conscious reality of accepting who one really is. A preeminent leader will see themselves for what they are and what they are not and accept the mutual encouragement and adjustments to produce change. In the book, *Emotional Intelligence 2.0*, the authors assert a plan for reshaping the contrarian attitude. "To be effective, we all need to discover our own arrogance—those things we don't bother to learn about and dismiss as unimportant. One person thinks apologies are for sissies, so she never learns to recognize when one is needed. Another person hates feeling down, so he constantly distracts himself with meaningless activity and never really feels content. Otherwise, they will continue down an unproductive, unsatisfying path, repeating the same pattern over and over again."

The aim for self-awareness is not being isolated from other people rather in the targeted relationships with whom they interact. The conditions are in the main source of relationships, thereby allowing leaders to learn about self-perceived emotion and the mind-sets that drive human behavior. As Boris Pasternak wrote in *Doctor Zhivago*:

> *Well, what are you? What is it about you that you have always known as yourself? What are you conscious of in yourself:*

your kidneys, your liver, your blood vessels? No. However far back
you go in your memory it is always some external manifestation of
yourself where you come across your identity: in the work of your
hands, in your family, in other people. And now, listen carefully.
You in others— this is what you are, this is what your conscious-
ness has breathed, and lived on, and enjoyed throughout your life,
your soul, your immortality—your life in others.

The significant practice of development comes into view when drawn from the composition of external manifestations of human interaction. The face of a true leader is to know what is appropriate and what is not for the given circumstance. The only kind of leadership is a display of conditions moving in a direction from a position of behavioral unconsciousness to a position of consciousness. Willard Barth said, "Life is not about the goals you have achieved; it's about who did you have to become to achieve them and what kind of impact did you make along the way."

It would seem consistent, in the compacted attitudes of a leader, that what a leader becomes is the full measure of their ability to accept personal responsibility for both expressed concepts of self-awareness and the arbitrary behaviors that properly expand healthy relationships. Unfortunately, according to this view, people live in a time when responsibility gives way to a disillusioned outlook that it is always someone else's fault. The vista from the seat of a number of leaders is to push blame to someone or something else. Society is witnessing a pulverization of ethics. The social mores are a false sense of security that trends along the lines of no responsibility or guilt for their own conduct even though they had behaved poorly and are clearly at fault.

By such perception, they abdicate their own conscience. The attitudes of the central theme are to manipulate the mind or to activate other areas of fault. Every excuse is conveniently bound in the propaganda of upbringing, parents, and how they were taught or the social fabric of their existence. In practice, the suitable justification is to inscribe irresponsibility on many other reasons—ultimately, in the varying degrees of belief and thinking that they did not act for themselves rather were acted upon as puppets by forces beyond their control.

The vital power of people is they are not a product of their environment, genetics, and psyche rather they stand-alone and independent from such settings. They have the ability to choose. In truth, there are countless opportunities to spring up to great heights and experience the full chambers of life. The utmost influence of a leader is the power of choice. They can choose their relationships, their friends, their careers, their behaviors, and their emotions. The power is derived from intelligence to act for himself or herself as opposed to being acted upon as an inanimate object or some other animal or plant organism. The most powerful instrument human beings have is wielding the tool of self-awareness to govern their life—hence the prospective leader to be courageous and be responsible for who they are and how to conduct themselves. Greek wisdom instructs to "Know Thyself, Control Thyself, and Give Thyself."

Gandhi once said, "Become the change you seek in the world." The wisdom of this quote leads to a vitality of ultimate control. Aside, even from all other influences, choice secures the foundation to build a stable environment. If one wants to be trusted, become more trustworthy. If one wants better relationships, be a better friend and more understanding. If one wants more responsibility, become more responsible. The institutional build of true character is constructed on the mortar and steel of human conduct principles; trust, understanding, responsibility, consideration, fairness and others among the framework to which individuals opt to live.

Mobilizing a leader, to a responsible position of strong influence, is to recognize the strengths and weaknesses from an individual perspective rather than raging war on other individuals' faults and insecurities by shifting blame to the weakest point of entry. Like those in many different leadership positions, the instinct is to protect the image and position of the one in charge thus forcing casualty upon the innocent bystanders.

Organizations, and by extension, societies reap the total benefits from the person in charge who resists the temptation to exploit others and accepts and acknowledges the full weight of responsibility. The ownership is placed squarely on the shoulders of whom they are, what they know and do not know; their boundaries of strengths and weaknesses through Knowledge, Skill-Sets, and Attributes rather than the tactics of pretending to Know, Do, and Be everything. The affliction is to pay the price and actually use the strong leadership concepts taught throughout history that great writers, leaders, thinkers and practitioners have built overtime to create greater leadership capacity. The letters of William James, a psychologist pioneer illustrates the moral attitude that defines a man's character, he said, "I have often thought that the best way to define a man's character would be to seek out the particular mental or moral attitude in which, when it came upon him, he felt himself most deeply and intensively active and alive. At such moments, there is a voice inside which speaks and says, 'This is the real me.'"

Much depends on the followership to pursue the leader. The removal of restraints is to be acutely aware of the immoral forces and produce a catalytic power of trust. The catalytic conversion takes place inwardly based on truth and authenticity and not pretending to be something they are not. The reconstruction of the leader is to yield to humility and to acknowledge what they still have yet to learn.

According to the natural affinities to master every competency and capability, the actual application is unrealistic. The declaration that one might need help and has gaps is a sign of a truly self-aware and trustworthy person rather than turning to the classic means of pushing fault. The whole idea of effective leadership is the advancement of such a theory that leaders have the ability to effectively lead regardless of personal weaknesses and deficiencies. Closely related to this view is that followers are forgiving and understanding and will not shun the leader when basic needs are met and acting out of a sense of purpose. History is filled with people possessing limitation. An unknown author wrote, "Homer could have squatted at the gates of Athens, being pitied and fed coins from the rich. He, like Milton the poet, and Prescott the historian, all had good alibis: he was blind, as were they. Demosthenes, greatest of all great orators, had a wonderful alibi: his lungs were weak, his voice hoarse and unmusical, and he stuttered. Julius Caesar, statesman and general, was an epileptic. Beethoven was stone deaf at middle age. They all had good alibis, but they never used them!" They were self-aware and mindful of their deficiencies, however, through the reflection of their needs greatness was still found.

As Will Rogers once said, "We are all ignorant only on different subjects." At times, leaders become followers and need to be led and coached. In a highly social competitive environment, this can seem counterintuitive. In fact, many people maneuver and behave under the paradigm or mind-set that one must appear as though they know everything all the time or else people will question their abilities, which diminishes their effectiveness to lead. So rather than being honest and straightforward, people conceal their weaknesses, which in turn actually highlights the deficiencies creating the perception of a lack of integrity and self-awareness. The uncompromising position is whether one acknowledges their weaknesses or not, everyone else sees them. The developing leader admits their weaknesses—it demonstrates their strength and those they lead do not threaten them.

Shakespeare describes an encounter in the playwrite *Julius Caesar* when Cassius shares with Brutus his lack of awareness and his offering to help: "Therefore good Brutus, be prepared to hear: And since you know you cannot see yourself, so well as by reflection, I, your glass will be, and will modestly discover things which you yourself know not of."

Such combinations of history and stories attempt to fashion the strong support of the obvious common sense of the interrelations of the leadership environment and the operational theory of improvement in terms of reality. The classic story of *The Emperor's New Clothes* highlights what one cannot see. The mirror of followership will draw attention to the brutal realities. In 1837, Danish author Hans Christian Anderson wrote a reflective fairy tale, titled *The Emperor's New Clothes.* It is a story of the ruler of a distant land who was so enamored of his appearance and his clothing that he had a different suit for every hour of the day.

One day, two rogues arrived in town, claiming to be gifted weavers. They convinced the Emperor that they could weave the most wonderful cloth, which had magical property. The clothes were only visible to those who were completely pure in heart and spirit.

The Emperor was impressed and ordered the weavers to begin work immediately. The Rogues, who had a deep understanding of human nature, began to feign work on empty looms.

Minister after minister went to view the new clothes and all came back exhorting the beauty of the cloth on the looms even though none of them could see a thing.

Finally a grand procession was planned for the Emperor to display his new finery. The Emperor went to view his clothes and was shocked to see absolutely nothing, but he pretended to admire the fabulous cloth, inspect the clothes with awe, and after disrobing, go through the motions of carefully putting on a suit of the new garment.

Under a royal canopy, the Emperor appeared to the admiring throng of his people—all of whom cheered and clapped because they all knew the rogue weavers' tale and did not want to be seen as less than pure of heart.

But, the bubble burst when an innocent child loudly exclaimed, for the whole kingdom to hear, that the Emperor had nothing on at all. He had no clothes.

Logical theory about a lack of self-awareness is a fundamental cause of pride. The central feature of pride is leveraging wealth, skill, intellect, personal looks, position, title, and all other worldly devices against others. C.S. Lewis adds his comments, "Pride gets no pleasure out of having something, only out of having more of it than the next man...It is the comparison that makes you proud: the pleasure of being above the rest." Leadership is not about feeling worthwhile based on the number of people below who are deficient. Pride is easily seen in others but not traditionally in one's self. The antidote for pride is a hard look in the mirror and an examination of one's self, which requires humility. The stabilizing opinion is reflected in the relationships people hold. The effectiveness of the social mirror allows the true self to be exposed providing an accurate depiction of the perception others have of them.

This theory of pride takes a stand upon the damaging consequences, which supplement and reinforce the harm of a lack of self-awareness. Some of the most devastating stories in history are because of a lack of awareness. An officer of the ill-fated Titanic once stated, "There was no fear of God, man or devil, because the Titanic was built so solidly that it could readily withstand collision with other ships or contact with any other force, including icebergs." The Titanic was in fact three football fields in length, 12 stories high, built from the finest steel. On that fateful night of April 14, 1912, other ships warned of ice ahead. Yet the Titanic continued to increase her speed cutting through the cold Atlantic Ocean. By the time the lookouts sighted the iceberg, it was too late, the Titanic could not turn out of its way in time. The iceberg scraped along the starboard side creating a series of punctures. Two hours and 40 minutes later the unsinkable Titanic sank to the bottom of the ocean. Over 1,500 people drowned.

To characterize self-awareness, an iceberg is one-eighth above the waterline and seven-eighths underwater. The largest portion of ice remains hidden much like the unaware leader who tries to cover their flaws and the forces of pride blind them in many situations. Leaders may try to escape the burden of the consequences but unfortunately; danger is lurking even when the leader attempts to mask the brutal reality of self. As it was with the ill-fated Titanic encountering the iceberg, there is hazard for anyone who is not self-aware of his or her own deficiencies and gaps of what they really know and who they are loses the ability to not only have healthy relationships but perhaps at the expense to influence others with honor. Not to risk overemphasizing self-awareness and pride unaware leaders simply make it hard for others to interact forcing them to manage their work, time, and energy around the leader's dysfunction.

The burden is to engulf awareness in the stream of behaviors, which flow from the conscious and unconscious mind-sets and attitudes. The complex issues are to understand the waves of the sea of paradigms or mind-sets that drive human behavior. People traditionally behave for a very good reason based on experience and conditioning—the key is discovering the balance of conditions for a manifestation of appropriate behavior. Countless of examples can be used to show the relationship between mind-sets and behaviors.

The Washington Post conducted a social study *Pearls Before Breakfast*.

> *The young man enters the L'ENFANT plaza station. He appeared to be like most young men dressed in a tee shirt, Levis and a baseball cap. There was not anything expressive about him other than the violin he pulls from its case to collect the money. The original owner of the violin was no other than, the Polish virtuoso Bronislaw Huberman that the young man purchased for $3.5 million dollars. He started his music with "Chaconne" from Johann Sebastian Bach's Partita No. 2 in D Minor. The young man of 39 years of age "played with acrobatic enthusiasm", his body leaning into the music and arching on tiptoes at the high notes. The sound was nearly symphonic, carrying to all parts of the homely arcade as the pedestrian traffic files past.*
>
> *Three minutes went by before something happened. Sixty-three people had passed, when finally; there was a breakthrough of sorts. A middle-age man altered his gait for a split second, turning his head to notice that there seemed to be some guy playing music.*

"Yes, the man kept walking, but it was something."

A half-minute later he received his first donation. A woman threw in a buck and scooted off.

His last piece played was "AVE MARIA" "To another thunderous silence."

Things never got better; "seven people stopped what they were doing to hang around and take in the performance, at least for a minute." And, of the other 1,063 people, twenty-seven gave money.

The performer in the Washington station was, Joshua Bell with his 1713 Antonio Stradivari Italian masterpiece violin. Joshua is an international acclaimed virtuoso selling out concert halls all around the world. He can command up to $1,000 per minute.

There was no ethnic or demographic pattern to distinguish the people who stayed to watch Bell, or the ones who gave money, from that vast majority who hurried on past, unheeding. Whites blacks and Asians, young and old, men and women, were represented in all three groups. But the behavior of one demographic remained absolutely consistent. Every single time a child walked past, he or she tried to stop and watch. And every single time, a parent scooted the kid away.

A fact of who a leader represents is very much a product of the complex structures of how one thinks in which not only influences behavior but ultimately influences results. The climb to self-awareness starts by understanding the complex structure of paradigms. People behave for a very good reason much like the parent scooting the child away based on perceptions, assumptions, and interpretation—a paradigm is how one understands the environment based on experiences and conditions.

The extent to which the person understands the profundity of paradigms, the greater the conforming will be to appropriate behaviors. However, central to people is the ability to challenge certain mind-sets. The process to challenge will allow for one to learn and unlearn new and old mind-sets, experiences, and develop new thought even if it closely mimics the current paradigm. The disparity between the parent and child is the parent's misaligned paradigm of the musician, Joshua Bell, playing in a subway terminal—a stereotype of a beggar needing assistance.

The children's attempt, without preconceived thought, was more about the music and less about the judgment of the musician, all of this contrasts with stereotypes driven by paradigms. Attitudes and behaviors are cultivated from the most inner parts of assumptions. More precisely, if a person sees or views a group or class of people as inferior, their behavior and actions of dismissal will naturally support and reinforce the paradigm and viewpoint of how they think. Paradigms are deeply imbedded into the thought processes, which make it difficult to act inconsistent with mind-sets very long. The real mentality of how one thinks will eventual represent the true character.

Behaviors are iterative and are exhibited even when they are no longer relevant and are not grounded in truth. Repetition is not necessarily bad, but when the behavior produces poor results and is misplaced, it requires a shift in how one thinks to influence behavioral change. One of the goals perhaps is to alter behavior, but by the extent to which the focus is solely on the behavior the value might yield little to no change. Regardless of how diligent one is to focus on changing behavior; the response will continue to manifest itself unless there is a shift in paradigms. This is not a straightforward linear process; many may not be able to make the shift from their current condition of behavior except through a conscious and challenged awareness of the influences.

Levels of Paradigms

Human behavior is very complex and requires a rigor of knowledge to understand the theories and applications. It merges arguably culture, attitudes, values, ethics, emotions, genetics, and other ranges to understand common, uncommon, acceptable, and unacceptable behavior. The emergence of paradigms, as expressed in leadership development, is to simply make sense of such weighty theory and apply the concepts for personal and organizational development. I crafted a simplistic watered down design to communicate three levels of paradigms to make sense of and how to follow through on its implementation.

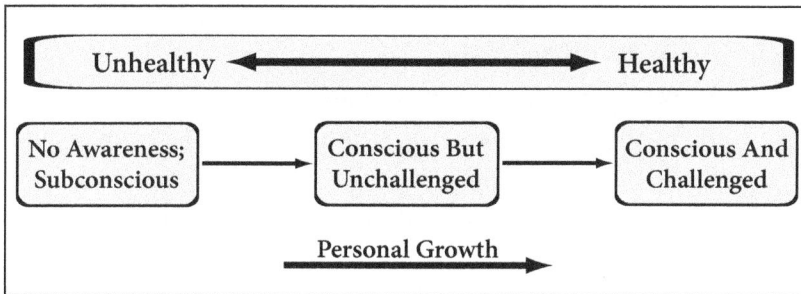

No awareness and subconscious paradigms: behaving but not having an understanding as to why one behaves a certain way.

Conscious but unchallenged paradigms: awareness of the behavior but continues to behave based on choice.

Conscious and challenged paradigms: awareness of the paradigm and the associated behavior. The paradigm is correct when the behavior produces a desired result. If the behavior is inappropriate and causes pain producing poor results, the paradigm needs to change to influence a new behavior.

The root of social and organizational conflict lies in the "No Awareness and Subconscious" paradigm that shade into the dysfunctions of all layers of life to the explicit ends of bad relationships, ineffectiveness, and organizational deficiencies. The test of "Conscious and Challenged" paradigms is noted in the sharper form of the result of the professional and personal ends such as healthy relationships, happiness, effectiveness, organizational speed, and countless other manifestations of positive forces.

Unhealthy Paradigms

Paradigm: people are inferior
Behavior: demeaning, selfish, unfair, rude, cunning
Results: bad relationships, sadness, ineffectiveness, organizational deficiencies, slow, bureaucratic

Healthy Paradigms

Paradigm: people are equal
Behavior: listening, sharing, leading, fairness, kindness
Results: healthy relationships, happiness, effectiveness, organizational efficiencies, fast, nimble

There are many examples throughout history and many more in today's society to illustrate the simple mechanics of paradigms and the influences they have on behavior.

Over 500 years ago, people had a mind-set of the old world. There was an understanding that, if you were to travel in either direction, you would fall off the edges of the world. An expert seaman and navigator challenged the whole mind-set and paradigm. Christopher Columbus (1451-1506) set sail west disputing the conventional understanding in hopes of discovering the West Indies. The new understanding and mind-set resulted in a breakthrough in world history.

Other renaissance individuals have had similar experiences challenging the old way of thinking, old paradigms, and mind-sets. There was an accepted theory of the Egyptian astronomer Ptolemy, that the earth was the center of the universe and had no movement. Copernicus challenged the old paradigm and proved that the earth did in deed have movement and the sun was the center of the universe. Well-versed astronomers and others considered his theory heresy.

In his writings, *De Revolutionibus Orbium Caolestium*, Copernicus wrote, "To ascribe movement to the earth must have seemed absurd to those who for centuries have consented that the earth is placed immovably as the central point of the universe. But I shrink not from any man's criticism. By long and frequent observations and by following a set of fixed principles, I have discovered not only that the earth moves, but also that the orders and magnitudes of all stars and spheres, nay, the heavens themselves, are so bound together that nothing in any part thereof could be moved from its place without producing confusion in all the parts of the universe as a whole."

One of the worst stamps ever placed on the history of the United States was segregation, which is closely related to the rise of many social issues of today. During the civil rights movement there were laws of segregation to divide the classes of people because the paradigm of one group was more superior to the other. Such laws drove and instituted different rights and privileges based on superiority. There was great awareness of the behavior and treatment, but the paradigm was not challenged until the civil rights movement of the 1960's. Over the course of time, there was a new mind-set and the Civil Rights Act was enacted in 1964. It is not without its challenges, but the social fabric has forever been changed because of a paradigm shift.

To hang a picture of simplicity, much like a car with a blind spot, people have blind spots as to their own mind-sets. In a mature and stabilized environment, it is easier and certainly more accurate for the social mirror of relationships to expose the lack of awareness of other people. The great juncture of devastation and catastrophe is an unchecked blind spot. Lives invariably are destroyed, relationships are deteriorated, and in due course, organizational strategies and processes are bogged down and the formidable acts on the corporate stage are completely halted because of inaccurate paradigms.

Part of life's journey is to discover new roads of self and what one ought to become. It can be argued that in times of trouble and adversity, one finds out what kind of steel they are made of and not through fragile efforts. Essential time, energy, and deep reflection needs to be spent thinking about the nature and core of who one is and the consequences of behavior. Nathaniel Hawthorne said, "No man for any considerable period can wear one face to himself, and another to the multitude without finally getting bewildered as to which may be true."

Joshua L. Chamberlain, a General Commander in the 20th Marine, Union Forces of the Battle of Gettysburg writes,

We know not of the future, and cannot plan for it much. But we can hold our spirits and our bodies so pure and high, we may cherish such thoughts and such ideals, and dream such dreams of lofty purpose, that we can determine and know what manner of men we will be whenever and wherever the hour strikes that calls to noble action...No man becomes suddenly different from his habits and cherished thoughts.

The essence of what manner a leader is prompts them to listen to the voice of consciousness. The centrality to know the noble action is to exert leverage to grow, stretch, and push forward for personal and professional greatness. The decision to fulfill a lofty purpose and nobility turns almost entirely to the persons aligned patterns of mind-sets to produce behaviors of good human conduct of integrity, fairness, kindness, understanding, patience, and forgiveness. In the words of William George Jordan, a literary and editor wrote, "Into the hands of every individual is given a marvelous power for good and evil—the silent, unconscious, unseen influence of his life. This is simply the constant radiation of what really is, not what he pretends to be." This is precisely on the ground for what is correct behavior as opposed to alternative courses of action. Effective leaders are far more attuned to principles of human conduct than their counterparts who rule by iron fists rather than out stretched hands.

Roger Merrill, who wrote the book, *First Things First,* taught me a very important principle. He said, "We become involved in an ongoing quest to understand and live in harmony with laws of life. We don't get caught up in the arrogance of values that blind us to self-awareness and conscience."

The indispensability of the laws of life and the conflict with toxic values is an important discriminator of leadership. Leaders do not retreat or adjust from such discipline to develop the human nature and science of leadership. The projection of the attitudes of today's society is trending towards the lines of choosing behaviors that produce immediate pleasure even at the expense and detriment of those who they attempt to lead.

Certainly, there are sharply increasing forces operating and pushing against the better judgment and the bursting points creating instability. The stabilizing position is the freedom to choose. Perhaps more than ever before, the supreme quality of leadership is not to heed to the enticing things of today rather on the foundational values of leadership. Influential leaders respect the central purpose of what the essence of leadership represents.

The broader reality is that leadership is deeply aligned to support and mentor those they lead with out stretched conditions to meet followership and organizational needs. The question remains: How does one balance the natural and unnatural tendencies of behavior? Psychiatrist M. Scott Peck addresses this issue, "Just because a desire or behavior is natural, does not mean it is…unchangeable…It is also natural… to never brush our teeth. Yet we teach ourselves to do the unnatural. Another characteristic of human nature—perhaps the one that makes us more human—is our capacity to do the unnatural, to transcend and hence transform our own nature."

The investment is high to do the unnatural, while the reverse of doing the natural is low. Some of the collective bankruptcy of effort to do the unnatural is the required discipline to change and the fear of potential pain. The quality asset is to bridle the natural tendencies for immediate gratification in place of one's transformed nature of self. A California philosopher, Eric Hoffer said, "Freedom from responsibility is more attractive than freedom from restraint." The compelling part of being human is the ability to do the unnatural, which transcends animal instincts.

Against one's better judgment, exercising 30 minutes a day pays dividends in the form of increased self-esteem, better health, and a greater quality of life. Unfortunately, many choose the natural tendency to do less pursuing the pleasures of rest.

Changing paradigms and behaviors require one to nurture the landscape of effort and awareness. I am reminded of the allegory of the Chinese Bamboo Tree and the lasting influence in the form of diligence. The Chinese bamboo tree is planted only after the ground is prepared and cultivated. What is most seemingly failure; the first four years has very little outwardly visible growth and change. The only noticeable change is a small sprout coming out. The substantial change is taking place underground to develop the root structure for support. Then, in the fifth year, the bamboo tree springs to eighty feet.

In sharp comparison, development and change requires people to pay the price of consistent and diligent effort. The allegory of the bamboo tree embodies little to no outwardly growth—one cannot see the immediate results of change. The non-visible growth is taking place in the cultivated human soul without the produced results to those around them. Gradually overtime, others will see the apparent fruits of an influential character springing forth and see them for whom they are and not what they were.

In the book, *The Scarlet Letter,* Nathaniel Hawthorne tells the story of Hester and the letter "A". In the 17th-century, in a Puritan village a young women name Hester Prynne was led to the town prison with a young child in her arms. An upper case "A" was written on her chest-representing adulterer, a symbol of her sin, a badge of shame, for all to see. While her husband was presumably lost at sea, she falls in love with the minister and conceives a child. She raises her daughter with honor in the midst of shame and ridicule. Her life was dedicated to a life of charity and serving others. At the time of her death, the once inscribed letter "A" that represented "Adultery" was now placed on her tombstone representing "Angel." The town folks have come to see her for who she truly was.

The complete circle of human behavior is not simply drawn with paradigms and mind-sets rather with paradigms, mind-sets, and principles along with systems and structures. The exhibited combinations characterize the manner, in which to close the broader circle of elements, producing human behavior.

Paradigms and Mind-Sets
Principles
Systems and Structures

Paradigms and Mind-Sets: things of understanding and how one interprets their environment. A perception of a group of people being either superior or inferior will drive an interaction of acceptance or contempt.

Principles: the values and beliefs one holds as truth. A religious and social belief that stealing is wrong will drive the behavior of paying for goods and services.

Systems and Structures: the Organizational Design, such as reward and compensation structures and measurement of metrics and numeric for performance. If a manager changes the metrics and numeric by rewarding a sales person by increasing the call volume, the new behavior will be to pick up the phone to talk with more people.

Closing the triangle between the elements of paradigms, principles, systems, and structures, with behaviors and results requires a gap analysis of pain and gain. There is an active link between results and the influences of human behavior, which generates the pace for change. When the pain is significant, people are willing to alter behavior in order to alleviate the pain in hopes of joy. Conversely, one might change his or her behavior in hopes of something greater such as, going to school in order to secure a better higher paying job. The conceptual challenge is to think through the negative and positive parts to the extent in which one can shake off or carry on through life.

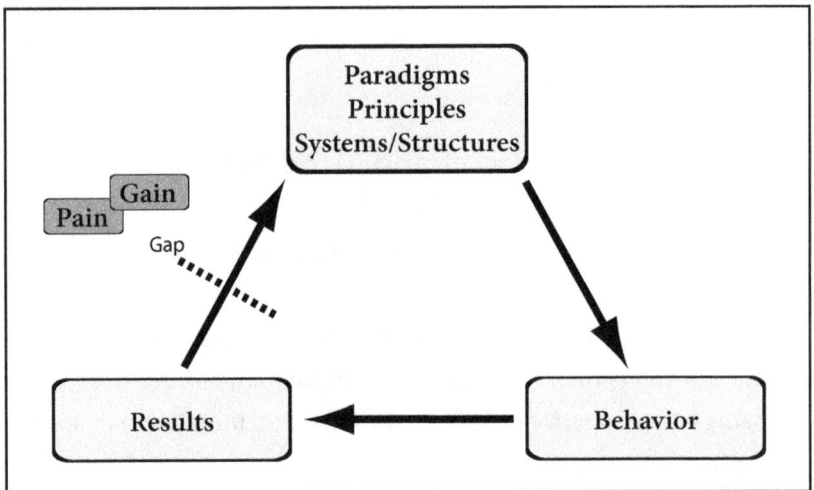

The larger question concerns the capacity of persons to change. Oftentimes, one will hear that a certain individual is "the same person they were years ago." However, that is not entirely true, people are getting older, their perceptions, and experiences are constantly changing although it might be insignificant. People might say, "You cannot teach an old dog new tricks" or "they were born that way." In reality, people are always changing their behavior in some fashion. The long-established theory is people have the intelligence to act and not to be acted upon—they have the freedom to choose how to behave and not at the dictate of environmental, genetic, and psyche determinisms.

The long and short of it is long-sustainable behavioral change takes place on conditions of paradigms, principles, and systems and structures, which influence actions rather than the focused piece meal of hit and miss on individual behaviors. The ambiguity rises in part from a misunderstanding of the focal point of change. It requires individuals to pass through a sequence of all three elements of the model. This concept brings to bear on the short-term impact of change when focus is on the behavior rather than the influence of behavior. The embattled smoker who merely tries to stop the bad habit or behavior will surrender to defeat sooner than later because the control of the behavior is in the condition driving actions. The most quantum influential change takes place on the condition and not on the behavior.

In optimal conditions, the distinctive competence of self-awareness enhances scruples to examine the realities of how people behave. The scale and quality can be exercised to study the values that are the function of life. The degree, in part on the appropriate corrections, will depend on self-awareness. The following poem by Portia Nelson reflects the attitude.

I walk down the street.
There is a deep hole in the sidewalk.
I fall in.
I am lost...I am helpless.
It isn't my fault.
It takes forever to find a way out.

I walk down the same street.
There is a deep hole in the sidewalk.
I pretend I don't see it.
I fall in again.
I can't believe I am in the same place.
But it isn't my fault.

It still takes a long time to get out.

I walk down the same street.
There is a deep hole in the sidewalk.
I see it is there.
I still fall in...it's a habit.
My eyes are open.
I know where I am.
It is my fault.
I get out.

I walk down the same street.
There is a deep hole in the sidewalk.
I walk around it.

I walk down another street.

The most considerable and visible part of a self-aware leader is taking responsibility for their own actions and who they are. It is of significance that they do not finger point and blame others for their own deficiencies and dysfunction forcing others to manage around them. They shoulder the responsibility for their failures and never shift fault to excuse their behavior. They carry the burden squarely on their shoulders.

When leaders are capable to admit their mistakes, they demonstrate profound self-awareness. They do not lead blindly rather they recognize errors and immediately accept responsibility to better position their ability to lead through their strength of character. When CEO, Joe Cullman, reviewed the decision by his company, Philip Morris, to buy 7UP in 1978 and sell it eight years later at a loss, he admitted that it was his mistake and it could have been avoided if he had listened better to the people who challenged the idea at the time.

Beyond the scale and scope of individual lack of awareness and blind spots, there needs to be the willingness to see the chronic organizational blind spots that exist. John Gardner spoke of this fact when he said, "Most ailing organizations have developed a functional blindness to their own defects. They are not suffering because they cannot resolve their problems but because they cannot see their problems." The same discussion of self-awareness applies to organizational-awareness.

Feedback

The fundamental process for continual personal development is called feedback. Feedback is the element that helps leaders create self-awareness about their performance and behavior. Each day, individuals arise and prepare for the day's activities. One must look into the mirror and comb their hair and upon leaving, one looks into the mirror to ensure everything is in order. It is difficult to be self-aware without the social mirror of feedback to monitor behaviors and performance. Feedback is one of the most important tools around. However, feedback is a double edged sword. Ethan M. Rasiel and Paul N. Friga, in their book, *The McKinsey Mind*, write, "On one hand, we have a strong interest in finding out what people think of us, as a means both to improve ourselves and to feed our egos. On the other hand, feedback can make us uncomfortable when it forces us to confront our weaknesses."

The conflict of asking for feedback appears to be an outwardly position of insecurity. However, this theory is on the contrary. The premise is sharply different; the very nature of seeking feedback demonstrates accountability, strength, and wisdom. Feedback ultimately turns on the nature that others do not threaten them—they empower themselves. It positions leaders for greater opportunity in their job, performance, advancement, and character development.

Not only is it important to receive feedback, it is equally important to provide feedback. The process of receiving and providing feedback requires deliberate thought and timing. An arbitrary approach will disrupt any reasonable balance to provide or receive constructive exchange with others. The origin of change is in the form of wanting to help rather than to hurt and damage relationships. Feedback is not to merely influence negative behavior rather of the extent to which it is to lift, support, and express the capacity to achieve better results. In the ongoing process for development, feedback is essential in all areas of human interaction even though the tenet is difficult and no one enjoys providing it. Winston Churchill said, "Criticism may not be agreeable, but it is necessary. It fulfills the same function as pain in the human body. It calls attention to an unhealthy state of things." In short, one cannot solve problems one does not see.

King George writes in his personal diary, July 4th 1776, "Nothing of importance happened today" reveals that revolutions can start which will forever transform the world and to a degree even kings fail to notice. Of consideration, there needs to be a mention that possibly King George was not aware of the signing of the Declaration of Independence due to the delay of communication and the deficiencies of methods.

To a long run effort to learn, people have varying volumes to summarize the concepts of self based observations and how others perceive them. The reflection of the social mirror of others is linked firmly to an understanding of self-improvement. Unfortunately, people attempt to fog the mirror to conceal the true essences of self. To the degree that people attempt to disfigure the truth, it is impossible to conceal one's weaknesses and gaps, because the authentic image is already highlighted to those around them. Others already see the deficiencies and gaps; it is nothing new to them. On the face of self-awareness is the humility to acknowledge what one still has to learn and unlearn and not become the hippo.

How the Hippo Lost His Hair

The first hippopotamus to walk the earth was not hairless like hippos of today. He had a beautiful fur coat and a mane so thick it was rivaled only by that of the lion. Although his coat had been inherited from his ancestors, Hippo took full credit for its beauty and luster and showed it off whenever he could. In fact, Hippo would grow quite ill-tempered at night because the darkness hid his coat from the envious glances of the other animals.

Thanks to his elegant fur; Hippo didn't need to sleep near the fire like the others—his coat kept him warm. Even so, each night Hippo would lie just a little closer to the flames. He wanted the light from the fire to shine on his fur so everyone could admire it twenty-four hours a day.

One evening Lion gave Hippo a gentle warning, suggesting softly that it might not be safe to sleep so close to the fire. Hippo ignored him. "Lion is just jealous," he thought. "Jealous because all the animals can see both day and night that my coat is better than his."

Jackal was also worried about Hippo's coat catching fire. Jackal, however, despite her great intellect, did not have great tact. "You big hairy oaf," grated Jackal. "Your inflated pride is matched only by your girth, and it's going to get you into trouble one of these days."

Hippo was indignant. "I didn't ask for her opinion! How dare she speak to me like that. When she learns how to treat me with respect, I will listen."

One night disaster struck. Hippo slept just a little too close to the fire. A stray spark flew into his fur and his exquisite coat burst into flames. Hippo made a desperate dash for the river, but by the time he got there it was too late. Although he couldn't see it in the darkness, his fur was gone.

He spent the rest of the night in the cool waters of the river.

When the sun rose the next morning, Hippo climbed onto the riverbank and shook himself off. He turned to admire his reflection in the water. Instead of a thick glossy coat, Hippo saw only charred flesh.

"If only I had listened to Lion, or even Jackal!" he wailed, then immediately plunged back into the water. To this day, to hide his embarrassment, Hippo spends the sunlit hours buried in the waters of the river. Only at night does he venture out, when he can eat without worrying who might catch a glimpse of his hideous hairless hide.

Assuming accountability for feedback is as easy as asking a few simple questions: "What feedback do you have for me?" "What should I know?" "Do you have any suggestions for me?" As David Brinkley once said, "Successful people are those who can lay a firm foundations with the bricks that others throw at them."

When most people receive the brick of feedback, they feel pressed to immediately act on the comments. There might be a need to address the issues that requires immediate attention. But generally, what needs to be communicated to the individual providing input is a simple "Thank you." This does not mean that what is provided is truth, accurate, correct or even insightful. One is simply saying, "thank you" for their willingness to provide a perspective.

I believe that one does not live life blindly, but through life, as one lives and breaths it and to find one's way through hard work and determination to better oneself. If leaders are unwilling to better or lead themselves, how can they possibly expect others to follow?

It is a matter of ethics accepting the good with the bad, the right and the wrong. Leaders who lacked the character to accept responsibility for their deficiencies have destroyed everything from relationships to major organizations. They believed their mistakes were best swept under the carpet or fed through the paper shredder. Denying oneself the opportunity to have complete self-awareness tears down the very nature and core of one's identity and existence.

Chapter 7

Role Modeling

Have you ever left your home to hear your mother say, "Remember who you are?" Did you wonder or ever consider why she said that each time you left? The question needs to be asked, "Who am I?"

Among all the learning and knowledge about human and leadership development, there is a continued search for personal and professional patterns of identity. The topic of development is essentially found in the finer points of theory and concepts, of which is the process of role models who represent moral and behavioral correctness, paving the path on which people can pattern their life.

Perhaps in the circumstance when formal authority is given, people look to others in search of a role model and a prototype of leadership. The new opportunity gives way to a moment of reflection to change, as if they are being transferred into a different reality requiring them to behave differently. Ira Chaleff, in the book, *The Courageous Followers: Standing Up To and For Our Leaders,* said, "As a newly elevated leader, they have no precedent for this experience, and they grope in the recesses of their minds for models to guide their behavior."

Underlying the conflict between being a newly elevated leader and the more critical question: Who will serve as the role model? Needs concrete answers. Choosing poor role models and unconsciously basing behavior on improper examples will eventually lead to isolation and leave others choosing not to follow.

The illustration of a newly elected U.S. Congressman who became abrupt and abrasive to his staff realized what was driving his behavior. During a leadership conference, he recognized his pattern of conduct was from a role model who was in Congress for many decades. The understanding was based on what he thought was acceptable behavior, of what a leader is and what a leader does.

Since the focus of leadership development rests essentially in the mechanics of business, many will give less time, less thought and less effort to being self-aware of: "Who am I?" Such a question is possibly the greatest influential trait of a leader. The aim for all leaders is to enlarge the targeted answer and the imprescriptible responsibilities for their own actions and to those they lead.

The sharp view of leadership is the required strict accountability of self in order to provide a much stronger landscape to hold others accountable for their own behavior and performance. People tend to perform and behave at the standards set by their leader. If a leader is not behaving or performing appropriately, it will be virtually impossible to hold others accountable for their own vista on behavior. On the outlook of modeling, is the raising of the standard, setting the direction, and the declaration of ethical goals, which need to be centered on fixed principles and truths rather than the emotional tides of circumstances and made up rules along the way.

In 2001, Ms. Watkins wrote an internal memo to Ken Lay, Enron's founder, detailing her concerns about the company's creative accounting methods. She warned that its improper practices were risky and that they might not withstand scrutiny. Her fear was that scandals were on the horizon requiring immediate change. History went on to prove Ms. Watkins' discoveries. Many thousands of lives were destroyed. Retirement accounts were lost and many employees lost their jobs. Those who lost sight of the set standards, the appropriate direction, and correct goals were eventually jailed.

The decisive move both away from fixed core values and towards the dictates of the latest cultural trends of behavior, creative financing, vulgar language or phrases, and styles and fashion are forces far more attuned to be in motion towards compromising positions. Modeling is all about behaving based on a fixed value system, stabilized on a footing of good principles of human conduct such as fairness, understanding, consideration, steadied with the espoused values of the organization such as hard work, providing exceptional products and value.

Jack Welch, who expanded General Electric's market value from $14 to $410 billion during his tenure, believed so deeply about living corporate values that those who were even high performers who violated the corporate values were terminated. In his book, *Winning,* he said, "To make values really mean something, companies have to reward the people who exhibit them and "punish" those who don't. Believe me, it will make winning easier. I say that because every time we asked one of our high-performing managers to leave because he didn't demonstrate the values—and we said as much publicly—the organization responded incredibly well. In annual surveys over a decade, employees would tell us that we were a company that increasingly lived its values. That made people even more committed to living them too. And as our employee satisfaction results improved, so did our financial results."

Where most leaders aspire to model various careers and strong work ethic, to supply supporting forces to those central jobs and do it superbly well, they must also do much more. Leaders must be committed to the most outwardly pronounced character ethics, which is the greatest sustaining power to those they lead. Unfortunately, most relationships are breached and violated because of unmet character expectations in the leader's behavior to the extent it creates uncertainty and weakness rather than strength and capacity.

During a presidential speech, Vice President Biden, was inadvertently overheard, by the reporter's microphones saying to President Obama, "This is a big F…en deal." Vice President Biden was referring to the passing of the healthcare reform bill and used possibly the worst word in the English language on the national stage. Philip Massinger, a play writer from the early 15th century shares his thoughts in his social and political themes, "He who governs others first should be a master of himself."

The theory of role modeling and the simplification of the issue are explicit and comprehensive. The enduring meaning is something far more profound when the appropriate role model serves as the example. The beleaguered and bewildered persons are those who choose to pattern their lives after poor role models in government, corporate enterprises, athletics, entertainment, and virtually all other fabrics of society. In some cases, they are the complete inverse of what is considered acceptable. Today, so many leaders are like chameleons; they change their hues to fit the situation, which tends to confuse those they lead. Such change burdens their followers to determine who the leader is and what direction is being pursued.

The dialogue of role models has a broader implication as to who are they. In the cynical age of today's leaders, are the problems springing forth from selfishness and self-centeredness. Selfishness and self-centeredness require others to figure out the demands of the leader in order to satisfy their large egos. This manipulative leadership style does not spring forth from fixed principles and truth rather a springboard of lies to use employees for their own needs and not the needs of others. In the name of some kind of cruel disillusionment, they feed off of and use others who are vulnerable and unsure of themselves for self-interest. The source of that idea may be to get subordinates off balance by making them feel they are always wrong and inadequate; taking pleasure in all kinds of reasons as to why people cannot succeed. On one hand, there is evidence that insecure leaders reinforce and support the follower's dependency mentality with the consequence of incapability in functioning adequately on their own. On the other hand, perhaps poor role models initiate communication in a way that is demeaning and suppresses the talents and capabilities, in order to control subordinates, forcing compliance with no allowance for dialogue, questions, or discussion. Some leaders will intentionally manipulate a situation where the subordinate is forced to agree on their directive causing them to question or resist, so the leader can show who is boss.

Perhaps, the final failure in the vast erosion of finding good role models are the burdens it causes people in being suspicious of authority even when the behaviors are appropriate. In many cases, the leader is very much behaving appropriately, but the subordinates have been conditioned to react negatively based on a mind-set that leaders are manipulative and inappropriate—some subordinates manage their time around the resistance to those in authority. Eyebrow raising employees can always find a reason why the desires of authority should not and cannot be carried out and it drives behaviors of struggle to undermine authority reinforcing their position that authority is wrong. It is from the person in authority that subordinates are trying to break free to demonstrate their own competency in a manipulative style.

The strap which binds role models in the ability to influence not only encompasses those they lead it also tightens entire masses and generations of societies. Some years ago, I was invited to attend an International Symposium where the wife of Anwar El- Sadat's, Madame Jehan Sadat, shared a story and spoke of Anwar's legacy.

He was a very popular president and extremely dedicated to the Arab world, the history, and philosophy of the people. As president of Egypt, he gave political speeches vowing to never shake the hand of an Israeli as long as they occupied Arab soil shouting "Never! Never! Never!" the crowd would shout back, "Never! Never! Never!"

Overtime, Anwar changed his position and took a change of heart. Stephen R. Covey, in his book, *The 8ᵗʰ Habit*, shares the story of his lunch with Madame Jehan Sadat. He asked, "What was it like living with Anwar Sadat—particularly at the time he made the bold peace initiatives of going to the Knesset in Jerusalem, a move that culminated in the Camp David Accord. She said she had a hard time believing his change of heart, particularly after all he'd been doing and saying. Confronting him directly in their living room quarters of the palace, she asked him,

"I understand you are thinking about going to Israel. Is this correct?"
"Yes."
"How could you possibly do this after all you have been saying?"
"I was wrong, and this is the right thing to do."
"You will lose the leadership and support of the Arab world."
"I suppose that could happen; but I don't think it will."
"You will lose the presidency of your country."
"That, too, could happen."
"You will lose your life."
He responded, "My life is ordained. It will not be one minute longer or one minute shorter than it was ordained to be."
She embraced him and said he was the greatest person she had ever known."

Anwar Sadat subordinated his ego in place of doing the right thing and became a role model to reform movement in the Arab world. The quality of leadership made a fundamental difference in the social foundation. His ability to model character traits of collaboration, win/win mentality, forgiveness, and other such transcendent attributes reverberated throughout the world. Anwar shared, "He who cannot change the very fabric of his thoughts will never be able to change reality, and will never, therefore, make any progress."

Anwar Sadat's leadership work is not the only solo performance rather there are many such acts of role modeling throughout history, by which to influence. Another historical account of being a role model was that of Mickey Mantle, an American baseball star who admitted to years of various forms of substance abuse. Upon receiving a liver transplant in an effort to save his life, he made an amazing statement. He said, "Do not use me for a role model." He also said that he was committing the rest of his life to being a better example. Mickey Mantle finally accepted the responsibility for his mistakes. Unfortunately, he died shortly thereafter. In all of his personal achievements, it was about moving beyond them and accepting responsibility to be a better example.

In World War II, troops were taught in officer training that the only appropriate answer when they made a life-threatening mistake was, "No excuse, sir." The shifting foundation is accountability for his or her behavior and any great personal or organizational accomplishments do not excuse leaders from leading in front.

Some of the crucial aspects of learning the role of modeling was when I was consulting a senior executive from Boston, Massachusetts. He said, "The best CEOs are those who know how to clean a toilet." The lesson taught was the small and simple things influence the large and significant elements. The cross-cutting work was not about the job as it was the power of leading in front and being a role model. The outgrowth is developing a culture of strong work ethic, teamwork, and a "can do" attitude—nothing is beneath the leader. Leaders are the superb mobilizers of the workforce.

The most decisive course of action is simply being the example, lighting the path of those who follow. It is not just about attitude, diligence, or skills of knowing what to do and how to do it rather about performing some of the most inconsequential jobs. If a leader can lead by example and do what is asked of others, their effectiveness and ability to lead will be tremendously enhanced.

The story of Sam Walton is a classic example of what modeling and humility is all about in a leader. A Brazilian businessman wrote to the top 10 U. S. retailers in the 1980's seeking permission to view their operations and make a personal visit. Many of the recipients either threw the letter away or simply replied "No thank you." All of them except Sam Walton.

The Brazilian businessman along with his colleagues deplaned and was greeted by a white haired gentleman. To which the guests said, "We're looking for Sam Walton," to which the reply, "That's me." Sam accompanied the men to his truck and introduced them to his dog, Roy. In route to their destination, the Brazilian billionaires were inundated with questions. You see Sam Walton loved to learn about constant process improvement and the value of breaking new ground. Sam later visited his friends in Sao Paulo. As the story goes, late one afternoon there was a call from the police. Sam Walton had been crawling around in the stores on his hands and knees measuring aisle widths and had been arrested for suspected burglary.

It is virtually impossible to inspire the employees to action if the Modus Operandi "MO" is "Do as I say, not as I do." I have found it much easier to buy the hearts and minds of people when leaders model "Do as I do, not what I say." There is no more powerful motivation, than a leader who walks the talk and leads by example. It speaks to the inner soul that energizes and directs behavior of others to follow. They must not only hear what they are expected to do, but also see what they are expected to be.

The role or roles a leader plays is determined on the whole character and purpose they design for themselves. The roles will vary tremendously, but never to the degree where they are phony and duplicitous in his or her behavior. An individual can have the surface signs of being an example; however, they are more related to being empty inside of the true character in personal and professional identity when the role is villain masked as a hero. Overtime, the person who is faking leadership will eventually be exposed and the mask of fraud will be revealed.

Leaders who do not live by their conscience of right and wrong will invariably not experience the true enjoyment of leadership. Doing the wrong things are not joy and happiness rather misery and desolation. Abraham Lincoln wrote, "It is the eternal struggle between these two principles—right and wrong. They are the two principles that have stood face to face from the beginning of time and will ever continue to struggle."

All the pep talks, speeches, and discussions of purpose are deemed worthless, if there is no example and modeling to represent the message— life is not lived dichotomously. One might suggest that they can belong simultaneously to both parts and be two different faces. That is simply masking life and others quickly see the masking as a failed performance. Leaders cannot expect to do right in one area and wrong in the other and anticipate having influence with those they lead. Life flows horizontally within all areas of life and vertically across them with all types of circumstances and environments as a whole person.

When those trying to lead behave in such a duplicitous manner followers ask: Why should we even trust you? Are you deserving of our trust? Why would any of us want to follow you? What have you done or not done to have us follow? Do you make the time and do you take the time to get to know us beyond the simple interactions?

Once again, there is the confronting of the essence of every leader to ask, "Would I choose to follow myself?" The apparent paradox in leadership is that the leader does not know who the leader sees standing in the mirror. The perceived leaders are those who reflect the capacity of Know, Be, and Do and mirror the needs and attitudes of those who choose to follow—poor reflective leaders have no followers. Unless leaders are willing to image their representation, they will be viewed as the reflective saying, "What you are doing rings so loudly in my ears that I can't hear what you are saying."

An appropriate comparison might be made between the gardener and the garden. The gardener will ask the questions: What is it going to take to grow my people? How do I weed the garden and care for it through the natural invasion of insects and subject to drought and wind? Everyday there is the constant care and responsibility to water, weed, and hoe. Much like the gardener the leader has similar responsibility to care and create the conditions to develop and grow their employees. If a leader does not like being the gardener, they need to get out of the garden. People deserve to be led by leaders who model all leadership traits and who enjoy the role, assignment, and responsibility.

I learned years ago, if one does not know the shape or even the location of the playing field—if one does not know the environment or the rules or even know if one exists—or the basics of how the game is played, just do not stand there, do something. They cannot expect to be coaching and leading from the sidelines or from behind. The simplest form of leadership is about being in front and being an example based on fixed principles of human conduct and truth.

Chapter 8

Visibility

Most would tend to agree that leadership visibility is a critical function of effective leadership, which at first is not often recognized as an important skill. The pattern is simple, but not easy to follow. There is a compelling responsibility to protect this skill because of the dividends received because of it.

The cluster of concepts and even the tiny matters of leadership development require an appeal for heavy consideration. The scale is whether or not to accept the theories. The strength of leadership is more the extent to which a leader lives the principles rather than merely learn the concepts. The missing piece of the leadership puzzle is the skill of visibility. A great leader walks and talks with those they serve; they are highly noticeable; they are not long distance and unseen. Similarly, they are not afraid and concerned of being in close proximity, in fear of disappointing those they guide. Leaders recognize the continuous force and endless responsibility to which they inspire, teach, instruct, and mentor out in front.

Centuries ago, a leader's place was up-front in the most visible position leading the way into battle astride their horse or in front of the chariot. Influential leaders show the way and never in the neutral place of the office. Alexander the Great, and Caesar inspired, cheered, and encouraged their warriors against all odds. Overtime, the new adopted model of leadership is managing from behind with a low profile. The hierarchy of the staff is an inverted model where the staff is now called front-line workers.

Leaders of today need to adopt the old style of leadership, by leading in front. The employees, customers, and all other stakeholders need to see the confidence of the one who is in charge. The battleground of competition, market share, and customer service requires an engaged leader drumming up support, and bugling the voice of optimism. Perhaps the external credibility can be converted into central influence for those they lead. The visible example brings the followers into the vision and process to shape, alter, and evaluate the anticipated needs of the employees. Leadership capital expands, when they understand the needs of the subordinates and walking along the side of them. They need to do more than being elusive in the same room; they need to be engaged and involved in the welfare of the folks whose lives they influence.

The subordinates and followers must not only hear, but also see the leader taking charge and assuming responsibility. It is impossible to assess too highly the influence of the leader who pays the price to understand the hearts and minds of those they lead. The latitude in which leaders take advantage of the teaching moments to inspire lasting impressions, are those who actively seek out others, provide vision and direction, nurture relationships, supply encouragement, hope, and strength to perform is the choice between devotion or abandonment.

To claim some of history's teaching moments, the 16th President of the United States, Abraham Lincoln served passionately with the troops. During the early stages of his first year and subsequent years he was dedicated to finding out the conditions, gather information and to know his people. Donald T. Phillips, in his book, *Lincoln On Leadership,* wrote, "One of the most effective ways to gain acceptance of a philosophy is to show it in your daily actions. In order to stage your leadership style, you must have an audience. By entering your subordinate's environment—by establishing frequent human contact—you create a sense of commitment, collaboration, and community. You also gain access to vital information necessary to make effective decisions."

A survey of leaders from Fortune 500 companies concluded that leaders need to get closer to their employees if they want to be good coaches. The majority of respondents, cited openness, trust, and friendship as key factors to successful relationships.

The central question: Why is so much time spent on meeting the needs of the direct reports or followers? Perhaps the decisive answer is they are simply the greatest resource. More persuasively, the people a leader meets in the parking lots, elevators, and elsewhere are those being asked to execute the vision and strategy of the organization—they are the ones who ultimately meet the needs of the stakeholders. Unless the employees can observe and notice the qualities of leadership, it would be difficult to move others down the path of superior performance. Leaders who exclude this character trait become strangers and the direct reports or followers will end up following someone else who can demonstrate the way.

The fixed conviction of a leader to influence and lead is abundantly all around. Those who do well and do not isolate themselves from the opportunities will have greater influence to show the way. Whatever the current leadership sphere is, it will naturally grow and eventually create critical mass for sustained superior performance. There are many people who are waiting for such visible authority to be trained, understood, and to build trust.

The behavior, as characterized in the theoretical description of visibility, will highlight the ennobling characteristics and qualities of mature emotional intelligence, strength, courage, vision, and all other leadership traits. On the other hand, unless others can see the full weight of the leader interacting, asking questions and listening, the natural consequence will be a weakened ability to being effective.

As long as the followers perceive their leader as a commanding figure, the greater the strength will be for followers to be more respectful and obedient. The more one gives their employees, the more they are willing to give. Imagine a leader responding more intensively to external contact through the simple tasks of picking up trash in the hallways, or greeting employees at the entrance of the building. This one trait will transform an unstable platform into a stable and durable structure for employees to stand with their leader. This type of seemingly indeterminate conduct has the ability to generate motivation and commitment to transform cultures the world over on a long-term basis.

Leadership is not so much of what takes place behind closed doors rather what happens on the floors and offices of the entire organization. Leadership is found in public areas out and about walking the floors and offices communicating and knowing their employees. This one behavior and skill will help transform a culture from silos to synergistic teams, breaking down walls and barriers, and ultimately creating trust and transparency. Leadership is essentially the process of venturing out front, going first, and blazing the trail, with the close following audiences of thousands. They do not hide behind the façade of the office and their titles, they are in front with the people. It might be expected in the final conclusion that the janitor who cleans the public areas and the private offices of the employees—the person who is possibly paid the least is the most visible.

In the world of leadership development, there are calculable and measurable properties with exponential return—such as the property of the power of 1 influencing the rest of the 99. By being a single enduring example, to 1 the rest of the 99 will be taught based on what they see the leader do. In the function of my career, I have opportunities to teach groups of students. It was obvious, from the first day of class, that there was one individual in particular who had difficulty making friends and fitting in with the others. In his attempt to be noticed, he would act out inappropriately, which only brought further unfavorable attention from the other classmates.

In his efforts to transition, I demonstrated many different leadership qualities in the extent to which patience, and understanding was given. In due course, the student became a part of the group no longer looking in from the outside. The teaching moment came when the rest of the students said, "We know in the event, if any of us were left out of the group, you would be there to support each one of us." The leader who has the most influence sets the hearts and minds afire of those they lead and makes the ordinary routine of being noticeable the vista for others to see and aspire to be—it is exponential.

Influential leaders have remarkable visibility and a noticeable voice. Bona fide, visible leaders are on a level of great importance which establishes the power to change the corporate culture. Visibility is profound, simple, and most of all, makes sense to those who care to listen. It translates to everyone; scientists, engineers, line workers, decision-makers, and many others. The duty of the leader is to be visible among those they lead and then act in all diligence, never being anything less than what a leader is and does. Visibility is a central role to set the tone of the culture, which produces organizational results.

The leadership responsibility will stretch and test the limits of any leader to do one more thing on top of all the other responsibilities being required of them. With such stretching, could lead to an expectation of feeling overwhelmed from time to time. That is okay, if compared to the analogy of developing muscle strength. Building muscle requires one to tear down the tissue to the point of exhaustion and pain to allow for growth. The leadership capacity is to push oneself to their potential limits, building influence and power through the strong concepts that great writers, thinkers, and practitioners have built and used over the course of human history to carry the burdens of leadership.

Chapter 9

Telling It Like It Is

One of the most difficult things of being a leader is "Telling It Like It Is" which is essential to the authority of a leader. Many of the influences to define a leader's ability to be effective are placed on high valued skills such as writing, speaking, critical thinking, problem solving, and many others. What tends to bury most leaders lay in the deeper soft skill-sets that crush the leader's effectiveness and ability to lead.

Such character traits of "Telling It Like It Is" are insufficient in themselves but when coupled with other leadership concepts they place the leader into paths of influence to communicate honestly. According to a 2005 Mercer Management Consulting study, 40 percent of employees trust that their bosses communicate honestly—

which means that 60 percent believe that their bosses are not being honest.

Most people have the skill-set to have basic communication interactions on a daily basis, but not the ability to communicate conflict, fear, anger, and disappointment. The analysis of the nature of candor is the difficulty to own personal emotions let alone managing the emotions of others. There is reason to believe that a central absence of candor forces people to push feelings into passive aggressive behavior to resent and complain. Even if one understands the skills to effectively communicate negative emotions, it is very difficult. The most obvious question: What makes it so uncomfortable and even painful to communicate such feelings in a direct approach?

From on high, are leadership commandments to steward, guide, and mentor their careers, performance, and effectiveness in the work environment. The obedience to such laws are easy when the employee is achieving all the measures of success, but much more problematic, when they are under-performing and experiencing difficulty in the workplace. Prolonging the inevitable hard conversation will not only compound matters for the employee, but also force other team members to question the leader's strength to resolve conflict and to effectively lead. The counsel is to approach the issues head on, balanced with consideration, which sends a strong message to the rest of the team the set standards of the culture.

The knot of both ends, in which leadership ties trust and truth, loosens when candor cannot be shared. A common poor knot is where organizations go to the extent of hiring an individual to be the "Corporate Bulldog" or an appointed friend because the senior personnel or persons either do not have the leadership muscle or the skill to have the hard obvious conversations. When corporate layoffs are to take place, at the dictates of a slow economy, the corporate bulldog would have the assignment to announce the downsizing, or rightsizing. The universal understood language is *"Don't shoot the messenger"* pushing blame somewhere else.

The setting off in peoples' minds is thinking a rush to Mercy instead of an appropriate charge to Justice—the thoughts are to protect from offensives and to shy away from correctness, even when it might be helpful. Unlike many ill-suited leaders, Abraham Lincoln wrote a letter to Major General Hooker holding him accountable for inappropriate behavior while maintaining a balance in integrity with his direct report.

January 26, 1863

Major General Hooker:

General,

I have placed you at the head of the Army of the Potomac. Of course, I have done this upon what appears to me to be sufficient reasons. And yet I think it best for you to know that there are some things in regard to which, I am not quite satisfied with you. I believe you to be a brave and skillful soldier, which, of course, I like. I also believe you do not mix politics with your profession, in which you are right. You have confidence in yourself, which is a valuable, if not an indispensable quality. You are ambitious, which, within reasonable bounds, does good rather than harm. But, I think that during Gen. Burnside's command of the Army, you have taken counsel of your ambition, and thwarted him as much as you could, in which you did a great wrong to the country, and to a most meritorious and honorable brother officer. I have heard, in such a way as to believe it, of your recently saying that both the Army and the Government needed a Dictator. Of course it was not for this, but in spite of it, that I have given you the command. Only those generals, who gain successes, can set up dictators. What I now ask of you is military success, and I will risk dictatorship. The government will support you to the utmost of its ability, which is neither more nor less than it has done and will do for all commanders. I much fear that the spirit, which you have aided to infuse into the Army, of criticizing their Commander, and withholding confidence from him, will now turn upon you. I shall assist you as far as I can, to put it down. Neither you, nor Napoleon, if he were alive again, could get any good out of an army, while such a spirit prevails in it.

And now, beware of rashness. Beware of rashness, but with energy, and sleepless vigilance, go forward, and give us victories.

Yours very truly
A. *Lincoln*

One of the central points of leadership is straightforward talk. Abraham Lincoln first affirmed (consideration) General Hooker, and his confidence in him and quickly followed up with the ground truth (courage) to hold him accountable for his behavior. He encouraged General Hooker to go forth and do the honorable thing. Regrettably, the idea of trying to improve people by creating fear and making them fearful is counterproductive. The consequences for leaders who are adversarial towards the soft-skill tools of leadership cultivate severally damaged environments.

General Hooker was so impressed with the letter that many months later he commented in a newspaper that Abraham Lincoln's communiqué was "just such a letter as a father might write to his son."

C.S. Lewis, in his book, *God in the Dock*: *Essay on Theology and Ethics* wrote, "The Humanitarian theory wants simply to abolish Justice and substitute Mercy for it...Mercy, detached from Justice, grows unmerciful."

What Abraham Lincoln had was much more than an understanding of accountability, he had the absolute conviction of the potential in all men to be their very best. The challenge is to return to the principle of *Telling It Like It Is*. How many have had the experience of a performance review, which was supposed to be an inevitable hard review, only to come out with the mixed message of " Wow, they think I am doing a great job." What should have been addressed and discussed quickly became a pat on the back with a few "Attaboys." The shattering impact of withholding information is not serving the person or organization in any shape or form—it is highly destructive and damaging. The leader becomes a misaligned force to enable dysfunction in others and it highlights their own incompetence.

Neal A. Maxwell, a lifetime educator and author of over 30 publications imparts his educational wisdom, "The leader who is willing to say things that are hard to bear, but which are true and which need to be said, is the leader who truly loves his people and who is kind to them. Nothing is more cruel than that leader who, in order to have the praise and plaudits of his followers, entices them from safety into the swamp out of which some may never return."

The analogy of a parent applies to the role of a leader. How many would sweep away the opportunity to have a serious discussion with one of their children knowing that the inappropriate behavior will naturally lead to self-destruction? The most obvious answer is no one would ideally sit on the sideline waiting for the inevitable train wreck to occur—there would be intervention and support. Unfortunately and to the demise of many, when addressing poor performance or dysfunctional behavior, the damage has been done. Through the heartache and pain many will hear, "If you knew what was going to happen, why did you allow me to continue?"

In most cases, it is difficult to share the hard ground truth of reality. It makes most individuals very uncomfortable. Unfortunately, most people confuse parenting and leadership as being a friend, as opposed to being a trusted parent and leader providing feedback and essential counsel. When feedback and counsel are simply withheld, in hopes of not offending, it will ultimately cause further harm to the individual and those around them. In a parent child relationship, it will be absurd to enable dysfunctional behavior in hopes of keeping the relationship intact. It is not about friendship, it has everything to do with leadership. A good parent will be a parent. A great leader will be just that, a leader. A good parent and leader will hold the children and employees accountable for their actions and set the tone and conditions of the family and organizational culture. By not addressing the issues head on, others will question the leader's authority and ability to lead. It is the wise leader and follower who can cope with the reproof of life.

Ram Charan, an acclaimed business advisor to some of the world's most successful CEO's, links truth telling to the quality of the dialogue and the quality of the corporate culture. He notes, "Dialogue…is the single-most important factor underlying the productivity and growth of the knowledge worker…dialogue shapes…the corporate culture…faster and more permanently than any reward system, structural change, or vision statement."

There are virtually many layered reasons why organizations must be dedicated to the cause and to demonstrate *Telling It Like It Is.* An organizational culture with the ability to share hard ground truth is much more likely to be effective. It cuts cost by eliminating poor performing employees, needless meetings, corporate blind spots of inefficiencies, which translates a significant financial return and impact to the bottom line.

Some years ago, I had an opportunity to quickly meet with Jack Welch, former Chairman and CEO of General Electric. I learned that he calls "Candor" the dirty little secret in business. Furthermore, he says, "Lack of candor blocks smart ideas, fast action and good people contributing all the stuff they've got. It's a killer."

Jim Collins, a student and teacher of enduring companies and author of the books *Built To Last* and *Good To Great*, writes, "Leadership is equally about creating a climate where the truth is heard and the brutal facts confronted. There's a huge difference between the opportunity to 'have your say' and the opportunity to be heard. The good-to-great leaders understood the distinction, creating a culture wherein people had a tremendous opportunity to be heard and, ultimately, for the truth to be heard." A lack of truth is absolutely damaging yet it is permitted to become an enduring part of the culture.

I am reminded of a poem that illustrates the principle of *Telling It Like It Is* and the interplay of growth and opportunity, when truth is appropriately shared.

> *"Come to the edge," he said.*
> *The people answered, "We are afraid."*
> *"Come to the edge," he said.*
> *They came.*
> *He pushed them.*
> *And they flew.*

While Winston Churchill served as prime minister during England's darkest days of war, he did not skirt the hard issues and brutal realities facing his country. During his first address to the House of Commons as Prime Minister on May 13, 1940 he said, "I have nothing to offer but blood, toil, tears, and sweat. We have before us an ordeal of the most grievous kind. We have before us many, many months of struggle and suffering. You ask, 'What is our policy?' I say it is to wage war, by sea, land, and air. War with all our might and with all the strength God has given us, and to wage war against a monstrous tyranny never surpassed in the dark and lamentable catalogue of human crime. That is our policy. You ask, 'What is our aim?' I can answer in one word: It is victory, victory at all cost, victory in spite of all the terror; victory, however long and hard the road may be, for without victory there is no survival."

Winston Churchill awakened the sleeping security and notified all Britains that threat was on the door step and disruption was about to challenge the status quo. The unexpected news was most certainly painful, and to say the least, very intense. Those in England could not ignore the wake up call to the brutal realities of truth. Such truths will invariably force everyone out of their comfort zones and place them into a disequilibrium.

Peter Drucker, the practitioner and theorist of how humans are organized across the boundaries of businesses, governments, and all other groups, acknowledges the need for high-quality communication and truth telling to the success of an organization. The 20th century leadership guru wrote, "At its most powerful, communication brings about 'conversion,' that is a change of personality involving values, beliefs, aspirations. But this is a rare existential event and one against which the basic psychological forces of every human being are strongly organized." The strength of a person's life is in interchange of truth enabling transformation to take place in behavior.

Colin Powell, a retired four-star general in the United States Army and former Secretary of State, wrote in his autobiography, *My American Journey*, "When we are debating an issue, loyalty means giving me your honest opinion, whether you think I'll like it or not. But once a decision has been made, the debate ends. From that point on loyalty means executing the decision as if it were your own. This particular emperor expected to be told when he was naked. He did not care to freeze to death in his own ignorance. 'If you think something is wrong, speak up,' I told them. 'Bad news isn't bad wine. It doesn't improve with age.'"

Truth has been a discussion for thousands of years. It is the heart and soul of philosophy and the liberator to set all men free from the incarceration of a false façade. The unrivaled Italian sculptor and artist, Michelangelo, was able to see the full potential in the raw material by carving away the rough walls. In the broadest meaning, truth chisels away the rough edges of behavior.

> *In every block of marble I see a statue;*
> *See it as plainly as though it stood before me,*
> *Shaped and perfect in attitude and action.*
> *I have only to hew away the rough walls*
> *Which imprison the lovely apparition*
> *To reveal it to other eyes, as mine already see it.*

As with any master's touch, the wielding tools are required to produce a masterpiece. The key is how a leader administers the skills to guide the conversation. The discussion does not need to be necessarily a despairing conversation rather a statement of the genuine deficiencies and an invitation to work on them productively. The lines of communication are sharply drawn by means of simple tools.

Once an issue has been highlighted, it is best to resolve the issue immediately. Separate the inappropriate behavior from the individual. Identify the behavior and speak to it and not the person. For example, your behavior is inappropriate as opposed to you are inappropriate.

Avoid being condescending; use language and a tone that is non-threatening. People understand a threatening environment. This will force an instinct of defense.

Influence with honor; this will allow the individual to be a willing participant to accept feedback as counsel as opposed to mandates of force and fear. The old industrial management style was to: "Give them hell, show them who is boss, set fear into them." This approach is manipulative and coercive to keep control. Overtime, this style of management will be the undoing of the leader. They will rebel.

Invest time to understand; individuals behave for a very good reason. All behavior flows from the most inner parts of self. It is based on paradigms, mind-sets, and espoused principles and values. The sustainable solution is not to focus on the nature of the behavior rather the reasons that drive the behavior.

Create conditions of safety; balance the environment with courage and consideration. Remember the metaphor of the head and the heart. Always lead with the heart first, validating the individual who is deserving of consideration followed with the head to share the realties of truth.

The capacity to move others along the path of development is to become a trusted advisor, who they will seek out for guidance and mentoring. Leadership is about leading in front showing the way. When asked what the difference between a sheepherder and a shepherd, the reply, "A sheepherder drives the sheep and the shepherd leads them." People cannot expect to force others to behavioral change rather they must demonstrate the new behavior and share the truth to assist others in their own development.

Chapter 10

Work Life Balance

The past 30 years has fueled a greater awareness around the subject of "Work-Life-Balance." The dictates of faster technology, personal ambition, family pressures, and market globalizations have attributed to the stresses of people. These stresses force an imbalance in how one lives life. People are experiencing the "burnout" factor.

The exhausting affects are having adverse consequences on organizations, families, and individuals. It is taking its toll virtually in all fabrics of society. It is becoming apparent that stress related symptoms are manifested physiologically and psychologically.

Lives are becoming consumed with a multitude of professional and personal activities that tend to confuse how to choose between what is good, better, and best and tying the decision to those for whom they have responsibility. The discipline is to abstain from the good things in order to choose those things that are better or best because they address the true purpose of life.

The intersection of the issue is people are required to do more things than what is possible to accomplish. The most visible and consequential learning is to balance the roles of an employee, spouse, parent, coach, churchgoer, and community advocate. Is it any wonder why so many are suffering either personally or publicly with outcries of burnout?

Doing mundane things that are identified as good might be an insufficient reason for doing them. Individuals can spend the allotted time and resource doing everything good and never focusing on those things that are better and best. When considering all of the choices available, individuals must recognize the reality of choices and the quality gradient between: good, better, and best.

One might consider spending time developing their golf game, studying a subject of interest, viewing television or spending their evenings coaching a community sports team. All of these activities are good and noteworthy endeavors to serve and to develop, but of those activities, not everything is worth that portion of life, to achieve it at the expense of those things that matter most. There will always be the competing activities that will need to be managed but never at the displacement of those activities over which one has full responsibility.

As a young man in my mid twenties, I graduated from college and accepted a job in Los Angeles, California, which was 800 miles away from home. Eight weeks before our move to California, my wife and I had a set of triplets who spent time in the hospital to receive proper care. The daunting responsibility to care for family, career, and myself, seemed impossible. Much like a young professional who is trying to remain competitive in the marketplace to support and provide for his or her family, or the mother trying to raise children and balance a career along with all other activities are encumbered to learn how does one enjoy life and not simply endure life.

The answers are almost invisible and certainly inconspicuous to work life balance. The response is not so much a discussion of time as it is a conversation of the priorities and purpose to focus on those things that matter most. Goethe, an 18th century writer and philosopher said, "Things that matter most should never be at the mercy of things that matter least." The true joy of life is to be used for a purpose that is worth living.

The central question that sharply affects choices is: To whom and what an individual wants to be. What is the purpose of life? What makes me and others happy? What is my distinctive contribution? What are my talents? What do I enjoy doing? Even though my particular choice of family and career was more costly in time, it was by far the best value I made in all of my decisions. My choice of family served my spiritual needs and the choice of career served my temporal needs.

The balance of spiritual and temporal needs creates purpose and meaning for people to live life. Real work-life-balance comes from temporal activities feeding real and vital spiritual growth to sustain purpose and a meaning in life.

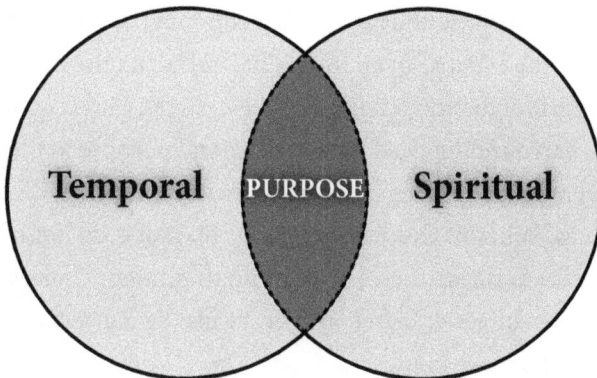

Without this perspective, work life balance seems to be balancing activities and ensuring that "buckets" of time are spent wisely. While this perspective (the "buckets") is useful for time management, it does not truly address balance and purpose in life. For example, a young father may work 60+ hours a week, constantly travel, and have the majority of his non-working time focused on volunteer service. One could argue his life is out of balance; however, if all activities serve to build the core of whom he is spiritually and his family benefits from his leadership and strength of character, he is a well-balanced and centered person.

The discussion is to understand what the core activities are at a temporal and spiritual level. The mind-set is not about giving equal time to all of the activities rather what are the most important activities to enjoy a full rich life. If individuals do not understand their purpose in life, regardless of the effort to achieve balance the attempt is futile.

In order to strike balance between temporal and spiritual life, people are often burdened to determine the choices between varied activities. One may need to say no to those activities for which there is no time or resources. For example, the idea of conducting numerous corporate meetings, focusing on too many goals, or enrolling the children in numerous sport activities may develop many results, talents, and skills. All of these activities serve a purpose and are worth mentioning; however, they should not be done at the expense of an individual's chosen pure purpose of life.

The important distinction needs to be between the activities and the much more surrounding need to have a general purpose in life. The purpose of life has an overriding influence on what one does with their time and resources. Without this perspective, individuals do not have an internal compass to direct their life, leading to random choices of activities. The choices of good, better, and best must be a direct consequence of a perceived purpose in life.

The imbalance between the temporal and spiritual is a long-standing problem that seems to be growing more problematic everyday. There is an exponentially larger gap due to the increase of self-gratification through the purchasing of material goods. The material goods are purchased at the expense of emotional and spiritual strength. Most anxiety, pain, and suffering could be spared if one possessed a greater balance between their choice of spiritual and temporal purpose of life.

One must learn that activities can be measured in qualitative and quantitative measures. Qualitative activities can be related to the quality of time spent to develop relationships, people, and things. In a materialistic society, much more attention is given to the quantitative activities of acquiring because they are easier to measure and quantify. They reflect direct material growth and wealth. The qualitative nature of activities becomes less important because the numerical measurement of relationships, development, and contribution, is harder to measure.

Based on my experience, those individuals who spent too much of their time in the temporal world of production and acquiring of material things will actually obscure the need for qualitative development in the spiritual world which will thwart the true purpose of one's life.

Activities that are not meaningful and have little significant value need to be subordinate to the strength of the purpose. There is a danger in trying to lead a balanced life when one feels they need to appear busy and overwhelmed all the time. The constant and notable causes that are put aside are those that distract from the balance of spiritual and temporal well-being. Doing too much of anything can create an imbalance in one's life as well as doing too little. Lin Yutang wrote, "Besides the noble art of getting things done, there is the noble art of leaving things undone."

Highly effective and balanced lives are those led by individuals who spend their time and energy focusing on the fixed activities that impact purpose. As the minutes of focused activities pass by, they produce an outcome, which results in purpose. Activities dictate either one's desired or a non-desired purpose. Balancing the time of temporal and spiritual activities ensures an impactful purpose and although happiness expands, it remains at the mercy of work-life balance.

Unless the activities and objectives are in accordance with the general purpose, a devastating consequence of inner conflict will be destructive and harm the balance of one's life. The surest and most productive life is the one that leads to a purpose.

From the age of twelve, Agnes Gonxha felt the desire to give herself completely to god. Later in life, she left Skopje and went to Calcutta dedicating herself to serving the poor in the slums. Mother Teresa taught school for twenty years, fed the poor, and cared for the sick and afflicted. Mother Teresa said,

> *The miracle is not that we do this work, but we are happy to do it.*
> *God has not called me to be successful. He has called me to be*
> *faithful. What we do is nothing but one drop in the ocean. But if*
> *we didn't do it, the ocean would be one drop less.*

Most people, at one point or another, have all experienced the burdens of coping with the complexity and diverse challenges of everyday life, which can momentarily disrupt the balance of spiritual and temporal balance.

The space shuttle has 7.8 million pounds of thrust. This is not an arbitrary number. In fact, the calculation is critical for the success of any mission for each of the space shuttles. The three main engines provide 1.2 million pounds of thrust and the two solid rocket boosters provide an additional 6.6 million, totaling 7.8 million pounds. During the first minute of flight, the shuttle burns one and a half million pounds of fuel to reach 1,000 mph. At two minutes, the shuttle is traveling 3,000 mph and the 6.6 million pounds of fuel contained in the rocket boosters have been burned. In order to lighten the load, the boosters are jettisoned into the Atlantic Ocean. It requires a disproportionate amount of fuel to travel the first 28 miles.

Much like the millions of pounds of thrust, life requires different energy and time throughout the course of living. Such variances of thrust put time out of balance but not the purpose of one's life. Everyone faces these kinds of challenges and imbalances from time to time. It is part of having the human experience. The demands of life weigh heavily on everyone. The key to success is to work within a framework of life's purpose, which will provide a pronounced direction to choose between good, better, and best.

Chapter 11

Decision-Making

Leadership is doing the right thing. Often, this requires making a hard decision that is frequently not immediately valuable to employees, peers, or beyond. However, real leaders identify and gravitate towards difficult circumstances that require their pronounced decision-making abilities.

Reaching back through the corporate annals of history, the story of Roy Vagelos of Merck & Company is a case in which doing the right thing was more important than potential profit. Vagelos' mission was to combat a persistent disease called river blindness. As recently as 1988, over 20 million people worldwide contracted the disease, of which one-third eventually went blind. The disease is caused by a waterborne parasitic worm. Vagelos discovered that a drug for heartworm in animals would kill the parasite. However, he was faced with an immediate dilemma in trying to bring the medicine to those in need. The dilemma was three fold: first, transferring a drug from animals to humans mostly failed, second, those infected would need annual doses for up to fourteen years, and third, this new product had little to no profit potential. Roy Vagelos funded the program personally in spite of shareholders concerns and outcries. Vagelos took the heat to commercialize the product that proved to be successful.

The intention is to not only meet the needs, but also exceed the needs of the broader community and all stakeholders. Most organizations have an institutionalized process and set priorities so they can make decisions and further design the policies to respond to needs and goals. This will produce a measure of confidence to operate within a relatively fixed and stable environment for predictable results.

Leadership perils are bent on the decision-making process. Leaders who trend away from the pressures of decision-making reduce their capacity to a mere bystander. President Warren G. Harding once burst out to a friend, "John, I can't make a damn thing out of this tax problem. I listen to one side and they seem right, and then... I talk to the other side and they seem just as right, and there I am where I started. I know somewhere there is a book that would give me the truth, but hell, I couldn't read the book. I know somewhere there is an economist who knows the truth, but I don't know where to find him and haven't the sense to know him and trust him when I did find him. ..., what a job." This is what leadership is about.

The former leader of Johnson & Johnson is legendary for the decision he made when an act of terrorism struck consumer products in the United States. In 1982, James Burke made the right decision to pull all Tylenol capsules off the shelves. Despite a likely very small amount that was laced with cyanide poisoning, he made the strong choice to pull all product. They recalled approximately 31 million bottles of Tylenol, retailing at more than $100 million.

Most do not like making the critical and most difficult decisions. It is not natural to place oneself at positions of heavy responsibility. The hard decisions rest entirely and squarely upon the shoulders of the leader and it become his or her full responsibility.

In 2001, the Texas Rangers signed Alex Rodriquez to an unprecedented contract of a quarter-billion-dollars. The following season, the Texas ball club started slow and with a poor start. Who do you think took the brunt and heat when the axe fell? Was it Alex Rodriquez, the club's franchise player? No, it was the manager. When a symphony loses its sound, who is to blame? Is it the first chair of the violin section? No, it is the Maestro or conductor who accepts responsibility. The point is that the leader makes the decisions. They hire the employees, they train the employees, and they create the conditions for success. They evaluate them and lead them. If employees fail, it is the leaders' responsibility. No one else owns the issue.

When faced with a decision, resist the urge to make the latest problem feel like an immediate crisis. Gather all of the information that has any relevance. Good leaders pay the price in short-term loss in order to completely understand all angles and consequences of their decision. They do their homework and do not rush a band-aid solution. They keep information flowing with the door open for new available input. When all information is gathered, they sit down and review what they have. When ready and recognizing that there will never be perfect information, they make the best decision based on what is known and what is right.

Great leaders ensure the entire team understands the decision and spend time explaining why the decision was made. They allow others to question the methods, but hold firm and insist they respect the position as the key decision maker. Encourage employees and your team to allow the effects of the decision to take root so new observations can be made to determine the decision's effectiveness.

If a leader is indeed dealing with a real crisis, they will still make decisions based on the best available information they have at the time.

Always recognize however, that unless the business is literally facing an enterprise ending possibility, most "crises" are simply dramatic turns of events that every organization faces.

When making appropriate decisions, it is important for leaders to surround themselves with strong and independent thinkers who are not simply yes men; someone who has an opinion and perspective beyond their own thoughts. Organizations riffed with yes men are ultimately doomed to failure. When cultures are stifled from thought, truth, and courage to speak up, bad decisions are allowed to become institutionalized processes or lack thereof. This is extremely expensive and will drive talented individuals out of the organization. Once a leader has made a decision he or she must carry out the appropriate actions, but up until that point, leaders make it clear that they will consider dissenting points of view. Award those who speak their minds. Encourage dissent through tactful spirited meetings. Allow employees from beyond management to be part of these exchanges.

Once a decision is made, the leader needs to become fully invested. A halfhearted effort will surely be disastrous and the decision is destined to be unsuccessful. If a leader gives less than a full effort, it would have been better not to make the decision in the first place. Leaders commit. Leaders take action. They have a determined path and execute.

In a *Time* article, "We're Going Down, Larry", yields to a more fundamental responsibility to exert proper decision-making rather than merely symbolic authority of being in charge. "As the snow swirled down on Washington that Wednesday afternoon, the drivers creeping past National Airport could barely see their way. Some even parked on the road and stepped out into the blizzard to clean their windshields of the sticky snow before driving farther. On the runways at National, the snow and ice were just as bad. Several of the idling jetliners returned to their bays, more than once, to be cleared of snow and ice and swabbed with glycol antifreeze.

The crew in the cockpit of Air Florida's Flight 90 was not oblivious to the freezing conditions; their plane had been de-iced twice. Yet the pilots' attitude about the buildup of ice on their Boeing 737 was at times casual, perhaps imprudently so, judging from their tape-recorded conversations released last week by the National Transportation Safety Board. Just after the joking stopped, the jet lumbered into the air, slammed against a bridge and plunged into the Potomac River, killing the pilots, 72 others aboard and four passing motorists.

The NTSB has not finished its investigation of the crash, but the pilots' conversation supports the leading line of speculation about the causes: the snowy, 24° weather. First Officer Roger Alan Pettit, 31, the copilot, initially expressed concern about the icy conditions, as he would again and again. Twenty minutes after the 737's last glycol wash, Pettit joked: 'Maybe we can taxi upside some [727] sittin' there runnin' [and] blow off whatever [ice and snow have built up on the wings].' Several minutes later Pettit remarked, 'It's been a while since we've been de-iced.' He remained astonished by the weather. 'See all those icicles on the back there and everything?' Minutes later Pettit said, 'Boy, this is a losing battle trying to de-ice those things. It [gives] you a false sense of security, that's all it does.' Replied the pilot, Captain Larry Wheaton, 34: 'That, ah, satisfies the feds.'

Unlike the pilots of several nearby planes, Wheaton and Pettit, neither of whom had had extensive experience flying in such weather, never mentioned to the control tower their concern about the ice each saw building up on the wings. Pettit said only to his pilot: 'This one's got about a quarter to half an inch [of ice] on it.' Despite the unequivocal federal regulation against flying with snow, frost or ice on the wings or engines, they taxied out to take off. Pettit was at the controls. 'Slushy runway. Do you want me to do anything special for it or just go for it?' he asked. Wheaton: 'Unless you got anything special you'd like to do.' Pettit then described his planned ascent maneuvers, with the final, jesting caveat, depending on how scared we are.

Reading the transcripts last week, one 737 pilot was surprised by the looseness of cockpit procedure. Said he: 'I can't imagine getting ready to roll and asking 'Should I just go for it?' Remarked another top airline pilot: My God. Either those guys were scared to death, or they hadn't the foggiest idea of what they were getting into.'

As the accelerating plane splashed down the runway, Pettit was alarmed by the instrument readings for engine thrust. 'God,' he said, 'look at that thing. That doesn't seem right, does it? Ah, that's not right.' Wheaton: 'Yes, it is.' Pettit: 'Naw, I don't think that's right. Ah, maybe it is. I don't know.'

The jetliner took off. Seventeen seconds later, already alerted to the danger of a stall by the rattle of the control stick, Wheaton tried to will Flight 90 aloft. 'Forward, forward. Come on, forward. Forward! Just barely climb.' Five seconds later Pettit knew it was over. 'Larry,' he said, 'we're going down, Larry.'

'I know it,' Wheaton said. Before he uttered his last word, the tape picked up the first sound of crushing metal."

There needs to be preconditioned responses set for proper decision-making. One must be prepared to make such vital decisions. There are warning signs to alert oneself to danger when going in the wrong direction. There were visible signs both for Wheaton and Petit to alert them to the improper decision to take flight but they violated their better judgment.

Employees easily see halfhearted and unsupported decisions. Leaders who exhibit this kind of weakness communicate unwittingly to their employees that the decision, and by extension, the leader's decision-making and problem solving abilities, are not really something they need to take seriously. Employees are left to their own devices, morale suffers, and execution and productivity falter. Real leaders understand that making the decision is just the first part of actually living the decision. Effective decision-making requires a leader to lead by their example in order to communicate the serious and deliberate nature of their leadership.

Hanging in the New York Jet's locker room, was Bill Parcell's message:

"BLAME NO ONE!
EXPECT NOTHING!
DO SOMETHING!"

Lou Gerstner in, *Who Says Elephants Can't Dance?*, says, "Decisions need to be made by leaders who understand the key drivers of success in the enterprise and then apply principles to a given situation with practical wisdom, skill, and a sense of relevancy to the current environment."

The best possible way for a leader to make the appropriate decisions is to make decisions based on what is best for the majority of those they lead and serve and will have the greatest impact.

William S. Kane, *Thriving in Change,* wrote, "In May 1962, Russian President Nikita S. Khrushchev conceived the idea to up the ante in the Cold War by constructing a storage/launch site for intermediate range nuclear missiles in Cuba, a mere 90 miles from the U.S. coastline. With Fidel Castro's blessing, the warheads were quickly and quietly installed. By October, President John F. Kennedy had been shown the photographic evidence from military reconnaissance that clearly delineated the missiles.

With such a nearby threat, JFK had a mandate for action, and he took it. While Soviet diplomats continued to deny the missiles' existence, JFK commenced an immediate flurry of correspondence between the two nuclear powers—including personal communication with Khrushchev. Clearly, JFK knew what was at stake, and he refused to bow to any Russian denial or demands. In an address to the American people, he outlined the nature of the threat, and true to his word, he ordered an immediate naval quarantine of Cuba, effectively blocking all shipments to and from the island. Finally, after a 7-day standoff, the Soviets ordered the missiles dismantled."

In many circumstances, the decision-making process is about calculating the consequences of risk. The moral reasoning decision-making is to perform the duty and action, which leads to the benefits of good, or harm, of individuals and the organization. Business leaders, scientists, politicians, and military leaders consistently weigh the resulting benefits and harm when making decisions.

When General Eisenhower decided the time to send the troops to Normandy Beach on D-Day, he considered the greatest benefits after the costs have been taken into account. General Eisenhower knew that many lives would be lost.

Eisenhower's concern was with the men. Twenty years later he said, "Goodness knows, those fellows meant a lot to me. But these are the decisions that have to be made when you are in a war. You say to yourself, I am going to do something that will be to my country's advantage for the least cost. You can't say without cost." Utilitarianism is a moral principle that embraces the right course of action that balances the benefits over damage for everyone involved.

Mayor Giuliani once said, "Often I make a decision knowing that I'll be criticized but feeling certain that I'll be vindicated. A leader has to have the confidence to think that his decisions will be proven correct. While trying to retain humility, you must accept that the reason you're making these decisions and other people are not is because, for now, you're in charge and they aren't. You do no one any good if like Hamlet; you cannot carry the weight of your convictions. Yes, you must guard against arrogance; but if you're doing your job and putting your motives and conscience through their paces, and accept that maybe you really do know better and can see a little further down the road than others."

Employees are more apt to follow a leader who is in control and can make the hard decisions. Decision-making accelerates corporate growth and translates into business results. It is widely regarded as one of the best and most effective competencies of leadership. Individuals will gravitate to those leaders who provide clarity and direction and do not delay a decision.

Chapter 12

Organizational Design

There are many clashing ideas and widely disseminating purposes of business. Peter Drucker, a management theorist and author said, "There is only one valid definition of business purpose: to create a customer."

If customers are the central focal point, why is it that many of the needs of all stakeholders go unsatisfied? Despite everything one has learned, customer focus continues to be elusive. Some have argued that customer service has decreased in recent years.

Arguably, poor customer service can be attributed to a lack of a unique position in the marketplace, competitive globalization, suppliers, inferior products, lack of financial return, and a myriad of other key measures. The most fundamental measure is financial, but it is closely followed by customer service. The central definition of a customer is those individuals who have a stake or invested interest in the success of the organization, including the employees. Customer-centered focus needs to be applied through the rank and file, whether the customers are outside or inside the company.

In their book, *Rules to Break and Laws to Follow*, Don Peppers and Martha Rogers write, "Customers have memories, they will remember you, whether you remember them or not." Further, "customer trust can be destroyed at once by a major service problem, or it can be undermined one day at a time, with a thousand small demonstrations of incompetence." Great customer service is the lifeblood of any organization. The quick fix of promotions, price-cutting, and gimmicks will not provide a long-term sustainable customer. The essence and key to customer loyalty is forming a relationship and meeting their needs consistently over time. The most accurate measure of any organization is customer satisfaction. A leader's central responsibility is to tie the ends of the needs of the customer and what makes them happy and loyal.

In any customer service environment, there needs to be a watchful eye on the conditions of rapid change taking place across the globe: frenetic transformations, market conditions, vendor suppliers, relationships, new domestic and international competition, and product integrity. Such examples are at the top of the list of meeting stakeholder needs.

Part of the roadmap for customer growth and satisfaction is the glaring signs of the customer's buying decisions. Many of the navigating questions: What matters most price or quality? Does policy have anything to do with the customer's ability to buy? Does the organizational mission and strategy support customer needs? How relevant is the product? What are the current market conditions? What are the trends? Where is technology going in the next one, two, or five years?

Part of the comprehensive plan is the voice of the customer, Fred Reichheld's book, *The Ultimate Question,* says, "Delighting customers requires insight and innovation—the continual development of your company's capabilities. The best process for generating these assets economically is to recruit the active involvement of customers and to listen closely to these conversations." Nothing increases loyalty more than inviting customers to have a seat at the table for process improvement and decision-making. It is not a position of privilege rather of necessity; the more fundamental cause is the satisfaction of the client. At Southwest Airlines, president Colleen Barrett upon receiving feedback from a customer, required appropriate responses with a thank you note and course of action to the feedback.

Change plays a common role in a company and can be difficult and labor-intensive for any leader. Viewing the problem as an opportunity for growth is very important. William S. Kane, in *Thriving in Change* wrote, "Change, even for the sake of change, can have many benefits beyond process improvement, market share enhancement, or greater profitability. It offers individual and collective learning opportunities. It may also heighten employee engagement and interest in work, thus increasing productivity and job satisfaction. Likewise, employees will have a greater sense of pride and ownership if they participate."

Many leaders typically assume what stakeholders want, and operate within their own structure that inevitably compromises and usually inhibits their ability to satisfy stakeholder needs. Change, in the end, is carried through the critical role of assessing needs. The long observed tendency to which hundreds of examples would attest are senior leaders being surprised to having lost a customer, and left scratching their heads in disbelief as to what went wrong?

Any system developed in an organization should take into account the nature of the specific needs of all stakeholders. Leaders should take the initiative to identify opportunities for customer growth and loyalty. Take the example of Harley Davidson buyers and riders being treated as part of the family. It is not coincidental that buyers identify themselves by branding the company logo on their arm. Customer loyalty is the key to success and sustainability for any enterprise.

The basic tenants for excellence are listening to customers, acting on what was heard, delivering on commitments for a great product, superior service, opportunities of innovation, and respect.

The rising stakeholder needs and expectations shift the planes for organizations to reengineer, reinvent, or transform to stay relevant in the world economy. Once market condition change has occurred, any organization will naturally shift to meet the new challenges and opportunities. Simply waiting for the change to happen is not often the route to success, if at all. History has shown that being slow to recognize the market conditions and staying current has been the downfall of some of the once most influential organizations in the United States: Woolworths, Sears, nearly IBM, and a countless list of others. It is staying ahead of the curve and anticipating the future market conditions that create long-term customer loyalty and success.

The hardest part of change is not the decision for change, the technology, the economic transformation, or the strategy and processes. Perhaps, the most difficult part is to know how to navigate the change process and connect the employees to the cultural shift. In most circumstances, change requires an entire cultural transformation of a new mind-set and competencies. It feels like taking a whale that has been held in captivity its entire life and releasing it into the wild and teaching it to survive. Those who can make the leap will stay relevant in the changing marketplace and world economy; those who do not will suffer along the side of those who do not know how or will not take the hurdle.

Cultural change turns on knowledge, systems, processes, research and development, decision-making, and reward systems combined with the intersection of specific values, attitudes, and leadership styles to rotate individual behavioral adjustments—collective behaviors produce cultural change. Leaders cannot expect to flip a switch and expect things to be fundamentally different. Change is to be well grounded in the mechanics of the organizational parts linked firmly to the needs and values of the culture.

The holistic approach is absolutely critical. The real core values of the organization are evident through the exhibited behaviors of those who are in charge of the organizational change efforts. The discernable values, in varying degrees, represent the culture of the organization. Consider the example of a corporate leader so consumed with his desires to cut costs and to hastily make change that he ultimately lost his way. "To the outside world, this gentleman had a most impressive educational and business pedigree, as well as a prior record of accomplishments. He traveled the globe, ate at the finest restaurants, went to the "right" shows and events, and carried a corporate title and compensation package worthy of it all. However, he was hardly out of central casting. Insiders were well aware of his Machiavellian approach and attitude. His caustic tyrants were rampant, and his volcano-like temper flared more than it settled. He had little patience, and he expected nothing short of "24/7 dedication from his team, treating them as if they were interchangeable parts. He ruthlessly closed plants, dramatically reduced the workforce, and sold off the businesses he deemed to be lacking—all in a manner of principle and practice that was contrary with the company's stated values."

Amidst all the ambiguity and insecurity to change, the dictates are in the external forces such as globalization, market conditions of supply and demand, new entrants, and supplier's competition, all of which dilates and dramatizes the volcanic forces for change. Overtime, like all other resources, they become old and antiquated. The assets, hardware, technology, knowledge, and skill-sets become largely out of step to the ever-changing market realities. Change is inevitable! It is the only surest constant. Apple computer, on April 1, 1976 never rested on their past successes with the first computer. Even in the moment of unparalleled achievement, Steven Wozniak and Steve Jobs recognized the need for process improvement to stay competitive and relevant.

To officially widen the scope for change, history has provided many illustrations of the old ideas, customs, methods, and traditions. Years ago, while attending school, a requirement was to take a word processing class. The company who provided the course material and content was none other than WordPerfect. Needless to say, the formulas and memorization made it difficult to learn the application. Albeit, it was coined as the new "killer application" revolutionizing technology, it was problematic for many users. Today, Microsoft dominates the world market with the intuitive windows application. Arnold Toynbee, got it right when he said, "Nothing fails like success." As leaders, they must avoid the pitfalls of the status quo mentality, which reduces their ability to survive in a frenetic changing world.

John P. Kotter, emeritus Professor of Leadership at the Harvard Business School said, "Too much past success, a lack of visible crises, low performance standards, insufficient feedback from external constituencies, and more all add up to: 'Yes, we have our problems, but they aren't that terrible and I'm doing my job just fine,' or 'Sure we have big problems, and they are all over there.'"

While the actual extent of change will vary broadly from organization to organization, the analysis is all enterprises must evolve and act in the vital transitional periods of its life cycle by exceeding the wants and purpose of all stakeholders. The representation of the recognizable wants and needs exists within a relatively fixed and predictable structure of the organization. At the root of change, lies the importance of defining the organization's distinctive contribution. This distinctive contribution to produce the results is found in the alignment of the Organizational Design. The importance of change lies behind such stories as the Boeing Company.

In the sharper forms of success, Boeing was critical in the achievement of World War II. Their manufactured products of planes not only helped, but also, at least to a large degree were the tipping point for victory in 1945; the nightmare of the most devastating war had come to an end. Out of all the celebrations came a heavy cost to Boeing. Their orders for manufacturing had dropped more than 90 percent. The need to produce bombers was no longer a want or a need. Overnight, their market was gone. The entire company and enterprise was built on one thing, manufacturing and producing bombers. Fortunately, for a competent visionary leader, Bill Allen saw the company as the leader of building and manufacturing the best flying instrument. In fact, Boeing is very much a product of, and remains always a part of the aviation business. In 1952, Bill Allen adapted to the new market conditions and entered into the commercial market. The public response was, "You make great bombers up in Seattle. Why don't you stick with that?" Against bad advice, the company redefined who they were and produced the commercial jet, the 707. Under the further direction and leadership of Bill Allen, Boeing built an organizational structure to produce the 707, 727, 737, and the 747. Great leaders such as, Bill Allen, will characteristically be the subjects of perhaps many leadership books.

Change is inevitable for continued existence. The barbed question is not a matter of if rather a question of when. The force towards change is confronting the hard ground truth and brutal reality. Certainly there are many forces behind change, but the catalyst of transformation is the power to accept truth. Leaders need to be "Reality Survivalists." Awareness and acceptance create the opportunities to enhance the competitive edge and help the enterprise to survive and grow.

Reaching back to the pages of history, some of the most influential stories of survival are told through the experiences of former prisoners of war and victims of catastrophe. The maneuvering techniques of survival are in the equipment to recognize brutal realities and conditions.

On the facade of survival, is the concept of "The Stockdale Paradox" which is named after Admiral Jim Stockdale who was the highest ranking U.S. military officer imprisoned in Vietnam. He was held in the "Hanoi Hilton" and repeatedly tortured over eight years. Jim Collins, author of *Good To Great*, describes going to lunch with Admiral Stockdale to understand how he survived eight years as a POW while so many died after just months in captivity. The truth of the matter is the discipline to confront reality. Admiral Stockdale shared, "This is a very important lesson.

You must never confuse faith that you will prevail in the end—which you can never afford to lose—with the discipline to confront the most brutal facts of your current reality, whatever they might be." Collins says, "The Stockdale Paradox is a signature of all those who create greatness, be it in leading their own lives or in leading others."

The sharp distinction from organizations that accept to those that reject reality suggests they are paralyzed by the lack of knowledge of how to navigate and address the current reality. When the global markets dictate change to reduce costs, increase prices, downsize, and better quality, most people will cling to the status quo and resist the present environment. The very nature of demurring from reality chokes the life out of any organization causing them to fail and remain irrelevant.

Anne Mulcahy reported in *Fortune* magazine soon after accepting her new position as CEO of Xerox, "The brutal facts were just that: brutal. Not only was Xerox losing money, they had enormous debt, high costs, and declining sales. They were in the midst of a liquidity crisis, and there had been a significant exodus of talent. On top of all that, they were facing an SEC accounting scandal, an outdated business model, and a staid product and service line. Prior leadership had put off the tough decisions the company needed to make in technology, product development and services. In addition, the overall economy was lousy. Xerox operated in a highly competitive industry, and in the prior year, the stock had fallen $63.69 to $4.43 per share."

These are certainly difficult situations for any one single organization to face. Rather then demur from the full weight of the responsibility for the one who is ultimately responsible, Anne Mulcahy rose to the challenge and resolved them appropriately. She resolved the issues without declaring bankruptcy even amidst advice from her advisors. She said, "Whatever you think the advantages of bankruptcy are from a financial standpoint, I think they are dismal and demoralizing for a company that desperately wants to turn around and regain its reputation." Out of the challenges of the organization emerged a strong competent figure, who would become a realist. She immediately went to work by closing divisions, restructuring costs, and among other things resolved the accounting scandals. The concept of telling the truth and sharing the brutal realities with others built capacity for leadership. As the stock fell her influence grew.

In spite of a strong tendency to remain in the comforts of the original organizational structure, the unremitting need to change is one of the most revealing aspects of an enterprise. Most important for the application of change are the clear and present questions of: Where does one start? How does one approach change?

Many organizations often announce ambitious growth strategies and mission critical goals then proceed to fail in achieving them. The consequential problem is change takes place in an ecosystem and not as individual parts. Most organizations are at the mercy of luck, or simply tamper in attempt to create sustainable change. The biggest mistake leaders make in trying to create change is to plunge ahead without a system.

The mechanics of the system are vision, employees, strategy, processes, and structures surrounded in the responsibility of execution and ultimately supported by alignment, technology, feedback, and culture. Such parts shape the corporate cultural behaviors and mores and ultimately pave the path for organizational results and success.

Newton's second law of thermodynamics basically states that any system left to itself will trend towards disorder. The role of the leader is to own the organizational system—the responsibility of the organizational system is placed squarely on the leader's shoulders. No one else can fulfill this responsibility. If, in the chain of command a message is sent to the leader for reengineering, the leader must know how to deal with change appropriately.

Reengineering or reorganizing requires an organization to have a scientific thoroughness to manage change. A systematic approach defines the boundaries for organizational change to take place without sacrificing current business results in place of future long-term sustainability. A great leader will find a way to tie the needed change with the results that will follow. Like any mathematical equation, organizations can calculate and predict business results based on the structure of the Organizational Design.

Take the example of Nokia. The company did not start off as a telecommunications company. Nokia was a paper company almost a century and a half ago. The company valued growth and the sustaining opportunity was in the process management of systems and structures for re-engineering, re-vitalization, and re-organization to occur. The 140-year company has become a trusted brand throughout the world. *Fast Company* said, "Nokia has gone from manufacturing paper to making rubber boots, then raincoats, then hunting rifles, and consumer electronics, until finally betting the farm on mobile phones. It's all part of an ongoing emphasis on renewal…Nokia is a company that refuses to grow big, grow old, or grow slow."

Much like any mechanical engine, there are parts that play a fundamental role in the operation and function of an engine; engines do not work without all of its parts. Each part is vital for combustion to produce power. Organizations have mission critical parts that serve a purpose to produce results.

The Organizational Design model, with all of its appropriate mechanical parts and internal and external mechanisms, will create stakeholder value. When an organization needs to create change, the leader should describe the change as a move away from the past to a better structure of opportunity. Ignoring any of the Organizational Design elements will create a misalignment, thereby throwing the system into disorder and paving the surest road to failure.

Organizational Design is the infrastructure that creates the economic performance to produce results for all stakeholders' needs. On the whole, the process is relatively simple, but the extent of it varies in the execution of all the concepts thereby strengthening the organization's ability to perform.

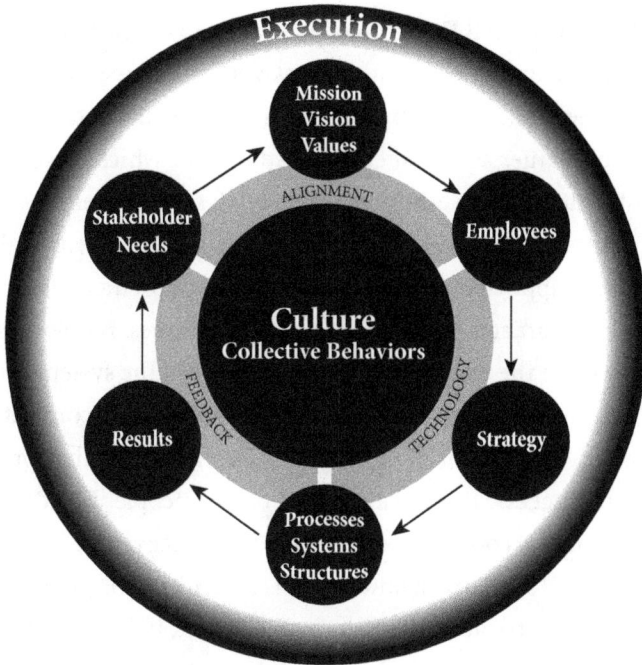

Vision:	Compelling purpose for existence
Employees:	The greatest resource of the company
Strategy:	Clearly stated and focused
Processes:	Infrastructure for work and production; vision translates to work
Structure:	A nimble, flexible, and flat organization
Results:	Outputs that produce consistent superior performance
Stakeholders:	Developing ecstatic customers
Alignment:	The interdependent relationships between all elements of the ecosystem
Technology:	Knowledge and tools to control and support environment
Feedback:	Understanding gaps to achieve intended results
Culture:	The collective behaviors of employees and the corporate atmosphere
Execution:	The control to get things done

The Organizational Design prefers to depend on the nature of an eco-system of cause and effect relationships with interdependence between the various elements, which produces results. The ultimate goal, the one to which companies are most committed and for which employees give their contribution, is meeting the needs of all stakeholders.

The manner and success, in which the entire Organizational Design elements are supported, are with the stable and predictable competen-cies and high character of the contributing employees. Employees are the medium to drive the perfunctory fundamentals of the system. What can be said broadly of the employees: they are hardworking, committed, pas-sionate, competitive, considerate, courageous, and truly the competitive edge for any success. It is always based on the people. Most often than not, organizations copy each other's vision, strategy, and other replicat-able systems and structures; however, it is difficult to copy and mimic the competency and character of the human element. If there is ever an argu-ment as to why leadership development is important, it is this one concept.

I started my career with Marriott hotels and resorts for 10 years. I learned a valuable lesson from CEO, Bill Marriott. Following in the foot-steps of his father, Bill became the successor of Marriott International Hotels and Resorts. Bill told me, "My father believed that if people were happy in their work they would take good care of the customer, and the customer would come back again and again. My father believed that concept, and he made it happen. My father had a tremendous loyalty to our employees, and I think we still do." Peter Drucker, a great lead-ership practitioner and theorist said, "Of all the decisions an executive makes, none are as important as the decision about people because they ultimately determine the performance capacity of the organization." If an organization is not built on good people, it will spark the dry timber of low morale, antiquated, disconnected, and slow moving misaligned strategies and systems; it will invariably burst into flames and destroy an organization. The success of the organizational enterprises rests on the power of the ecosystem. Each consequence or result is caused by the distinctive sense of balance between the parts of vision, employees, strategy, processes, structures, results, stakeholder needs, alignment, technology, feedback, culture, and execution.

Over the course of time, the elephant has evolved into a strong significant force as a bulldozer to modify and clear the savannah landscape in which it resides. At first glance, observing the behavior of elephants knocking down trees appears to be self-destructive. The very nature of the tree's vegetation is not only a food source, but also a shield to block the smoldering sun from all other animals. What is most outwardly damaging is merely a part of the elephant's survival, which is essential to the ecosystem of the savannah. One of the most intriguing aspects of the system is the conversion of the savannah to grasslands. The elephants act as a seed dispenser through their fecal matter. The dung beetle rolls the dung along and below the surface of the ground causing the soil to become more aerated and further distributing the nutrients for additional vegetation. As much as 80 percent of what elephants consume is returned to the soil as scarcely digested fertile manure.

In the broadest meaning, ecosystems are an absolute and all-encompassing stability to any organization. What would have happened if the elephants were restrained from the assumed destructive behavior of knocking down trees? Overtime, the entire population of other animals would die out because of the display of what would have seemingly been appropriate when it should have been left alone creating an imbalance. The giraffes that depend on the fallen trees to reach their food supply would pass away along with other living species that are dependent on the elephant's contribution to the ecosystem.

Similarly, like all other organized infrastructures such as an orchestra, the instruments of the ensemble are organized into the boundaries of four categories: Strings, Woodwinds, Brass, and Percussions. Each category's structure exists with their own distinct sound and tone. The beautiful sounds of the orchestra rests essentially in the system of how it is organized. Eliminate one of the four families from the orchestra will ostensibly change the entire output of the sound.

Underlying the conflict between the ends of leading and managing change is an even more critical question: How to fine-tune the system to produce sound results? What is essentially a best effort to create stability, unfortunately misalignment takes place in one of two ways: First, not understanding the Organizational Design elements, and second, tampering with the system with a quick fix solution.

In a participatory process, many tamper with the Organizational Design by tinkering with one of the elements, throwing the otherwise successful organizational ecosystem towards an inferior condition and dysfunction. What appeared to be a seemingly perfect solution, by removing the elephants from the savannah, would have ultimately destroyed the ecosystem.

Organizations who understand the interrelationships throughout the ecosystem of elements is able to out perform their competition, which enables flexibility and versatility to meet the demands of the changing environment. Out of the landscape of the Organizational Design blossoms organizational principles, which are consistent in truth. Such principles create controlled adjustments as opposed to complete destruction of constant misaligned changes and modifications.

The 1980's became the era of reengineering and process improvement driving leaders to tamper with the Organizational Design, ultimately giving way to failure. Perhaps in most circumstances, the employee's work shifted and now they were left to themselves to figure out how they fit into the new strategy and direction of the company.

The episode and ensuing problem with a customer order becomes mixed up. Jane Doe, who is the customer service manager catches notification of the mix up and with her best judgment mistakenly intensifies the problem by implementing her layers of change and in fact institutionalizes the means or unstable system to further complicate the problem. During the following months, Jane gets promoted and John Doe becomes the new replacement and experiences some new problems of his own and further compounds the problem by incorporating a few new ideas and thoughts. Soon, you have James Doe and Bruce Doe with their own bits and pieces to address the issue. In short order, the bureaucratic dysfunctional system makes no sense to anybody; it is so elaborate and problematic that it requires a full time engineer to manage the once simple system.

The complex systems in turn force the 21st century leader to not only attempt to understand, but also execute on the complex mechanics and tie the ends of change and process improvement together. The role is distinct from those of other individuals and the view is an explicit and consistent simplification and execution transforming from bureaucratic to a simple flat non-bureaucratic enterprise.

The Sears tower alongside Lake Michigan in Chicago is a perfect case in point of the bureaucratic hierarchy of layered systems and processes. The hundred-story tower was the world headquarters of Sears, the perfect representation of bureaucracy. In contrast, the world headquarters of Wal-Mart in Benton, Arkansas is a flat building and comparatively speaking, is a flat organization. Bureaucratic organizations are sluggish, lethargic, and exhausting. Dissimilarly, non-tower organizations are fast, agile, and nimble. The apparatus of managing change is in the fundamental core within the framework of the Organizational Design.

In the mid 1990's, Dell Computer redefined the massive computer market. Most, if not all, of the computer giants were competing on the manufacturing front by offering a faster and more powerful memory capacity. Dell understood the new opportunity and challenged the previous successes of the industry by influencing the purchasing and delivery experiences of buyers. By defining the strategy, to grow the market through lower prices, and the process of direct sales, Dell cut cost up to 40 percent. The delivery time for Dell was four days while the competitors took 10 weeks. Furthermore, the availability of the online and telephone ordering system allowed customers to customize their machines. Dell is a significant leader in computer manufacturing. Sales in 1995 hit $5.3 billion and grew to $35.5 billion in 2003.

The voice in the theory of change can be also characterized in the call for such influences to shift from supply to demand, from archaic systems to innovation. The boundaries of limitations are in the minds of leaders and practitioners who are in charge of the overall structure. The demands of change depend on the expressed vision in the realm of possibilities and significant "killer applications" which is the new revolutionary idea. The decisive and consistent mentality is to break through the barriers of limitations and learn that demand exists and growth and opportunity is abundant. One of the more general questions is how to generate it.

Part of the equation and answer for growth and stability is in the forces of competition. The fundamental nature of the strategist and leader is to define the parameters of competition and the science strictness behind it. Most often than not, leaders define competition too narrowly. The global market is much greater than the rival competition. There exists a worldwide market outside of a leader's industry that participates in the influence of market competition.

Michael E. Porter, of Harvard University, in his book, *The Five Competitive Forces That Shape Strategy*, outlines five forces:

Rivalries Among Existing Competitors—The strongest competitive force or forces determine the profitability of an industry and become the most important to strategy formulation.

Bargaining Power of Suppliers—Powerful suppliers capture more of the value for themselves by charging higher prices, limiting quality or services, or shifting costs to industry participants.

Threat of New Entrants—New entrants to an industry bring new capacity and desire to gain market share that puts pressure on prices, costs, and the rate of investment necessary to compete.

Bargaining Power of Buyers—This is the direct opposite of suppliers. Powerful customers can capture more value by forcing down prices, demanding better quality, or providing more service.

Threat of Substitute Products or Services—A substitute performs the same or similar function as an industry's product by a different means. Video conferencing is a substitute for travel. Plastic is a substitute for aluminum and email for express mail. When the threat of substitution is high, profitability suffers.

Porter says, "Understanding competitive forces, and their underlying causes, reveals the roots of an industry's current profitability while providing a framework for anticipating and influencing competition and profitability over time. A healthy industry structure should be as much a competitive concern to a leader as their company's own position. Understanding industry structure is also essential to effective strategic positioning."

Marriott started its business by providing root beer in Washington, D.C., which quickly grew to the restaurant business for travelers ordering food on the way to the National Airport. The restaurant business grew to the airline catering business and eventually to the hotel industry. In addition, Marriott branched out from the hotel industry to other similar offerings such as cruise ships, theme parks, travel agencies, real estate and retirement communities. Marriott's diversification allowed for joint effort of food procurement and distribution channels. As a result, Marriott earns 50 percent higher margins on food services than any other hotel company. Marriott's diversification strategy is based on acquisitions for similar opportunities and geographic expansion. The parts that do not support the strategy are spun off or disposed. Of note, those acquired businesses that were similar in nature, but where the skill-set was not transferable, they were divested.

Equally important to the Organizational Design process are the five competitive forces in which the leadership pendulum hangs in the center. Such an approach is holistic instead of gravitating to one element, which is simply tampering.

The judgment of history will place W. Edward Deming as one of the great thought leaders of process improvement and lean theory. Subsequent to World War II, he spent time developing better processes and more effective systems for production and manufacturing. His theories came to bear on the Organizational Design that systems, structures, and processes influence employee's performance within the cultural framework producing results.

In his explanation, the classic "Red Bead" experiment demonstrates his concept towards system design. The individuals were asked to deliver white beads, and only white beads, to a fictitious customer. Each participant was blindfolded and instructed to draw fifty beads from a large bowl filled with a combination of red and white beads. As they each drew a handful of fifty beads, they were then recorded noting the number of red and white beads. With each draw, Deming would use the traditional management techniques for better performance. He would use methods of intimidation for those who did poorly and awards systems for good performance to influence the outcome. Clearly, anyone observing this exercise would see the futility of management. Despite the fact that the customer would only accept white beads, it was inevitable that a portion of the drawn beads would be red.

One of the tying conclusions of performance is tied directly to structure and not necessarily to the employee. The first assumption for non-performance is a misalignment in the conditions of systems, structures, and processes. If the systems are aligned, then it becomes the responsibility of management to ensure that employee skills-sets are appropriate for performance. Of all the decisions a leader makes, none is more critical than selecting the right people. People determine the performance capacity of the organization, which is central to the entire Organizational Design—human capital supports and drives all of the elements.

The interplay of culture produces the results and infinitely addresses stakeholders' varied needs. Culture is defined by the collective behavior of all the people that cannot be manipulated or influenced by simple initiatives, programs or rousing speeches from leaders. Culture is driven from the point of view of vision, mission, and shared values of the organization and the aligned mechanics of the system, structures, and processes. Culture is a derivative of these forces producing actions and behaviors exhibited in people. If people are producing appropriate behaviors the systems are perfectly aligned.

The single aspect of results measure, at least in a preliminary way, the forces at work in meeting stakeholder's needs. The ultimate test of satisfaction is understood in the flow of results. To catalogue results, gaps require any organization to redesign. This complexity does not happen independently of one another or in a vacuum. It must be a holistic approach because of the nature of the ecosystem of Organizational Design. All of the parts are fluid and interdependent of one another. Tinkering and meddling will unquestionably do more harm and throw the organization into chaos.

Organizations are similar to a machine that produces some form of output or result. Whether it is horsepower from a vehicle, a manufactured product, or meeting other needs of stakeholders; there is the existing order and integration of all components for production capability. The design will enlarge the ability to be more analytical in dealing with change. Perhaps the best analysis is to place the organization up on the racks and examine each part through the model of Analysis, Back, and Construct "ABC".

Analysis: The process of identification or process of elimination to learn and receive knowledge based on logic and experience to determine the cause and effects of problems.

Back: The plan to support the building processes towards the production of a natural system to produce results.

Construct: To produce effective alignments to create a more effective Organizational Design ecosystem.

The organizational transformation must be anchored in a controlled environment governed by principles of change. Jack Welch CEO of GE, and Dr. Noel Tichy, who served as GE's manager of education, imparts their wisdom. "Mr. Welch's insight, which was not widely shared in business at the time, was that leadership was not the province solely of the CEO in his or her senior executive team, but had to be institutionalized throughout the company. A globalizing economy meant that a business world long characterized by stability, autocracy, and strictly bounded processes would have to become more change embracing which would require the development of nimble, adaptable leaders up and down the company hierarchies. That in turn meant building the capacity for teaching men and women not only how to manage change, but how to create it."

The foundation of this kind of control lies in adaptable leaders to manage and create change appropriately to improve competitive strength in the market place. Organizations will be required to manage the forces of micro and macroeconomics to reduce head count, control cost, experience growth, create demand, and produce product superiority. If leaders do not know the guiding principles to facilitate change, reengineering bogs down, growth initiatives fail, acquisitions are not incorporated appropriately, and strategies are not executed.

Change is virtually impossible without the full support of the hierarchy of leadership. A single individual or small group of change agents will never have the critical mass to create transformation, no matter how competent, talented or how strong the business case is. Countervailing forces will undermine the best efforts to change. These and other findings suggest the importance of the guiding principle of vision to direct and inspire employees to change behavior. Without vision for change, it will further push people to greater resistance and deeper into the traditions of the status quo, sabotaging all best efforts. Organizational change will invariably degenerate into a list of confusion, needless projects, and incompatible work assignments. Individuals will eventually suffer along the side of the organization.

In many transformation efforts, the direction becomes too complicated and buried much deeper than the basic elements of the Organizational Design ecosystem. Without the structure to manage change and create process improvement, the progression will dissolve into a never-ending debate of how to approach transformation. The Jefferson Memorial illustrates just how straightforward change and process improvement can be. The stones in the Jefferson Memorial were deteriorating badly. The initial, knee jerk plan was to replace the stones with fresh ones hauled up from a quarry in southern Virginia. This would cost millions of dollars and require closing the memorial to tourism for several months.

So, some simple questions were asked: Why were the stones deteriorating? Because they were frequently cleaned with harsh chemicals. Why was this cleaning necessary? Because pigeons were leaving too many calling cards. Why all the pigeons? They fed on the heavy spider population. Why so many spiders? They were attracted by a huge moth population. Why all the moths? The monument's lights attracted the moths during their twilight swarming frenzy.

Solution: Turn on the lights one hour later.

This is systems thinking, examining the big picture to reveal the multiplicity of cause and effect relationships for performance. What might have been a seemingly painful and costly effort became an inexpensive and simple solution. Out of these elemental, yet concrete concepts emerged the ability to manage change. The concept is explicit enough to put forward that the competitive edge to direct change lies in the mechanics of Organizational Design.

Maintaining a steady course of change is the preserved foundation of vision. The communication of vision is extremely important, whether it is setting the direction of the organization or reform movements for improvement. The unswerving purpose seems to drive the force that sustains the will power to continue when all else seems lost and the nature of work is no longer understood.

During World War II, the failed attempts to soften the beaches that would become known as the beaches of Normandy never raised objections from the importance of the vision; the vision of defeating the German expansion throughout Europe. The victory laid in the outcome of the B-17's responsibility to bomb the beaches to form craters and bluffs to be used as foxholes for the infantry. The failed strategy of bombardment was too short and in every case missed the intended targets. June 6th 1944, D-Day, there were over 2,600 dead in the early morning dawn. The imperiled strategy was subordinate to the vision. The mission moved forward, ultimately ending the war.

Organizational effectiveness is by no means a solo performance of one element of the design process. The trapeze act is to balance all the parts. However, the mounting failure and frustration in many organizations rests in the arrayed forces of spending too much time and energy in one area.

The struggle for leaders, in large part, is over strategizing. All the theories, the talking points, the worlds finest presentations, and certainly the stack of insurmountable data will only lead to a complex mess and disrupt the ability to execute on the wildly important vision. The exact absolute focus is extremely important in each area, but not to the extent in which there is a diminishing return of effectiveness. Leaders tend to end up stuck in the weeds of detail. It is not about the details as it is about setting the directions and executing with precision. Even if an organization has a mediocre strategy, the immense success comes in the execution of the strategy. The main concept expressed is, "It is better to have a 'B' strategy and an 'A' execution than to have an 'A' strategy and a 'B' execution."

Ransom E. Olds', of Oldsmobile, direction appeared to run toward the perpetual demand for the innovative horseless carriage. The strength of vision to address the growing market demands for greater transportation produced the assembly line concept in 1901. Prior to the assembly line, it required skilled workers and a slow and expensive procedure. The expansion of industry and the modernization for assembling cars enabled the Oldsmobile Company to more than quadruple the factory output. The rising needs and expectation shifted production from 425 cars in 1901 to 2,500 in 1902. The new revolutionary process improvement was aligned to drive strategy, ultimately fulfilling the vision.

There is a far more striking example in Henry Ford's vision to enhance transportation and produce an automobile that was within the economic reach of the average American. He came to recognize the potential and indispensability of a simple, reliable, and affordable car. His more mature concept of the assembly line enhanced the original design by putting conveyor belts in the process. He did not design the concept; rather he perfected it. What used to take one and a half days to fabricate one car now only required ninety minutes. His vision, strategy and processes increased the efficiency of manufacturing and decreased cost, which profoundly transformed the automobile from a luxury to a conventional American staple.

The Model T made its first appearance in 1908 with a purchase price of $825. Over ten thousand were sold in the first year and four years later, after the introduction of the conveyor belt assembly line the price was $575. By 1927, there were over 15 million Model T cars sold.

The ultimate goal, the one to which Henry Ford was committed and for which the employees gave their contribution, was centered on the Organizational Design ecosystem. All of which produced the appropriate set of consistent patterns of behaviors to provide results with a high degree of predictability and customer satisfaction.

Henry Ford and the Model T

<u>**Vision**</u>:	Enhanced Transportation
<u>**Employees:**</u>	Character and Competence
<u>**Strategy:**</u>	Affordable Entry
<u>**Processes:**</u>	Assembly Line
<u>**Results:**</u>	Increased Production
<u>**Stakeholders:**</u>	Ease of Transportation
<u>**Alignment:**</u>	Production Processes
<u>**Technology:**</u>	Conveyor Belt
<u>**Feedback:**</u>	Make Appropriate Adjustments
<u>**Culture:**</u>	Employees Assigned to One Job
<u>**Execution:**</u>	Consistent Performance

As a leader, Henry Ford demonstrated a grasp of the Organizational Design in all its subtlety and complexity as well as the power to produce results. The fine tactical elements undoubtedly broaden the ability to meet stakeholders' needs. Vision is the central bolt to the stability of any organization. It tightens all other elements of the organizational ecosystem. Overtime, a concise vision and consistent strategies and processes will fuse behavioral patterns of action, commitment, and motivation.

In the expression of the Organizational Design and other relevant resources, there remains the counter pressure of any leader. One of the countervailing forces for most leaders is complacency. When complacency is part of the cultural fabric, change is nearly impossible. It is simply naive to assume that what has been accomplished, as the perceived final destination will continue to drive the employees to perform. The world economy is changing at alarming rates. Research and development never sleeps nor dies. The need for constant process improvement and redesign is paramount for sustainability and relevance. Henry Ford lost his market position because the gap between results and stakeholder needs widened. The market wanted a variety of colors and Henry Ford would only produce the black Model T.

Business enterprises are started because of profound visions and strategies. The McDonald brothers, Richard and Maurice, recognized the quantum opportunity because of the changing face of life. After World War II, families had more discretionary income, and the automobile became more prevalent for most families. The social fabric was looking for opportunity. In 1937, they opened the first tiny drive-in in San Bernardino, California. Overtime, they operated consistently based on the ecosystem of the Organizational Design for process improvement. It is customary that no matter where people go throughout the world, french fries taste the same. McDonald's believed in uniformity in every restaurant; the strength of the brand depended on it. The accomplishments in the food service industry are likened to those of John D. Rockefeller in oil refining, Andrew Carnegie in steel manufacturing, and Henry Ford in automotive assembly.

The implication of corporate culture experienced by such leaders as Rockefeller, Carnegie, and Ford is the output and influence of executing on the vision, strategy, processes, and the expressed values, attitudes, and beliefs of the organization. On a wider front of change and organizational effectiveness, are the decision-making processes, reward systems, written and unwritten rules, and human interaction between team and department members. Employees are expected to assimilate the cultural behaviors and mores of what to do day in and day out at work.

People are the most significant asset of any organization; it is the outlier of any enterprise. This is the whole crux of why leadership is so important. Everything hinges on it. Without the people and great leadership, everything else fails.

Chapter 13

Execution

There are parallels in the strengths of any organization. The unifying atmosphere that marks success is strategy and execution. In looking back in recent years, the fundamental alterations to the parallel lines have created perpendicular business issues. Many leaders spend significant time developing strategy but fail to execute on the strategy. The classic view of "execution is secondary" has yielded defunct organizations.

The assumed fundamental of leadership is not the sole concept of strategy rather the varying concepts broken down to execution. The extent to which leaders can execute on such concepts of vision, strategy, process, and all other resources exemplifies the strength of the leader. The displacement of success is rarely in those concepts rather in the ability to execute around the elements. Ram Charan, coauthor of, *"Execution: The Discipline of Getting Things Done"*, says, "Seventy percent of strategic failures are due to poor execution…it's rarely for lack of smarts or vision." Additionally, he says, "Execution is the major job of a leader and must be a core element of an organization's culture."

The pursuit of organizational results through execution is the newest leadership theory in recent times moving quickly to broaden the leader's utility to systematically address the execution gap. Within the framework, the complexities depend on concrete organizational goals and strategies and employee competencies and capabilities. The dilemma is to what extent are the employee's competencies and capabilities aligned to the strategy?

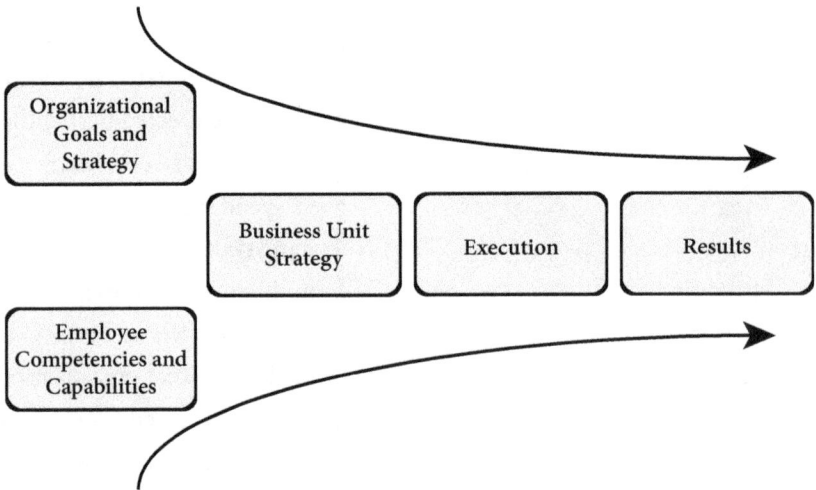

Executing as a leader starts in the exercise of strategy, which is the calculated design to achieve a particular goal. The function and responsibility is to deal with the rival competing current and unforeseen needs centered on the vision. Initiatives require well thought out stratagems and processes to extend and maintain organizational focus and success in relationship to response time in the changing markets, environments, and the unexpected.

Strategy is the thought and plan. Execution is the action and discipline to see it through. The barbed problem is strategy means nothing without the execution behind it. The conflict remains over the priority of time and energy and where to seat it among strategy and execution. Furthermore, strategy is duplicated from organization to organization. The thoughts and ideas are traditionally the same and are within the realm of what everyone else is doing. The volcanic energy that is traditionally spent in strategy would be better served in the thrust of how to execute.

The significant force of execution requires the strategic human capital; knowledge, skill-sets, attributes, talents, and behaviors along with the Organizational Design of an organization. Arguably, linking employee's competencies and capabilities to the broader organizational strategy can be very challenging. Furthermore, connecting the employees' daily work to the organizational goals is even more complex.

The relationship between current human capital and the current strategic business rests essentially in the alignment to produce the expected business results. Underlying this alignment between ends leaders must ask: What are the production capabilities of the workforce to produce the expected outcomes?

Leaders must prepare and implement individual and corporate development plans to close gaps in current human capital. Revealed gaps and development plans must be specific on a function-by-function and a job-by-job basis. A leader's concern, while extremely critical and complex, is the development of strategy but the superior challenge is how to execute the strategy with the people in the organization. Leaders cannot be like the violinist who always wanted to play, but spent their practice hours merely stringing and unstringing the bow. There comes a time when all strategy needs to be acted upon and executed. Leadership is not a position; it is action.

Take the example of the retail sector in the early sixties. Sam Walton was not the only entrepreneur who saw potential in the discount retail business. In 1962, S.S. Kresge started Kmart, Dayton Hudson opened Target, and Woolworth launched Woolco. Within five years, Kmart had

250 stores with revenue of $800 million compared to Wal-Mart's 19 stores and $9 million in revenue. In spite of losing the revenue and market share battle, Sam Walton stuck to his strategy and executed on smaller markets. The other discounters had the same carbon strategy and eventually beat each other up over the diminishing larger markets. The strategy of Wal-Mart moved beyond the traditional cyclical description of stratagem and moved towards their distinctive contribution and executed the mission of the organization.

The sharp distinction of execution is in the structure to facilitate the various entities of the Organizational Design. Proper structural alignment will optimize the vision and mission, tying all other elements together. The strength of the leader stems from the capability to execute at all levels, to identify and set in motion the employee capital to produce results. Given the need to execute, Ram Charan and Larry Bossidy stated, "No company can deliver on its commitments or adapt well to change unless all leaders practice the discipline of execution at all levels. Execution has to be part of a company strategy in its goals. It is the missing link between aspirations and results." Additionally, they put their stamp on the profundity of execution by saying, "Leadership without the discipline of execution is incomplete and ineffective. Without the ability to execute, all other attributes of leadership become hollow."

Most decisive for the course of any leader is to address what I call the "Five Principles of Vision Realization." As I have studied a vast number of organizations throughout my organizational development career, all great companies have a fundamental understanding, and more importantly, discipline to execute not only on strategy but all of the elements of the Organizational Design model, which ultimately addresses the purpose of the vision.

Louis Gerstner of IBM states, "All of the great companies in the world out execute their competitors day in and day out in the market place, in their manufacturing plants, in their logistics, in their inventory turns— in just about everything they do. Rarely do great companies have a proprietary position that insulates them from the constant hand-to-hand combat of competition." Execution is not just about doing the appropriate things. It is about out performing your competitors. It is about being faster, better, and more effective in the marketplace.

Despite the staging of execution, the awkward position might simply be that leaders do not recognize the existence of the governing principles, which handicaps the performance of the enterprise.

Five Principles of Vision Realization

The most successful leaders are those who respond to the Five Principles of Vision Realization in which case, presumably, the organization will become more effective in achieving the strategy and ultimately realizing the unique and dynamic aspects of the vision. To capture the aspect, necessitates an analysis within the categorical framework of the model.

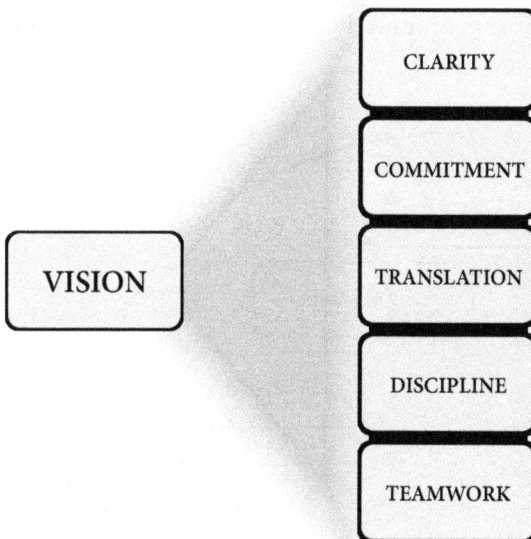

Clarity

Clarity is the ability to draw on and support the best interest of the vision. In the apparent genuine effort, most organizations have a vision and mission statement hanging in a beautiful frame; however, the conceptual problem is despite the best of efforts to draft the document, the consequential aspect is to activate, mobilize, and motivate all employees to the purpose of the vision—vision gives meaning to work, buying the hearts and minds. The function of a clear vision provides the sustaining power to execute in the most difficult times and conditions; it provides the strength to work. One of the most critical roles of a leader is communicating, re-communicating, explaining, and making sense of the vision. Employees should not be burdened to determine what the vision is and how their jobs contribute. In all the varying responsibilities of an employee, in context within the job function, interpreting the job is not one of them. The effectiveness of vision is sharply affected by the extent of the clarity in the communication channels. The natural consequence of confusion around the vision will increase operating expenses and erode profitability.

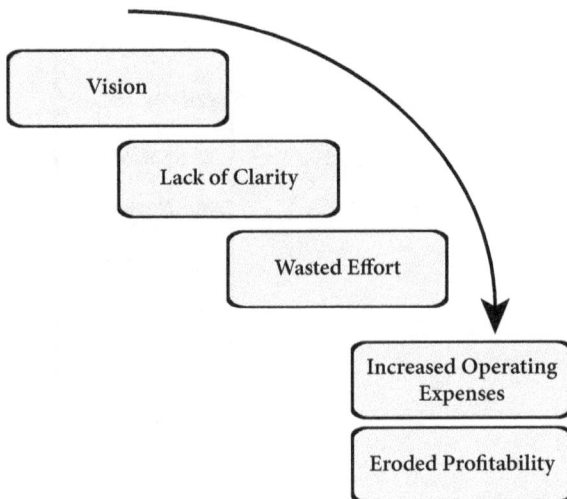

The power is to define the relationship between vision and the employee's contribution of work and milestones to organizational results of metrics and numeric. Execution of vision is the first responsibility to allow the systems, structures, processes, and culture to evolve freely. It allows the employees to understand how their job fits into the Organizational Design, creating daily work, production of tasks, and projects resulting in organizational success.

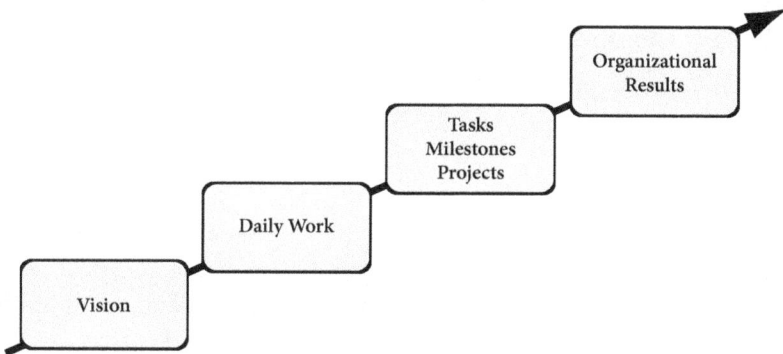

```
                                          ┌──────────────┐ →
                                          │Organizational│
                                          │   Results    │
                            ┌─────────────┤              │
                            │   Tasks     └──────────────┘
                            │  Milestones │
              ┌─────────────┤  Projects   │
              │ Daily Work  └─────────────┘
  ┌───────────┤             │
  │  Vision   └─────────────┘
  │           │
  └───────────┘
```

Much, if not the entire burden, rests on the shoulders of leadership to lay the clarifying support to exert direct personal influence and capacity to every employee. The essential and demanding call is voiced in such a way to link human capital to the purpose and goal of the organization.

Commitment

One of the vital pieces in the model is commitment, which is traced back to the vision. The key to understanding commitment lies in the deep purpose of both areas of the organization and individual. To cast a wide net, commitment converts into aspirations and motives for the cause in which they serve. When employees are uncommitted, they are disengaged and suffer along the side of the organization and everything fails.

Many of the extended observations of commitment are demonstrated in the environment of adversity. Epicurus, the ancient Greek philosopher stated, "…a captain earns his reputation during the storms." The successes and victories of human nature and organizations will invariably give way to difficulty and misfortunes; however, the strong point to face adversity and hardship is unwavering commitment.

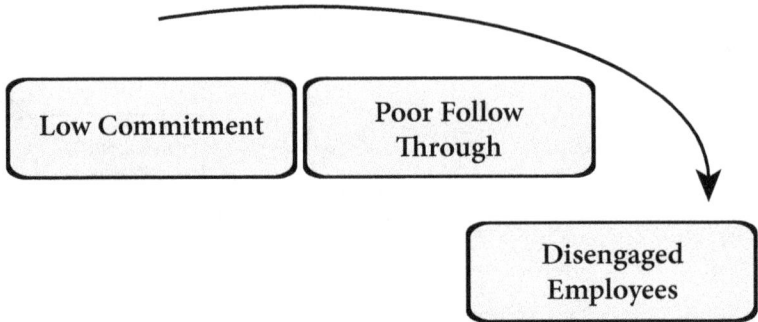

Low Commitment	Poor Follow Through

Disengaged Employees

The dynamic, in large part as a result of commitment, opens up the discussion to *The Principle of Compensation*. For every loss experienced during the times of trial and tribulation, there will be a return. Peering through the lens of experience the view of the swimmer who swims at 4 a.m. before school, the track sprinter who shows up early and stays late after practice, and the employee who works 10-hour days to finish a project, receives the greater compensation. The very presence of adversity broadens the dividend of over 100 times. Those that pay the price of hard work, obedience, and sacrifice are the victors. For the various forms of difficult adversity that requires personal strength, the outlook demands commitment, persistence, determination, willpower, and deep resolve. Organizations must never become blind because of the endless pressure of circumstance rather having a perfect focus on the things that matter most will serve the organization.

One of the biggest fabrications in business is that people are committed to their jobs solely because of money or compensation. The more money they earn, the happier they are. The idiom "carrot and stick" is about the driver who tied a carrot on a string attached to a long stick and held it in front just out of reach of the donkey. The donkey was committed to getting the carrot and proceeded to move the cart and driver forward. In today's environment, the certitudes of the carrot not only represent monetary compensation; it is more along the lines of being a part of a vision and purpose belonging to something much larger than oneself. Employees are looking for other basic tenets of life: security, pride, purpose, and meaning. By and large, it is vision and purpose that provide the commitment to engage the employees and the human spirit.

Answers to commitment are found in some of history's most central events such as the crossing of a small stream in northern Italy. What seemingly appeared to be insignificant changed the course of history marking the emergence of European culture.

Julius Caesar, with unrestrained political ambition, tried to fashion a coalition wide and deep to maneuver his way to control the consul of Rome in 59 BC. Caesar's harnessed superior skills strengthened his own political position thereby becoming governor of Gaul. Behind the protection of formal authority and power, he systematically and rubically acquired personal wealth and military power. The supreme and immediate goal was to shore up his position of power by controlling the native Celtic and Germanic people. Caesar's culmination and caricature of power threatened the power of the Senate and Pompey. The implication of his growing power broadened the immense insecurity of power in Rome, thereby calling upon Caesar to denounce his domination and dissolve his army or jeopardize being declared an "Enemy of the State". The lost command and control within the executive leadership in the Senate and structure required sharp enforcement of the edict.

The main goal, the one to which Caesar was most committed and for which his army had given themselves, was power. In January 49 BC, Caesar's fine tactical qualities undoubtedly positioned himself to overthrow the existing government. Caesar was optimistic and expedient in his attitude by positioning the troops in the northern Italian city of Ravenna in preparation to throw the Roman Republic into a gruesome civil war.

In his arrogance, he defied the ancient Roman law, which forbade any general from crossing the Rubicon River and entering Italy; such an act was treason. The preeminent crossing would mark the point of no return.

In seeking to change any layer of structure, a leader must not merely address the surface attitudes of people, systems, and processes rather thrust themselves into the full purpose and cause that represents the very nature of existence. They must see the ramification and not merely hear the steps of the change process. The sounding of "Advance" must not only incite action on attitudes and beliefs but to the essential needs, wants, aspirations, and desires of the followership. The rallying cry to "Advance" penetrated the inner soul and they all crossed to the other side. Caesar cried out, "Let us go where the omens of the Gods and the crimes of our enemies summon us!" Caesar declared, "iacta alea est," THE DIE IS NOW CAST!' He led his army over the river and called on the troops to pledge their fidelity. It was the point of no return. The ultimate test of the decision is rooted in the commitment to the values and goals in achieving power for their leader.

A superb organizational structure has the ability to stabilize itself from the inside out on the commitment centerpoint of engaging employees to remain productive. On the same wide front of leadership, leaders need to remain conscientious and vigilant in making the connection between vision, strategy, and work.

Translation

Although the goal of a leader is comprehensive, the inclusive skill of translating must be present to effectively communicate one to another. For effective translation, there needs to be discipline surrounding the grammatical rules. The translator and the receiver need to function within the borders of the governing principles of communication. Like the art of translation, in the literary and spoken communication, it is critical for any organization to translate the vision, and strategy according to job function.

Questions that strengthen the line of translation: Do employees understand what is required of them? Do they know how to translate the goals into action? Does it make sense to them? Is there a line of sight between vision and their jobs? How many are left to their own understanding to figure out the translation of the vision and strategy and how it is relevant to their job? It must feel something like this:

I want to quickly say thank you for making it to the meeting. I know it is tough to break away from work.

We are going to discuss company strategy and how it impac**ts you**花

冃来楼　零花楼零来冃　零花来楼　冃楼来　零

楼花来零冃　　楼 Does that sound good? You on board? 来

花零楼　来冃　楼冃花来零冃　花零来　楼

来楼零花冃　零来花楼 Any questions? If not, *let's do it!*

The critical problem concerns the implication of a failed translated message. The impaired line of translation needs to be repaired through the solutions to such questions: Does the connection between job, role, and strategy feel confusing and problematic? No matter how hard the leader or manager tries to motivate employees to understand, or offer a speech of encouragement, the translation is still not discernable. It does not matter how long one looks at the Chinese characters; it still does not make sense. The leader might even ask employees to change their attitude. Would that help? In most situations, the employee attempts the best efforts and intentions, but the barriers of translating the vision and strategy remain unclear. The solution is the leader's responsibility for the reshaping of communication as required by the vital message and translation to ensure that employees understand their jobs and how they map to the strategy and vision of the organization. If employees do not know the translation, they are presumably muddling their way through the workday and faking the job. Warren Bennis, a scholar, organizational consultant, and author said, "A leader is someone who translates intentions into reality and sustains it."

Some of the influences of history are placed in the pantheon of historical figures. Napoleon, it was said, could look upon a battle scene of unimaginable disorder and see its coherence for his advantage. President Jefferson was the visionary and Madison knew how to translate Jefferson's grand concepts into law. The original question can be answered only in the context of translation and the commitment that captures people's best effort.

Within the mechanical structure of translation, are the nuts and bolts of cascading goals. The tightening of such parts allows for superior performance in an organization. The instructional design aligns the entire organization from top to bottom—downwardly all employees have clarity of the direction, strategy, and goal, and upwardly individuals, teams, departments, and divisions realize results and profit.

On the face of all analogies, the old proverbial football sport correlation is subject to the theory of cascading goals. The team's goal is to ultimately win and score as often as possible while keeping the opponent from doing so. Divisionally, the offense and defense have designed schemes and objectives that must be executed in order to allow the greatest possibility for winning on both sides of the ball. Within the offense and defense, are smaller teams with specific assignments—comprising of linemen, running backs, linebackers, wide receivers, and defensive backs that have a specific function. Furthermore, individually every position on the team has an assignment within the various schemes. Needless to say, one missed assignment and the entire play breaks down.

Bill Hewlett and David Packard in 1937 had their first business meeting to discuss starting a company; their partnership was formed in 1937. One of the many key factors of success was their management philosophy centered on cascading objectives. "We thought that if we could get everybody to agree what our objectives were and to understand what we were trying to do, then we could turn them loose and they would move in a common direction."

Before Bill Hewlett and David Packard turned employees loose and moved them in a common direction, they first translated the jobs, roles, and interdependent relationship with the various parts of the Organizational Design's unique balance of mission, vision, values, strategy, processes, and culture producing results for all stakeholder needs. The question is whether the existing organization has learned the efficiencies of the mechanics.

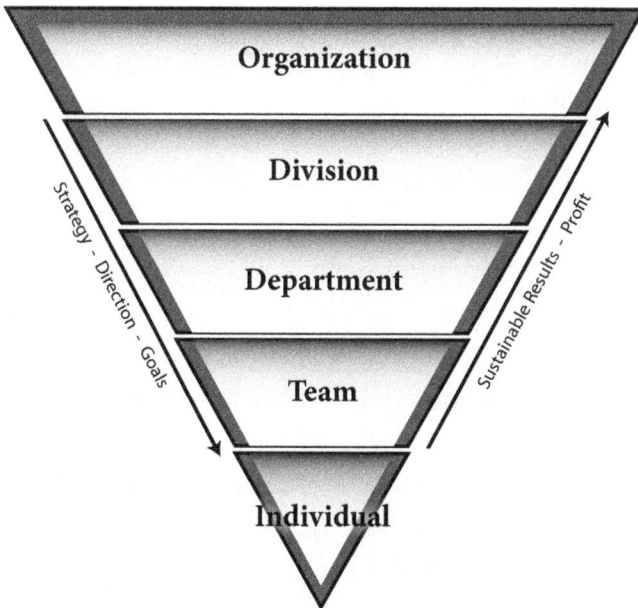

In the rivers of organizational flow, cascading goals are those goals that originate from the top and flow down to every employee. When the employee's efforts are focused on one goal and one purpose, the cascading force creates greater focus and a concentrated effort to produce better and sustainable results for stakeholders.

One of the most important stakeholders is the employee. Invariably, employees need to know what is in it for them. It goes beyond the banks, of traditional needs of a paycheck and a secure work environment; it streams to purpose and contribution. It is one thing to communicate the goals and an entirely different thing to collect employee commitment. After all, employees are the energy to execute the strategic goals.

The erosion of the organizational riverbed lies in the weakened theoretical and philosophical structure of cascading goals, which are not institutionalized, causing resentment and silos between departments. The misaligned and fragmented goals invariably create behaviors of acting independently, forcing competition, scarce mentality, and empire building among divisional leaders. Individuals, teams, departments, and divisions suffer along the side of the organization. Leaders should be bridge builders and not silo architects.

Discipline

Within the machinery to execute vision, a relevant piece is discipline. Organizations must have a broad and deep base that can widen the work ethic of everyone; everything tends to translate into hard work. A discipline that demands so much from each person is physical, mental, and emotional lifting and requires the skill to choose wisely. EM Gray said, "The successful person has the habit of doing the things failures don't like to do...they don't like them either necessarily, but their dislike is subordinated to the strengths of their purpose."

Leaders must be strong examples of discipline and avoid the pressure of being anything less than what they should and ought to be which will only increase their ability to lead effectively. The one in charge sets the standard and those who choose poorly hold their own perils to lose the followership. The measures of confidence are within the narrowly agreed boundaries governed by discipline.

In a world of ideally rational thought and actions, organizations have moved towards decayed and lost identity because the organizational culture has lost the discipline to work hard and stay focused. Such irrational thoughts and actions of tenure has its perks without accountability for actions. Disciplined athletes do not play $3^{1/2}$ quarters in basketball, 8 innings in baseball, or sprint 90 yards in a 100-yard dash—it is with reason that championship horses are retired and poor behavior is punished with steep fines and suspension. Winston Churchill said, "Discipline without purpose is torture; discipline with purpose is joy." Discipline must be a constant characteristic at all levels of the organization; it does not discriminate within the framework of where people contribute.

Scott Peck M.D, in his book, *The Road Less Traveled,* addresses the four basic concepts of discipline:

Delaying Gratification—The willingness to experience pain first, enables us to go on to experience the pleasures of life.

Accepting Responsibility—Not placing the blame for problems on others; being willing to solve our own problems.

Dedication to Truth (Reality)—Seeing the world as it is in order to effectively deal with it.

Balancing—The flexibility to give something up in order to gain something of transcendent importance.

Discipline ⟷	Results

— Stay Above the Line —

Lack of Discipline ⟷	Poor Results

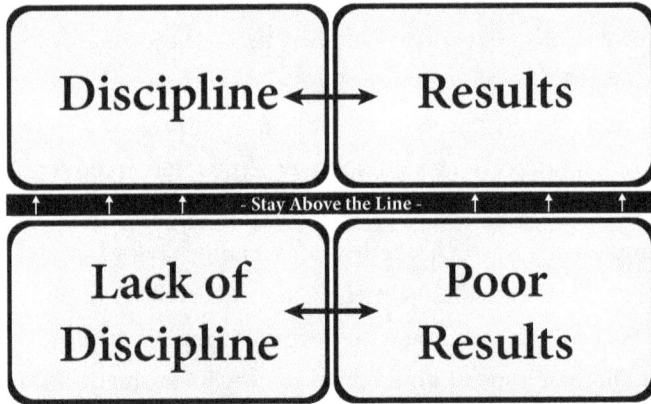

In August of 1776, General George Washington arrived in Brooklyn to check on the troops. He was outraged by what he saw in the discipline and conduct of those present. He wrote, "All 'irregularities' must cease at once. The distinction between a well-regulated army and a mob is the good order and discipline of the first, and the licentious and disorderly behavior of the latter." All great leaders must uphold the set standards and hold everyone accountable.

To take the lead, is to act in terms of values, purpose, and exemplifying strong standards; it is certainly not about friendship and charisma. Leaders must build a culture of discipline based on accountability and set standards and not through oppressive punishment of the fist rather with the outstretched hand to develop and mentor those they lead.

Marie Curie spent much of her life in an effort to discover radium. After the 487th experiment had failed, her husband Pierre threw up his hands in despair and said, "It will never be done. Maybe in a hundred years but never in our day." Marie Curie faced up to him and said, "If it takes a hundred years it will be a pity, but I will not cease to work for it as long as I live."

No horse gets anywhere until he is harnessed.
No steam or gas ever drives anything until it is confined.
No Niagara is ever turned into light and power until it is tunneled.

No life ever grows great until it is focused, dedicated, disciplined.
Henry Emerson Fosdick

It is the discipline to behave in such a way to accomplish a task even though there are more appealing activities. The short-term pleasure is subordinate to the long-term accomplishments. Self-discipline becomes foundational to a leader's life.

Teamwork

The concept of team compensates for the weakness of others and can be the most solid, durable, and highly structured in human society. Scott Peck, an American psychiatrist, defines community as a group of individuals "who have learned to communicate honestly with each other, whose relationships go deeper than their masks of composure, and who have developed some significant commitment to rejoice together, mourn together, to delight in each other, and make conditions their own."

The range of characteristics is wide. At the opposite ends of the spectrum is steadfast loyalty and at the other end valuing the difference of all points of view of all members. Team members work through their challenges and come to share the different dimensions of each situation. The extraordinary nature of the teamwork is diversity to produce better results. General George Patton, of World War II said, "If everyone is thinking alike than somebody isn't thinking."

Leaders merge a dense network of inclusion at all levels. They have an ability to form and create cohesive effective relationships by connecting people together giving appropriate voice and influence to all members.

Ms. X had sat at dinner between Mr. Y and Mr. Z.
Mr. Y and Z were renowned individuals; Z in particular.
When you sat at dinner with him, you came away believing that
he was perhaps the smartest individual you'd ever met.

About Mr. Y, the truly successful one,
she said, "When you sat at dinner with Mr. Y, you came away
thinking that you were the smartest person on earth."

In David McCullough's book, *John Adams*, he broadens the importance of team concepts. He describes the role and the important nature of John Adams in American history. The Rushmorian fathers' movement embraced both single-issue liberty and rights during a precipitous and tenuous time period in America. The new nation required various leaders of vital skills that are most exacting for leadership such as: John Adams, Thomas Jefferson, George Washington, Tom Paine, Alexander Hamilton, and James Madison . They possessed many of the same as well as very different skill-sets. Eliminate just one from that list and the colony of Great Britain might have lingered. The animated strengths of each character were the extraordinary conjunction of forces that rescued America.

The same principle of team applies to an enterprise. You need the person who is visionary, the team member who can work well with the accounting personnel, the individual who can relate with the hard hats and lunch pail labor force; it takes diverse individuals to create successful teams.

Peter Senge of MIT and author of the book, *The Fifth Discipline*, shares this perspective of team, "When you ask people about what it is like being part of a great team, what is most striking is the meaningfulness of the experience. People talk about being part of something larger than themselves, of being connected, of being generative. It becomes quite clear that, for many, their experiences as part of truly great teams stand out as singular periods of life lived to the fullest. Some spend the rest of their lives looking for ways to recapture that spirit."

The 1980 U.S. Olympic hockey team displayed what has come to be seen as the classic Miracle on Ice in Lake Placid, New York. The spirit of teamwork is not a series of single linear acts rather a sequence of behavior: work ethic, communication, valuing differences, skills, and attributes. The string of behaviors enables the power to be an effective team. This was a team from a diverse background comprising of amateurs and collegiate players unifying the atmosphere of synergy. The law is one plus one does not equal two rather it equals three or greater. Exponential results produce a great deal more than an individual's own production. In an exhibition game, at the Madison Square Garden, the Soviet Union crushed the young inexperienced team. The final score on February 9, 1980 was 10-3 with the Soviet Union standing strong on top. Thirteen days later, on February 22, 1980 the United States assembled the same team to accomplish the unthinkable during the Olympics. They beat the largely viewed stronger Russians and went on to win the gold medal by winning their final match over Finland. The old proverbial team analogy applies; the team wins or loses together. Great teams value all roles and celebrate everyone's accomplishments regardless of where and how they serve.

The team breakdown is based on a discussion of dysfunctions related to several key pieces of the workplace and beyond. Judging teams along the following list of failures can greatly assist teams with their development to build effective teams. According to the book, *The Five Dysfunctions of a Team*, Patrick Lencioni suggests there are five dysfunctions of a team:

Absence of Trust

Fear of Conflict

Lack of Commitment

Avoidance of Accountability

Inattention to Results

Leaders are largely viewed as the practical administrators who oversee the execution operation or other evolved processes of the organization. For any system to have real value, leaders will ultimately need to lead the charge. Execution does not happen from the comforts of the executive offices. Usually, the leaders role devolves into ensuring all employees perform in their assigned roles and job functions. Many have tried a feeble attempt to provide stump speeches, mandatory meetings, or to redraft the corporate mission statement declaring the new culture of performance. It simply does not happen that way. Once it is understood how employees' behaviors are affecting teams and the broad enterprise, training and actions plans will be relatively easy to identify on all aspects of the organization.

Chapter 14

Removing Barriers

Change is more than a topic, it is the catalyst for sustainability and growth. The important question is whether it will be thrust upon oneself or whether one will lead the force in a productive direction.

In December 1967, the very first heart transplant was conducted in Cape Town, South Africa. The very nature, beyond the control of many, the malfunction of a diseased heart requires a replacement to be sewn into the person. The change of a new heart can prolong life and sustain a quality life who would other wise die from heart failure. What is seemingly in the best interest of one to receive a new heart, the natural tendency for the body is to reject the change.

Just as the need to change a heart for a transplant recipient, many organizations need to change to remain competitive and relevant in the world economy; every enterprise will experience some form of change in order to survive. There are many factors that influence organizational change, which is attributed directly or indirectly to the composition of the global economy. It is the globalization of multilateral organizations of production and consumption, emerging markets, finances, labor force, and national and international policy. Unfortunately, most will demur from the necessity of change, settling for the status quo not responding to the external and internal change and emerging markets, which leads to antiquation and dysfunction.

Two of the greatest fallacies are the old sayings, "If It Is Not Broke Do Not Fix It" and "Go With The Flow." People in general tend to accept that, if a lot of people are working and getting some form of result, the system must be working or the focus is on the right project. The "Go With The Flow Mentality" is damaging and leads to failure by degrees. Leadership and the organization will be burdened to determine the failure of their success.

Products, services, and technology are becoming obsolete at an extremely fast pace, faster than ever before in the history of the world. In order to survive and compete, organizations need to innovate, improve, and modify. Change is becoming the most important part of the business. The economy is shifting and the market demands are greater than ever. There is an old saying in Silicon Valley that illustrates the rampant change in which one lives, "Eat lunch and you are the lunch." Change creates the opportunity, but only those organizations who recognize and understand how to manage change will ultimately win.

As Conrad Hilton said, "If you want to launch big ships, go where the water is deep." Many organizations have grandiose ideas requiring a phenomenon of building complex systems and processes to manage the various elements of change. Any change effort must be balanced with the opportunity of return, equal to or greater than risk. The risk of change might lead to complete failure but not at the expense of complete destruction. Too many organizations try to launch carrier size change efforts in shallow water.

Change efforts should be tied to market needs whether they are current or anticipated. The whole mind-set of great organizations rely on their own ability to create market demand. One must not operate inside or outside the limits of defining change opportunities too narrowly or broadly, it requires a change effort centered on realities of market consumption and organizational need.

No matter the proportion or reason to change, there will always be a sector in the employee population who will resist change—it is the nature of human behavior. Many leaders stumble in the pitfall by making the assumption that once a decision has been made for change, everyone will naturally get on board. People tend to see change as a threat to their current environment. Most will never see the change as being good personally even though it is good for the organization. They will start to "attack the heart". Some of the resistors will be in open defiance and object or refuse to cooperate and others will be a dissenting passive voice. Change forms behaviors out of those who are for or against the effort. There will be early bureaucratic turf wars forcing individuals to turn inwardly to attack each other. The efforts and energy becomes an internal fight, political posturing, and adding fuel to the rumor mill.

Compounding the change effort is the moral decay of leadership. The culture is to distrust leadership and to be suspicious of their motives. They expect leaders to be duplicitous in their behavior by showing concern for their welfare and serve their best interest at the same time re-writing job descriptions, cutting back hours, or downsizing the workforce.

The workforce needs an explanation and understanding of the situation. It is insufficient for upper management to be aware and hold all the pertinent information. The change effort needs to be communicated and cascaded down to the lower levels so there is a common voice and direction. This will reduce alienation and divisiveness. Simply acting on the speed of change to find solutions by cutting the fat and also the flesh, and by cutting back resources and activities, might hinder the organization to deliver on current and future results. The employees will be left confused, bewildered, resentful, and without direction encumbering them to focus on the current reality as opposed to the future direction.

Those who are in charge of leading the change efforts will see themselves in a no-win situation. They will question their ability to lead and why they accepted the responsibility in the first place. They become disliked, targets of criticism, exhausted, and disempowered. The turbulence of change sends morale spiraling downward.

The practical impact of organizational change is to have a healthy culture which is accustomed to anticipate change and adapt to market conditions. Organizations that are better prepared to deal with change will be faster and more nimble when change is announced.

Change must take place within the controlled environment of the Organizational Design ecosystem. The process is applied in a certain sequence with the appropriate emphasis to produce the desired outcomes. *(See Organizational Design)* The foundation and the ground work is already in place and it becomes a matter of executing around the elements rather than managing the corporate politics and turf battles. Although the Organizational Design has a sequential pattern, the timing and effort spent with each element will be at the dictates of the unique organizational needs.

There is a sequence to implement change. The classic doctor and patient metaphor is used to diagnose the illness prior to prescribing a solution. The theoretical change framework of Assess, Decide, Propose, Implement, and Measure is put into operation at each element of the Organizational Design to address specific issues.

Assess: a systematic approach to understand the impact of change

Decide: organizational success in respect to short and long term goals

Propose: a solution to address issues and changes

Implement: the integration of the solution into the existing structure

Measure: the analysis of the affects of the decision

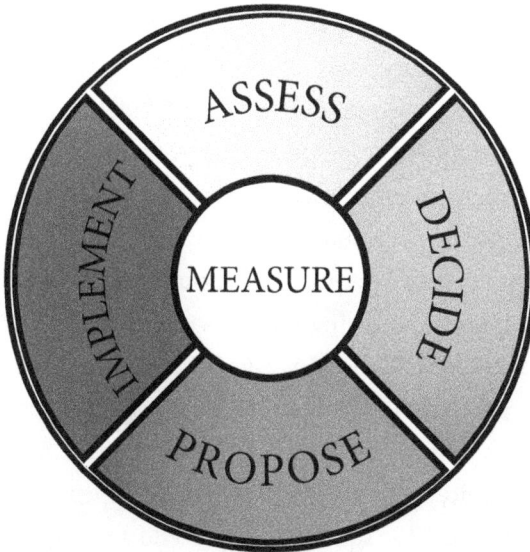

This method is a practical framework to assist organizations to solve simple and complex issues in a more comprehensive approach to produce more meaningful organizational changes. Clearing the path to allow change is an important function for any leader to systematically remove problematic processes, decision making, relationships, old mind-sets, and an insecure culture. Removing the obstacles that hinder and bog down organizational speed and growth is a critical and a survival function for effective change.

The leader's responsibility is to focus on the most leveraged activities that produce disproportionate results. Peter Senge explains in, *The Fifth Discipline,* the analogy of the trim tab on a rudder. Imagine an individual at the helm of an ocean liner moving through the water. How is it possible for one individual to change its course? A single person turns the steering wheel, which maneuvers the rudder. The rudder is very massive, many stories tall. What moves the rudder? The trim tab, which is much smaller in comparison to the rudder, moves to one side to create the energy to move the larger rudder assisting in the maneuvers of the ship.

When making change, whether at an individual or organizational level, it is the small things that have tremendous impact. Mayor Rudolph Giuliani of New York City was looking at solutions to address the safety issues in the city. Most people were looking to address the social issues, reduce the murder rate of 2,000 people per year, or tackle crime. He said, "We attacked crime immediately, but we knew it would take time to show results. And reducing the number of crimes wouldn't be enough: people had to see improvement, not just hear about it. If crime went down but the existing amount of pushing and shoving, urinating on the streets, and other quality-of-life issues remained the same, we could never have a convincing case that life was better." The city focused on the squeegee men. "At the time, there were men who would wander up to a car at the red light or in traffic, spray the windshield, and wipe it down…After the unsolicited "cleaning," the squeegee man would approach the driver and "request" payment. Drivers who refused might have their windshields spat on or their car doors kicked." When the squeegee men stepped off the curb, they were immediately given a ticket for jaywalking. The focus of working at a small trim tab problem gave way to address some of the larger issues of New York City. Crime was reduced by some 5,000 felonies per week. The leader in any organization is the trim tab creating conditions for quantum success to take place.

Barriers are those things that make it problematic for the employees to be not only efficient, but also effective in their jobs. Most organizations, if not all, have a myriad of processes, institutionalized policies, and procedures that make getting their responsibilities completed really heavy. One must ask themself, "how much red tape do I have to go through to get something done?" One has heard the terminology of making people jump through hoops. In all of my years of teaching and consulting, I have experienced that when things are difficult to accomplish, people will resent the leader or organization. The burden is just too weighty for people to be effective in their job and erosion of morale takes hold.

Effective leaders remove barriers that slow down real progress. They reduce the unnecessary red tape by eliminating pointless paperwork, complicated policies and procedures, antiquated bureaucratic systems and structures, the chain of command for decision-making, and a multitude of other meaningless, misaligned, and fragmented systems and practices.

When Lou Gerstner took over IBM many people ridiculed the decision because he lacked the industrial understanding and technical conditions. IBM was known for its "great customer service" but over the years, they had forgotten their core fundamental beliefs and lost sight of their customers. The company had become a bully. Gerstner visited their customers and asked them one questions, "What was IBM's problem?" Lou fixed the problems.

Lou Gerstner got it right. He rolled up his sleeves and got to work understanding the barriers for exceptional customer service. He did not start discounting prices and adding another layer of promotional gimmicks. He understood the barriers and removed the bully mentality.

The leader's prime role is to understand the restraining forces and barriers that suppress growth and success and remove them. It is the trim tab mentality. The leader's responsibility is to focus on the most leveraged activities that produce exponential results, by first focusing on the small that influences the large. It is about clearing the path and allowing immediate observable success to take place. In fact, it is much better to have a more manageable problem so that everyone can see that change can take place and that it is much more than rhetoric.

In the debate of healthcare reform, it was discovered that $1.2 trillion dollars is being leaked out of the system. According to PricewaterhouseCoopers' Health Research Institute, that is half of the $2.2 trillion the United States spends on health care each year.

One of the largest barriers to an effective healthcare system is "defensive medicine." Doctors are motivated to avoid malpractice suits ordering tests and procedures not based on need rather protection from liability.

As leaders, do they make themselves available? I have seen at the expense of millions of dollars a year where employees have been assigned a significant project only to find out that they could never get the appropriate time with the leader to make critical decisions and get approval. Or, being asked to provide world-class customer service and not having the empowerment to provide appropriate solutions to customer needs.

One of Kurt Lewin's initial and noteworthy studies about driving forces and restraining forces came as a result of a commission from the United States government. His task was to influence the buying, cooking, and eating habits of American housewives during World War II. The goal was to encourage women to buy and cook more of the visceral cuts of meat, the organs, and less of the good cuts of meat in order to support the troops abroad.

The effort was to promote driving forces along the lines of patriotism, sense of duty, availability, and presenting the fact of meat consumption. Much to their dismay, the consumption of visceral cuts of meat was nominal. The United States government had undervalued the strength of the operating restraining forces at play. The housewives were not accustomed to purchasing the stomach, and intestines, let alone cooking it. As it is with most organizations, to create change and resolve issues, one tends to focus on the driving forces. They have a propensity to develop new programs, greater incentives, and reward systems.

The conditions apply to the whole enterprise within which employees are working hard, resolving problems, and finding new opportunities. Regardless of how diligent an organization is at instituting driving forces in the environment of change, the efforts will be marginalized. Vast change and problem solving happens by eliminating the barriers and restraints that hinder development and progress.

In such a system to create change, there needs to be a flow of information and opportunity to express points of view and opinions. Everyone is faced with constant change, which requires one to understand how to make decisions. If there were no change in the environment, there would not be a need to make so many decisions. Everything that happened yesterday or in the past would be status quo, requiring no new decision other than the quality of the decision made.

The world is based on decision-making. Some of the decisions are more critical than others. The decisions leaders make will determine, to a large extent, how successful and relevant the organization will become. Good decision-making should be based on the organization's ability to deliver results balanced with their own needs. They should not be made when yielding to the pressures to satisfy someone's own ego or self-interests. Strong leaders do not go against their better judgment to do what is right. They stand on solid ground of sound principles to govern their decision-making; no decision for change is justified when being dishonest, unethical or cheating. Doing the wrong thing should never be reasonable. There is no justification even when everybody else is doing it. The moral decay in leadership should not distort the truth.

Many decisions need to be made based on a timeline. Unfortunately, many people have difficulty making the hard decisions. A psychiatrist once asked, "Do you have problems making decision?" The patient said, "Well...yes, and no." It requires a sense of courage to squarely place the consequence of the decision on one's shoulders. If a decision is delayed, it could mean a lost opportunity.

Decision-making is easier when there is a strong sense of identity in who the leader is and what the organization represents. The control for change should reside with the decision makers and not at the dictates of others who do not have the organizations best interest at heart. To make informed decisions, the procedure works relatively well when all the available information is based on evaluated facts, representing all sides of the issue.

Showing the way means making decisions for change. Making no decision at all could be just as toxic as making the wrong decision. Organizations who possess the mind-set that, if one does nothing long enough, they might become the leader in the company. When organizations stop changing, they stop moving towards the needs of the environment, and when they stop responding, they become dead.

Chapter 15

Metrics and Numeric

Part of a leader's responsibility is to ensure that every employee has well quantifiable metrics and numeric relating to the job and role. Accurate measurement is the first step to improve performance not only for the individual, but for the entire organization. Often leaders do not fulfill this role, not because they choose not to, but because they do not know how to develop and craft systems of metrics for superior performance at all levels of the organization. In a world of ideally sound theory and thought, the importance and economic value is relevant to any leadership role.

The practical purpose behind measurement and balanced scorecards is to reduce uncertainty to an expressed quantity and outcome. It allows for the appropriate attention and focus to be centered on the mission critical aspects of the company. If one wants to accomplish something, measure it. When one measures it, people will focus their attention to get it done.

The most fundamental measurement is financial, but it is followed closely by measurements of customer service, effectiveness of internal process innovation, and learning. In today's economy, organizations are finding it critical that they measure and understand all aspects of their industry and business to ensure success. Organizational success is built on the collection of individual employee performance. It is the culture that drives results.

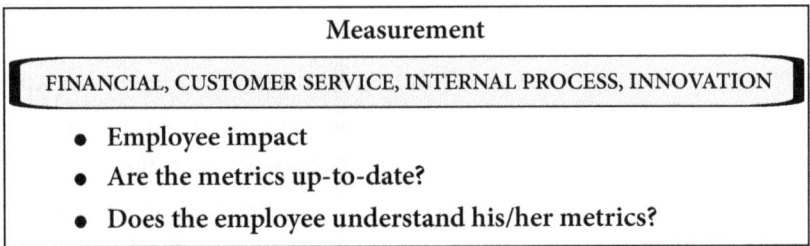

Measurement

FINANCIAL, CUSTOMER SERVICE, INTERNAL PROCESS, INNOVATION

- **Employee impact**
- **Are the metrics up-to-date?**
- **Does the employee understand his/her metrics?**

For improving and developing employees, measuring how individual performance ties to organizational goals can lead to quality employee development to improve their contribution in the organization. The most accurate measurement of an employee's contribution shows how an employee's work advances the organization's financial goals, improves customer service, improves the effectiveness of internal processes, reduces costs and waste, and whether their work is advancing innovation in the organization in new ways to support and grow the business. The process of individual employee performance improvement relies on quality measurement of their contribution.

A balanced scorecard is a strategic tool and management system. It now serves a purpose from a simple performance measurement to a strategic element for organizations to execute strategy.

Kaplan and Norton say, "The "new" balanced scorecard transforms an organization's strategic plan from an attractive but passive document into "marching orders" for the organization on a daily basis. It provides a framework that not only provides performance measurements, but also helps planners identify what should be done and measured. It enables executives to truly execute their strategies."

```
┌─────────────────────────┐        ┌─────────────────────────┐
│  Improved Competencies  │        │                         │
│     and Capabilities    │───────▶│  Improved Financial     │
│       (Resources)       │        │      Performance        │
└─────────────────────────┘        └─────────────────────────┘
```

Part of the difficulty in developing balanced scorecards is the cause and effect relationships between the strategy and the key performance indicators (KPIs). It is one thing to draft strategy and an entirely different task to boil the strategy down to appropriate KPIs that drive the strategy into logical step-by-step connections between the strategy, mission, and vision of the organization. The largest consideration to the holistic scorecard approach is in the Organizational Design to translate the vision and strategy into actions and tasks around the internal business processes transforming performance into stakeholder's needs.

Kaplan and Norton share the organizational perspective through financials, "That one must view the organizational perspectives through the lens of financial, internal business processes, learning and growth, and customers and to develop metrics, collect data, and analyze for scorecards."

Fred Richheld said, "Accountability is one of those magic words in business. Any experienced manager will tell you that where there is individual accountability, things get done. Measurement is another magic word: what gets measured creates accountability. With no standard, reliable metrics for customer relationships, employees can't be held accountable for them and so overlook their importance." I would conclude that good metrics and numeric apply to everything an employee does. It is how they contribute.

Measurement should be an iterative. It can be adjusted as the environment changes. The most important thing is to simply get started. It should be intuitive as opposed to a strong rigor of science. It is better to be approximately correct than to be completely wrong by not doing the exercise. Douglas W. Hubbard in his book, *How to Measure Anything*, highlights useful measurement assumptions:

Measurement Assumptions

The problem is not as unique as you think.

You have more data than you think.

You need less data than you think.

There is a useful measurement that is much simpler than you think.

In measuring employees, finding department and even position level metrics can be a difficult task. Some work is easier to measure than others. For example, measuring the impact of a sales associate or an operational position is usually easier than measuring the impact of an HR generalist or marketing specialist. Additionally, Hubbard provides a structure to breakdown the complexity in the clarification chain: If the measure is detectable even in the smallest amount, it is measurable.

Clarification Chain

If it matters at all, it is detectable/observable.

If it is detectable, it can be detected as an amount or range of possible amounts.

If it can be detected as a range of possible amounts, it can be measured.

There is a misguided perception of the value of measurement when one cannot observe it. Charles Handy, in his book, *The Empty Raincoat*, stated, "The first step is to measure whatever can be easily measured. This is OK as far as it goes. The second step is to disregard that which can't easily be measured or to give it an arbitrary quantitative value. This is artificial and misleading. The third step is to presume that what can't be measured easily isn't important. This is blindness. The fourth step is to say that what can't easily be measured really doesn't exist."

The key is to breakdown the job to observable relevant components that the employee is expected to perform. Many things a manager might consider immeasurable are actually measurable.

Job function and roles are important to an organization's success. Both positions affect the business in ways that measuring can help one understand the desired versus actual results. From these understandings, an employee's performance can be grown through the organization's employee development process. Customarily, there is a department of Corporate and Organizational Development to assist in the development of Knowledge, Skill-Sets, and Attributes. If a position is less obvious to quantify, asking the following questions can help define metrics:

1- What circumstances change or adjust based on this employee's performance?

2- What would happen in the business if this position or employee left?

3- Is it easier to see how this position affects the business if viewed over a longer term? Monthly, quarterly, twice a year, more?

4- What does superior impact look like (A+) versus negative impact (F-)?

Answers to such hard pointed questions should help build simple metrics. It is important that metrics be simple, understandable, clearly affected, controlled by an employee's performance, and reviewed often.

Considerations when Measuring Employee Performance:

1- Metrics should be simple and easily understood.

2- Employee buy in is critical; managers should ask themselves if their employees should have had a role in crafting their own metrics.

3- Review whether the metrics capture the employee's value and contribution to the organization. Roles within job descriptions shift often.

4- If metrics are not updated, employee morale and productivity can suffer.

Past Royal Statistical Society President, Leonard Courtney, said, "After all, facts are facts, and although we may quote one to another with a chuckle the words of the Wise Statesman, 'Lies—damned lies—and statistics, still there are some easy figures the simplest must understand, and the astutest cannot wiggle out of…'"

Measurement instruments are like most tools that provide benefit to the user; simple mechanical tools to provide an advantage. It is work done with mechanical advantages, much like a system of pulleys moving a heavy weight. The simple instruments much like the tools of a telescope and thermometer of Galileo and Fahrenheit to measure their environments.

The heavy weight one faces in organization life is the amazingly difficult nature of building and developing employees. Measuring individual performance leads directly to grow the employee's skills, address performance gaps, and develop the employee's capabilities.

The best key performance indicators are based on leading measures and indicators that actually address the goals of the individual and organization. Leading measures and indicators predict the outcome of performance and lagging measures and indicators reflect the performance of success or failure. Thinking strategically, about measurement and focusing on leading measures, will provide critical information that will assist leaders with strategy and execution while providing time to make adjustments before delivering on strategic commitments.

Take the example of financial leading indicators, of the cycles of prosperity and depression, to provide advanced warning of the economic fluctuation of growth or slowdown. Managing to leading indicators such as the Consumer Price Index (CPI), the so called term spread the difference between long-term and short-term interest rates on government debt and a multitude of other leading indicators financial institutions use to measure the projected failure or success, will allow sufficient time to make the appropriate adjustments in the economic activity.

Lead Measures	Lagging Measures
-- Predicts goal achievement	-- Measures goal achievement
-- Is easier to influence	-- Is harder to influence
-- Is harder to measure	-- Is easier to measure

Leading Indicators	Lagging Indicators
-- 25 prospecting calls a day	-- $100k sales goal
-- 5 safety classes	-- $25k monthly safety budget
-- 10 yard gain	-- 7 point TD

Crafting a measurement system based on leading indicators as opposed to lagging indicators will offset the risk of error. The environment will provide leaders control to recalibrate the environment for which they have influence. The system of metrics and numeric will also assist to detect behaviors that are reasonably undetectable.

Those leaders who are left to their own devices for assessment and measurement create inconsistency. Measurement systems generally create consistency in a culture where humans have limitation and error of their own. The tools can be supportive and improve the productivity and performance of all employees.

RESOURCES

LEADERSHIP

P. 2   **Managers and Leaders**: Abraham Zalenik, "Managers and Leaders: Are They Different" *Harvard Business Review on Leadership pp.* 61-87.

P. 2   **"One of the difficulties:** John P. Kotter, "What Leaders Really Do" *Harvard Business Review on Leadership* pp. 37-40.

P. 2   *Time* **asked in:** "Who's in Charge?" *Time*, November 9, 1987.

P. 3   **He lost his mother:** Donald T. Phillips, *Lincoln On Leadership: Executive Strategies For Tough Times* (New York: Hachette Book Group, 1992), p. 5.

P. 3   **Not even a bed:** King James Bible, Mathew 8: 20.

P. 4   **"Leadership is leaders:** James MacGregor Burns, *Leadership* (New York: Harper& Row Publishers, 1978), p. 19.

P. 4   **The new leaders':** Jan Carlzon, *Moment of Truth: Today's Strategies Consumer-Driven Economy* (New York: HarperCollins, 1989), p.x.

P. 4   **"Leadership does not:** Rudolph Giuliani, *Leadership* (New York: Hyperion, 2002), xii.

P. 5   **"Leaders have a significant:** Warren Bennis, *On Becoming A Leader* (New York: Perseus Books Group, 2009), p. 1.

P. 6   **There are many:** Jim Collin's *Good To Great*, James MacGregor Burns' *Leadership*, John Kotter's, *The Leadership Factor*, and Warren Bennis's *On Becoming a Leader.* Jim Collin's *Good To Great*, John Kotter's, *The Leadership Factor*, and Warren Bennis's *On Becoming a Leader.* Jim Collins, *Good-to-Great Why Some Companies Make the Leap... and Others Don't* (New York: HarperCollins Publisher, 2001); James MacGregor Burns, *Leadership* (New York: HarperCollins Publisher, 1978); John Kotter, *The Leadership Fac-*

tor (New York: Free Press, 1988); and Warren Bennis, *On Becoming A Leader* (MA: Reading, Addison –Wesley, 1989).

P. 6 **Early leadership practitioners:** Barbara Kellerman, *Followership* (MA: Harvard Business Press, 2008), p.14; Mary Parker Follett, "The Giving Order," *in Mary Parker Follett: Prophet of Management,* ed. Pauline Graham (MA: Harvard Business School Press, 1995), pp. 121-140. Also, Chaester I. Barnard, *The Functions of the Executive* (MA: Harvard University Press, 1938), chapter 12.

P. 6 **Global leadership awakening:** Zbigniew Brzezinski, *Second Chances: Three Presidents and the Crisis of American Superpower* (New York: Basic Books, 2007), pp. 201-205.

P. 7 **"I use the word *management*:** Henry Mintzberg, *Managers Not MBAs* (San Francisco: Berrett-Koehler Publishers, Inc.), p. 6.

P. 8 **"Great leaders move:** Daniel Goleman, Richard Boyatzis, and Annie McKee, *Primal Leadership: Realizing the Power of Emotional Intelligence* (Boston: Harvard Business School Press, 2004), p.3.

P. 8 **When Jack Welch was:** For additional notes on the relationship between superiors and subordinates in corporate America, see Abraham Zaleznik, "The Dynamics of Subordinacy," *Harvard Business Review,* May-June 1965, p. 119-120.

P. 9 **Abraham Zaleznik:** Abraham Zaleznik, *Leadership: A Behavioral view,* Compact Classic, Inc. 1994.

P. 10 **"Ego Boy:** Jan Carlzon, *Moment of Truth: Today's Strategies Consumer-Driven Economy* (New York: Harper Collins, 1989), p. 8.

P. 10 **"The company was:** Jan Carlzon, *Moment of Truth: Today's Strategies Consumer-Driven Economy* (Harper Collins, New York, 1989), pp. 8-9.

P. 10 **"Imagine then a:** Plato, The Republic, Book VI Written 360 B.C.E.

P. 11 **"Security is not:** Stephen R. Covey, A. Roger Merrill and Rebecca A. Merrill, *First Things First* (New York: Simon & Schuster 1994), p. 72.

P. 12   **"Leadership is not a gene:** James M. Kouzes and Barry Z. Posner, *The Leadership Challenge* (San Francisco: Jossey-Bass, 1995), p. 23.

P. 16   **Only having knowledge:** Alan Weiss, PhD., *Organizational Consulting* (New Jersey: John Wiley & Sons, 2003), p. 16.

P. 18   **Trait Theory: Great Event Theory: Transformational Theory:** Bernard Bass, *Stogdill's Handbook of Leadership: A Survey of Theory and Research* (New York: Free Press, 1989), pp. 37-54.

P. 19   **The example of Katharine Graham:** Jim Collins, "The 100 Greatest CEOs Of All Time. What These Extraordinary Leaders Can Teach Today's Troubled Executives" *CNNMoney.com Fortune*, July 21, 2003.

P. 20   **"What combination of:** Blaine Lee, *The Power Principle: Influence with Honor* (New York: Simon& Schuster, 1997), p. 259.

P. 20   **"The genius of leadership:** James MacGregor Burns, *Leadership*, p.19.

P. 21   **Environment Determinism: Genetic Determinism: Psychic Determinism:** Stephen R. Covey, *The 7 Habits of Highly Effective People* (New York: Simon & Schuster, 1989), pp. 67-68.

P. 22   **"At first, as a student:** Nelson Mandela, *Long Walk to Freedom* (Boston: Little, Brown and Company, 1994), pp. 543-544.

P. 25   **Level 5 Leadership builds:** Jim Collins, *Good-to-Great: Why Some Companies Make the Leap... and Others Don't* (New York: HarperCollins Publish, 2001), p. 20.

P. 25   **I am not under:** Stephen E. Ambrose, *D-Day* (New York: Simon & Schuster Inc., 1994) p. 195.

P. 26   **"I now leave:** Springfield Farewell Speech February 11, 1861.

P. 27   **"What I deal with:** Donald T. Phillips, *Lincoln On Leadership: Executive Strategies For Tough Times*, p. 62.

P. 27   **With malice toward:** Lincoln's Second Inaugural Address, March 4, 1865.

P. 27   **"Great leaders never wanted:** Jim Collins, *Good-to-Great: Why Some Companies Make the Leap... and Others Don't*, p. 28.

P. 28 **"Whatever era, whatever:** Barbara Bush, reported in *The Washington Post,* June 2, 1990, p. 2 (from a speech to graduates of Wellesley College).

P. 29 **"great person in charge:** Larry Bossidy, "What Your Leader Expects of You: And What You Should Expect in Return," *Harvard Business Review,* April 2007, 58-65.

P. 29 **"…senior executives seem:** "Charm Offensive," *BusinessWeek,* June 26, 2006.

P. 29 **"A couple of years ago:** Arthur Levitt Jr., "The Imperial CEO is No More," *Wall Street Journal,* March 17, 2005. Also, Barbara Kellerman, *Followership: How Followers Are Creating Change and Changing Leaders,* pp. 46-47.

P. 30 **There's a common:** James Blanchard, *There is a Common Thread:* James Blanchard speech at the Beta Gamma Sigma International Honoree Luncheon, April 22, 2005, as reported by the Beta Gamma Sigma International Society and available at betagammasigma.org.

P. 31 **"The most important:** Peter F. Drucker, *Management Challenge for the 21st Century* (New York: Harper Business, 1999), p. 135.

P. 31 **The main assets:** Stephen R. Covey, *The 8th Habit: From Effectiveness to Greatness* (New York: Simon & Schuster, 2004), p. 14.

P. 32 **"The information age:** Stuart Crainer, *The Management Century* (San Francisco: Jossey-Bass Publishers, 2000), p. 207.

P. 32 **"In a few hundred:** Peter F. Drucker, Managing Knowledge Means Managing Oneself, Leader to Leader, 16 (Spring 2000), pp. 8-10.

VISION

P. 37 **Vision is a love affair:** Tom Peters, *Re-imagine!: Business Excellence in a Disruptive Age* (London: Dorling Kindersley Ltd., 2003) p. 339.

P. 37 **Where there is:** King James Bible, Proverbs 29:18.

P. 37   **"Leadership is at its:** Michael Useem, *The Leadership Moment* (New York: Three Rivers Press, 1998), p. 4.

P. 40   **"As you shape your:** Harvard Business Essentials "Your Mentor and Guide to Doing Business Effectively" Manager's Toolkit (MA: Harvard Business School Publishing, 2004), p. 195.

P. 41   **The birth of Joan:** James MacGregor Burns, *Leadership* (New York: Harper & Row Publisher, 1978), p. 242.

P. 41   **I know this now:** Maxwell Anderson, "Joan of Lorraine" New York: Dramatists Play Services, 1946

P. 43   **Let every nation know:** John F. Kennedy inaugural address January 20, 1961.

P. 44   **$405 billion in net:** WalMart 2010 Annual Report.

P. 44   **1945 when he invested:** Sam Walton with John Huey, *Made in America: My Story* (New York: Doubleday, 1992) p. 27.

P. 45   **less than $30 billion:** Jim Collins, "The 100 Greatest CEOs Of All Time. What These Extraordinary Leaders Can Teach Today's Troubled Executives", *CNNMoney.com Fortune*, July 21, 2003.

P. 45   **The Boston Consulting Group:** Jena McGregor, "The World's Most Innovative Companies", *BusinessWeek*, April 24, 2006, pp. 63-76.

P. 45   **$150 billion:** Adam Lashinsky, "How Jobs transformed Apple," *Fortune*, November 5, 2009.

P. 45   **A shoe factory sends:** Rosemund Stone Zander and Benjamin Zander, *The Art of Possibilities* (New York: Penguin Group), p. 9.

P. 47   **"Human beings need:** Barbara Kellerman, *Leadership* (New York: McGraw Hill, *2010), p. xiv.*

P. 48   **"It's up to the:** Rudolph W. Giuliani, *Leadership* (New York: Hyperion, 2002), p, 298.

P. 48   **"Suppose Churchill had walked:** Ibid., p, 297.

P. 49   **The last human freedoms:** Viktor Frankl, *Search for Meaning* (Boston, Beacon Press, 2006), p. 66.

P. 51   **"If we are not careful:** Spencer W. Kimball, "The Message: There is Purpose in Life", *New Era,* September 1974.

P. 51   **"What for?!":** Gavin Mortimer, *The Great Swim* (New York: Walker Publishing, 2008), p. 150.

P. 52   **Sears & Roebuck:** www.searsarchives.com/history Pulled February 22, 2011.

P. 54   **Hewlett, Packard, Merck,:** James C. Collins and Jerry I. Porras, *Built To Last* (New York: HarperCollins), p. 76.

P. 55   **"In everyone's life:** Albert Schweitzer Humanitarian, Nobel Laureate

P. 55   **James Burke of Johnson & Johnson's:** Jim Collins, "The 100 Greatest CEOs Of All Time. What These Extraordinary Leaders Can Teach Today's Troubled Executives", *CNNMoney.com Fortune*, July 21, 2003.

P. 56   **Men wanted for Hazardous:** William J. Bennett, *The Book of Virtues* (New York: Simon & Schuster, 1993), p. 493.

P. 57   **"Setting the mission:** Jack Welch, *Winning* (New York: HarperCollins, 2005), p.16.

P. 57   **Corporate storytellers:** Eric Ransdell, "The Nike Story? Just Tell It!" *Fast Company.com.*, December 31, 1999.

FORMAL AND INFORMAL AUTHORITY

P. 59   **reward power:** Barbara Kellerman, *Followership* (MA: Harvard Business, 2008), p.63. Also, John R. P. French Jr. and Bertram Raven, "The Bases of Social Power," in *Studies in Social Power*, ed Dorwin Cartwright (Ann Arbor, MI: Institute for Social Research, 1959).

P. 60   **"Power is the:** Joseph S. Nye Jr., *Soft Power: The Means to Success in World Politics* (New York: Public Affairs, 2004), p. 2.

P. 60   **Manhattan hotelier:** Amy Joyce, "Big Bad Boss Tales," *Washington Post*, May 29, 2005.

P. 60   **"This category suggests:** Blaine Lee, *The Power Principle: Influence with Honor* (New York: Simon & Schuster, 1997), p. 9.

P. 61   **"He was only twenty-one:** Ibid., p. 328.

P. 61 **"In his attempt:** Nathan Stoltzfus, *Resistance of the Heart: Intermarriage and the Rosenstrasse Protest in Nazi Germany* (New Jersey: Rutgers University Press, 2001), p. 671.

P. 62 **Hitler had been:** Ibid., p.754. Story retold in Barbara Kellerman, *Followership*, p.111.

P. 64 **"In the movie:** Blaine Lee, *The Power Principle: Influence with Honor*, pp. 272-274. Story Retold

P. 66 **I claim to be:** Easwaran, *Gandhi the Man*, p. i.

P. 67 **"a pencil in the:** Jose' Luis Gonzales-Balado and Janet N. Playfoot, *My Life for the Poor: Mother Teresa of Calcutta* (San Francisco: Harper & Row, 1985).

P. 67 **Among the news items:** James E. Talmage, *Improvement Era*, October 1914, 1108-9. spelling, punctuation and words modernized

P. 69 **"Day by day:** David O. McKay, "Man's Soul Is As Endless As Time," *Instructor* Jan. 1960), pp. 1-2.

P. 70 **"What drove these:** Kristen Renwick Monroe, *The Hands of Compassion: Portraits of Moral Choice During the Holocaust* (New Jersey: Princeton University Press, 2004), p. x.

P. 70 **"How did you decide:** Ibid., p. 23.

P. 70 **"So how did:** Ibid., p. 30.

P. 70 **"Bystanders observe:** Barbara Kellerman, *Followership*, p. 97.

P. 71 **"In what direction are:** Richard Evans, *Quotebook* (Salt Lake City: Deseret Book, 1988).

P. 72 **"what it feels:** Robert E. Kelley, *The Power of Fellowship: How to Create Leaders People Want to Follow and Followers Who Lead Themselves* (New York: Doubleday, 1992), p.1.

P. 73 **"intelligence, independence:** Ibid., p. 12.

P. 73 ***Journey to the East:*** Barbara Kellerman, *Followership*, pp. 79-80. Story Retold.

P. 73 **"The group, it:** Robert E. Kelley, *The Power of Fellowship: How to Create Leaders People Want to Follow and Followers Who Lead Themselves*, p. 25.

P. 73   **"exemplary follower:** Barbara Kellerman, *Followership,* p. 80.

P. 73   **"into parity":** Ira Chaleff, *The Courageous Followers: Standing Up To & for Our Leaders* (San Francisco: BK Business book, 2009), p. 1.

P. 73   **"contribute to leadership:** Ibid., p. 3.

P. 74   **Responsible for maintaining:** George Orwell, *Shooting an Elephant,* in *New Writing* (London: GB, 1936). The quotes in this section are from the story. The story is retold in *Followership.* Barbara Kellerman, *Followership,* pp. xv-xvi.

P. 75   **"staff rebellion:** Krishna Guha, "The Marathon Man," *Financial Times* (London), June 2, 2007.

P. 75   **The president must:** Jeannine Aversa, "Bank Staff Asks Wolfowitz to Resign" *Washington Post* Associated Press, April 12, 2007.

P. 75   **clear and decisive actions:** Steven R. Weisman, "Wolfowitz Loses Ground in Fight for World Bank Post," *New York Times,* April 27, 2007.

P. 76   **"In an attempt to:** Blaine Lee, *The Power Principle: Influence with Honor,* pp. 168-169. Story retold.

P. 77   **"There was nothing unusual:** Eknath Easwaran, *Gandhi the Man: The Story of His Transformation* (Tomales, California: Nilgiri Press, 1997),* p. 11.

P. 77   **"I used to be:** Ibid., p. 13.

P. 77   **I am not a visionary:** Ibid., p. 1.

P. 77   **Imagine what it would:** Sterling W. Sill, *Leadership* (Salt Lake City: Bookcraft, 1958).

P. 78   **"A new moral principle:** Robert K. Greenleaf, "The Servant as Leader," *Servant Leadership: A Journey into the Nature of Legitimate Power and Greatness,* 25th anniversary ed. (New Jersey: Paulist Press, 2002), pp. 22-24.

P. 79   **"32 percent:** Barbara Kellerman, *Followership,* p. 55.

P. 80   **"He moves about:** Bob Herbert, "Cometh the hour, Cometh the mayor", *New York Times,* September 21, 2001.

P. 80 **"When the fever:** H.A. Guerber, *The Story of the Greeks* (New York: American Book Company, 1896), pp. 240-241.

P. 81 **"You have a dream:** Robert K. Greenleaf, "The Leader as Servant," in *The Company of Others: Making Community in the Modern World* (New York: Putnam, 1993).

P. 82 **...you have not:** Doris Kearns Goodwin, *Team of Rivals: The Political Genius of Abraham Lincoln* (New York: Simon & Schuster, 2005), p. 747.

EMOTIONAL INTELLIGENCE

P. 84 **"IQ offers little:** Daniel Goleman, *Emotional Intelligence: Why It Can Matter More Than IQ* (New York: Bantam Dell, 2006), p. 35.

P. 84 **"There is no known:** Travis Bradberry and Jean Greaves, *Emotional Intelligence 2.0* (TalentSmart, 2009), p. 17.

P. 85 **"Emotional Intelligences:** Ibid., p. 17.

P. 85 **"There's an old Chinese:** Ibid., p. 245. Story Retold

P. 85 **"Anyone can become:** Aristotle, The *Nicomachean Ethics*

P. 86 **"The ability to monitor:** Salovey P and Grewal D, The Science of Emotional Intelligence. Current Directions in Psychological Science, Volume14 –6, p. 281, 2005.

P. 87 **"You can't talk:** Stephen M. R. Covey, *The Speed of Trust: The One Thing That Changes Everything* (New York: Simon & Schuster, 2006), p. 127.

P. 88 **"Reactive people build:** Stephen R. Covey, *7 Habits of Highly Effective People* (New York: Simon & Schuster, 1989), p. 72.

P. 89 **"Often, however, the:** Ira Chaleff, *The Courageous Follower: Standing Up To & For Our Leaders* San Francisco: Berrett-Koehler Publisher, 2009), p. 127.

P. 89 **"Emotional competencies are:** Richard E. Boyatzis, Daniel Goleman, Kennth S. Rhee, Cluster Competence in Emotional Intelligence: Insights from the Emotional Cometence Inventory (ECI), 2000.

P. 90   **"…a United States Army:** Ira Chaleff, *The Courageous Followers: Standing Up To & For Our Leaders*, p. Dedication.

P. 92   **"We who lived in:** Victor Frankl, *Man search for Meaning* (Boston: Beacon Press, 2006), p. 65.

P. 94   **"The Shu Ching indicates:** Chungliang A. Huang and Jerry Lynch, *Mentoring: The Tao of Giving Wisdom* (San Francisco: HarperCollins), p. 45.

P. 94   **"Loving kindness towards:** Ibid., p. 44.

P. 95   **"For star performance:** Daniel Goleman, *Working with Emotional Intelligence* (New York: Bantam Books, 2001), p. 26.

P. 95   **"And now here is:** Antoine de Saint-Exupery "The Little Prince" (Gallimard, 1943)

P. 98   **"The visionary leader:** Polly Labarre, *"Do you Have the Will to Lead?"*, *Fast Company Magazine* 32 (March 2000), p. 222. Also, Stephen R. Covey, *The 8ᵗʰ Habit: From Effectiveness to Greatness* (New York: Simon & Schuster, 2004) p. 67.

P. 98   **Travis Bradberry & Jean Greaves in their book:** Travis Bradberry & Jean Greaves, *Emotional Intelligence 2.0*, p. 23-50.

P. 100 **"malice toward none:** Lincoln's Second Inaugural Address, March 4, 1865.

LEADERSHIP MORAL DECAY

P. 104 **For example, some define:** Barbara Kellerman, *Followership* (MA: Harvard Business Press, 2008), p. xx.

P. 105 **Tom Peters reported:** Donald T. Phillips, Lincoln on Leadership: Executive Strategies for Tough Times (New York: Hachette Book Group, 1992), p. 52.

P. 105 **Such as Boeing:** Barbara Kellerman, *Followership*, p. 22.

P. 105 **"The Boss on:** David Henry, Mike France, and Louis Lavelle, "The Boss on the Sidelines: How Auditors, Directors, and Lawyers Are Asserting Their Power", *Business Week*, April 25, 2005, pp. 88-94.

P. 106 **CEO Turnover in Overdrive:** Nanette Byrnes, "The Great CEO Exodus," BusinessWeek, October 30, 2006, p. 78.

P. 106 **Bill Allen's story of Boeing:** Jim Collins, "The 100 Greatest CEOs Of All Time. What These Extraordinary Leaders Can Teach Today's Troubled Executives", *CNNMoney.com Fortune*, July 21, 2003. Story Retold

P. 106 **"Long before Enron:** Warren Bennis, *On Becoming a Leader* (New York: Basic Books, 2009), p. 156.

P. 107 **"Leaders may come:** Ira Chaleff, *The Courageous Follower: Standing Up To & For Our Leaders* (San Francisco: Barrett-Koehler Publishers, 2009), p.128.

P. 107 **Believing that the activity:** Harry Levinson, "Designing and Managing Your Career" Why "Good Managers Make Bad Ethical Choices by Saul W. Gellerman (MA: Harvard Business School Publishing, 1989), p. 280.

P. 108 **Amitai Etzioni, professor:** Ibid., p. 281.

P. 108 **"Do you mean:** Ibid., p. 281.

P. 108 **"When one has reached:** James C. Humes, *The Wit and Wisdom of Winston Churchill* (New York: HarperCollins, 1994), p. 75.

P. 109 **"Medicine is for people:** "Medicine: What the Doctor Ordered" *Time Magazine*, August 18, 1952.

P. 110 **"Corporations are not responsible:** Michael E. Porter, *On Competition* (Harvard Business School Publishing, 2008), p. 499.

P. 111 **"A man who gives into:** C.S. Lewis, Mere Christianity (New York: Simon & Schuster, 1980), pp. 124-125.

P. 112 **"Trust is a function of:** Stephen M. R. Covey, *The speed of Trust* (New York: Free Press, 2006), p. 30.

P. 114 **Herb Kelleher, chairman:** Robert K. Cooper and Ayman Sawaf, *Executive EQ: Emotional Intelligence in Leadership and Organization*

(New York: Berkley Publishing Group, 1996), p. 88. Story Retold

P. 114 **"If you look at:** Warren Bennis, *On Becoming a Leader*, pp. 159-160.

P. 115 **"To thine own self:** Hamlet, I, iii, 78-81.

P. 116 **"Gandhi spent every moment:** Eknath Easwaran, *Gandhi, the Man*, 2nd ed. (Nilgin Press, 1978), p. 140.

P. 116 **"The principles you live:** Blaine Lee, *The Power Principle: Influence with Honor* (New York: Simon & Schuster, 1997), p. 1.

SELF-AWARENESS

P. 119 **"I think, therefore I am:** Rene' Descartes, Discourse on the Methods of Rightly Conducting the Reason and Seeking for Truth in the Sciences, pp.75-76 Sutherland & Knox, 1850.

P. 121 **"To be effective:** Travis Bradberry and Jean Greaves, *Emotional Intelligence 2.0* (TalentSmart, 2009), p. 69.

P. 124 **"I have often thought:** Gerald E. Myers, *William James: His Life and Thought* (Connecticut: Yale University Press, 1986), p. 49.

P. 124 **"Homer could have sat:** Author unknown

P. 125 **"Therefore good Brutus:** Shakespeare, *Julius Caesar*, Act 1, Scene 2.

P. 127 **"Pride gets no pleasure:** C.S. Lewis, Mere Christianity (New York: Macmillan, 1952), pp. 109-110.

P. 128 **The Washington Post conducted:** Gene Weingarten, "Pearls Before Breakfast," *Washington Post*, Sunday, April 8, 2007.

P. 133 **In his writings "De Revolutionibus Orbium Caolestium:** Stephen R Covey, *Principle Centered Leadership* (New York: Simon & Schuster, 1990), pp. 67-68.

P. 134 **"No man for any considerable:** Elizabeth Knowles, ed., "The Oxford Dictionary of Quotations, 5th ed. (Oxford: Oxford University Press, 1999), p. 503.

P. 134 **"We know not of the future:** Alice R. Trulock. "In the Hands of Providence" Joshua L. Chamberlain and the American Civil War (Chapel Hill: University of North Carolina Press, 1992), p. 62.

P. 135 **"We become involved in:** Stephen R. Covey, A. Roger Merrill and Rebecca R. Merrill, *First Things First* (New York, Simon & Schuster: 1994), p. 72.

P. 135 **"Just because a desire or behavior:** Scott Peck, *The Road Less Travel* (New York: Simon & Schuster, 1978), pp. 213-214.

P. 136 **"Freedom from responsibility:** Eric Hoffer, *True Believer: Thoughts on the Nature of Mass Movements* (New York: Harper & Brothers, 1951), passim.

P. 136 **In the 17th-century:** Nathaniel Hawthrone, *The Scarlet Letter* (Ticknor & Field, 1850).

P. 140 **When CEO Joe Cullman:** Jim Collins, *Good-to-Great: Why Some Companies Make the Leap... and Others Don't* (New York: HarperCollins, 2001), p. 77.

P. 141 **"Most failing organizations:** Stephen R. Covey, *The 8th Habit: From Effectiveness to Greatness* (New York: Free Press), p. 19.

P. 141 **"On one hand:** Ethan M. Rasiel & Paul N. Friga, *The McKinsey Mind* (New York: McGraw-Hill, 1999), p. 151.

P. 142 **How the Hippo Lost His Hair:** Nigel J.A Bristow and Michael-John Bristow, *Where's the Gift: Using Feedback to Work Smarter, Learn Faster and Avoid Disaster* (Utah, LCI Press, 2010), pp. 10-12.

ROLE MODELING

P. 148 **"As a newly elevated:** Ira Chaleff, *The Courageous Followers: Standing Up To & For Our Leaders* (San Francisco, Berrett-Koehler Publishing, Inc. 2009), p. 107.

P. 149 **In 2001, Ms. Watkins:** Frank Pelligrini, Person of the Week: Enron Whistleblower, Sherron Watkins, *Time Magazine* in partnership with CNN, January 18, 2002.

P. 149 **market value from $14:** Ron Coddington, "Business' Most Notorious", *USA Today*, July 30, 2007

P. 149 **"To make values really:** Jack Welch, *Winning* (New York: HarperCollins, 2005), pp. 20-21.

P. 150 **During a presidential speech:** Mark Silva, "Still Not Covered By Health Care: Biden's Mouth", *Chicago Tribune* March 23, 2010.

P. 150 **"He who governs others:** Philip Massinger, Timoleon, in: The Bondman, act 1, sc.3 (1624), Poems of Philip Massinger, P. Edwards and C. Gibson, eds. (1976).

P. 152 **"What was it like living:** Stephen R. Covey, *The 8th Habit: From Effectiveness to Greatness* (New York: Simon & Schuster, 2004), pp. 56-57.

P. 153 **"He who cannot change:** Anwar El-Sadat, *In Search of Identity: An Autobiography* (New York: Harper and Row Publishers, 1978), p. 303.

P. 153 **"Do not use me:** James E. Faust, "Acting for Ourselves and Not Being Acted Upon" *Ensign*, November 1995, p. 45.

P. 154 **The Brazilian businessman:** Jim Collins, "The 100 Greatest CEOs Of All Time. What These Extraordinary Leaders Can Teach Today's Troubled Executives", July 21, 2003 *CNNMoney.com Fortune.* Story Retold

VISIBILITY

P. 159 **"One of the most:** Donald T. Phillips, *Lincoln On Leadership* (New York: Business Plus Hachette Book Group, 1992), p. 25.

P. 159 **A survey of leaders:** John Rosemond, *Parent Power: A Common Sense Approach to Parenting in the 90's and Beyond* (Kansas City: Andrews and McMeel, 1990), p. 7. Also, "Don't Be Shy," *Business Ethics,* January, 1996 p. 15.

TELLING IT LIKE IT IS

P. 163 **According to a 2005:** Mercer human Resources Consulting, 2005 *What's Working Survey,* New York, 2005.

P. 165 **Major General Hooker:** Donald T. Phillips, *Lincoln on Leadership: Executive Strategies for tough Times* (New York: Hachette Book Group, 1992), p. 46.

P. 166 **just such a letter:** Donald T. Phillips, *Lincoln on Leadership: Executive Strategies for tough Times* (New York: Hachette Book Group, 1992), p. 46.

P. 166 **"The Humanitarian theory:** C.S. Lewis, *God in the Dock: Essays on Theology and Ethics* 1970, p. 294.

P. 167 **"The leader who is:** President N. Eldon Tanner, *Ensign*, November 1975, p. 74.

P. 168 **"Dialogue…is the single-most:** Ram Charan, *Conquering a Culture of Indecision*, (Boston: Harvard Business School Press, 2002), p. 146.

P. 168 **"Candor" the dirty little secret:** Jack Welch, *Winning* (New York: HarperCollins, 2005), p. 26.

P. 168 **"Leadership is equally:** Jim Collins, *Good-to-Great: Why Some Companies Make the Leap… and Others Don't* (HarperCollins Publisher New York, 2001) p. 74.

P. 169 **"Come to the edge:** Guillaume Appollinaire, "Le Larron," Alcools et Calligrammes, edited by Claude Debrone (Paris: Imprimerie National, 1991), pp. 108-113.

P. 169 **"I have nothing:** L. Snyder, *The War: A Concise History, 1939–1945,* (New York: Julian Messner, Inc., 1961), p. 8 & 9. First speech as prime minister, House of Commons, 13 May 1940.

P. 170 **"At its most:** Paul Wieand, Drucker's Challenge: Communication and the emotional glass ceiling. *Ivey Business Journal Online*, July/August 2003, p. 2.

P. 170 **"When we are debating:** Colin Powell, *My American Journey* (New York: Random House 1995), p. 319.

P. 170 **In every block:** Sterling W. Sill, *Leadership* (Salt Lake City: Bookcraft, 1959), p. 174.

WORK LIFE BALANCE

P. 178 *"The miracle is:* Jose Luis Gonzales-Balado and Janet N. Play-foot, *My Life for the Poor: Mother Teresa of Calcutta* (New York: Ballantine Books, 1985).

DECISION-MAKING

P. 181 **Roy Vagelos of Merck & Company:** Michael Useem, *The Leadership Moment* (New York: Three Rivers Press, 1998), pp. 10-42.

P. 182 **"John, I can't:** James MacGregor Burns, *Leadership* (New York: Harper & Row, Publishers, Inc., 1978), p. 410.

P. 182 **They recalled approximately:** Tamara Kaplan, "The Tylenol Crisis: How Effective Public Relations Saved Johnson & Johnson," Pennsylvania State University, 1998.

P. 183 **In 2001, the Texas:** Tom Peters, *Re-imagine!* (London: Dorling Kindersley Limited, 2003), p. 338.

P. 184 **"As the snow:** We're Going Down, Larry, Monday, *Time,* in Partnership with CNN, February 15, 1982.

P. 187 **"Decisions need to be:** Louis V. Gerstner Jr., *Who says Elephants Can't Dance?* (HarperCollins, New York, N.Y., 2003), p. 200.

P. 187 **"In May 1962:** William S. Kane, *Thriving in Change* (New Jersey: Pearson Education, 2008), pp. 30-31. Retold.

P. 188 **"Goodness knows, those:** Stephen Ambrose, *D-Day* (New York: Simon Schuster, 1994), p. 189. Walter Cronkite interview with Eisenhower

P. 188 **"Often I make a:** Rudolph W. Giuliani, *Leadership* (New York: Hyperion, 2002), p. 226-227.

ORGANIZATIONAL DESIGN

P. 190 **"Customers have memories:** Peppers, Don and Martha Rogers, Ph.D. (2008), *Rules to Break and Laws to Follow,* New Jersey: John Wiley & Sons 2008), p. 24.

P. 190   **"Delighting customers requires:** Fred Reichheld, *The Ultimate Question: Driving Good Profits and True Growth* (Boston: Harvard Business School Press, 2006), p. 173.

P. 191   **At Southwest airlines:** Ibid., p. 91.

P. 191   **"Change, even for:** William S. Kane, *Thriving in Change* (New Jersey: Pearson Education, Inc., 2008), p. x.

P. 193   **"To the outside:** Ibid., p. 6.

P. 194   **"Too much past success:** John P. Kotter, *Leading Change* (Boston: Harvard Business School Press, 1996), p. 5.

P. 195   **"You make great:** Jim Collins, "The 10 Greatest CEOs Of All Time. What These Extraordinary Leaders Can Teach Today's Troubled Executives", *CNNMoney.com Fortune* July 21, 2003.

P. 195   **"This is a very important:** Jim Collins, *Good to Great: Why Some Companies Make the Leap...and Others Don't* (New York: Harper Business, 2001), p. 86.

P. 196   **"The Stockdale Paradox:** Ibid., p. 86.

P. 196   **"The brutal facts:** Betsy Morris, "The Accidental CEO," *Fortune,* June 23, 2003. Also, Stephen M. R. Covey, *The Speed of Trust* (New York: Simon & Schuster, 2006), p. 186. Retold

P. 196   **"Whatever you think:** Ibid.,p. 186. Retold

P. 198   **"Nokia has gone:** Ian Wylie, "Calling for a Renewable Future," *Fast Company,* May 2003, p. 46.

P. 200   **"Of all the decisions: Peter Drucker,** *Peter Drucker on the Profession of Management* (Boston: Harvard Business School, 2003), p. 34.

P. 203   **Dell Computer redefined:** W. Chan Kim and Renee Mauborgne, *Blue Ocean Strategy* (Boston, Harvard Business School Publishing, 2005), pp. 202-203 and *MSN Money*, March 4, 2010 Retold

P. 204   **The Five Competitive forces:** Michael E. Porter, *On Competition* (Boston: Harvard Business School Publishing, 2008), pp. 8,13, 14,17.

P. 205   **Understanding competitive forces:** Ibid., p. 4.

P. 205 **Marriott earns 50:** Michael E. Porter, *On Competition*, pp. 159-160.

P. 205 **Marriott's diversification:** Ibid., pp. 159-160.

P. 206 **Red bead:** W. Edward Deming, *Out of the Crisis* (Cambridge: MIT, Center for Advancement Educational Services, 1982). P. 446.

P. 208 **"Mr. Welch's insight:** Randal Rothenberg and Noel M. Tichy, *The Thought Leader Interview, Strategy+Business Magazine* (Spring 2002), p. 91-92.

P. 210 **B-17's:** Stephen Ambrose, *D-DAY* (New York: Simon & Schuster, 1995), p. 323.

P. 211 **425 cars in 1901:** http://www.ideafinder.com/history/inventions/assbline.htm. Pulled March 12, 2011.

P. 211 **By 1927, there:** http//www.modelt.ca/background.html. Pulled March 12, 2011.

P. 213 **In 1937, they:** John F. Love, *McDonald's: Behind The Arches* (New York: Bantam Books), p. 12.

EXECUTION

P. 216 **"Seventy percent of:** Ram Charan and Geoff Colvin, *Why CEO's Fail, Fortune,* June 1999.

P. 216 **"Execution is the major:** Larry Bossidy and Ram Charan, *Execution: The Discipline of Getting Things Done* (New York: Crown Business, 2002), p. 21.

P. 217 **In 1962:** Jack Covert and Todd Sattersten, *The 100 Best Business Books of All Time* (New York: Penguin Group, 2009), p. 211

P. 218 **"No company can deliver:** Ibid., p. 34.

P. 218 **"Leadership without the:** Ibid., p. 19.

P. 218 **"All of the great:** Louis V. Gerstner, Jr., *Who Says Elephants Can't Dance?* (New York: HarperCollins Publishers, 2002), p. 230.

P. 223 **"Enemy of the State:** "Julius Caesar Crosses the Rubicon, 49 BC," EyeWitness to History, www.eyewitnesstohistory.com (2002). Also, Duruy, Victor, History of Rome vol. V (1883); Suetonius "Life of Julius Caesar" in Davis, William Stearns, Readings in Ancient History (1912). Story Retold

P. 226 **Napoleon, it was said:** James MacGregor Burns, *Leadership* (New York: Harper & Row, Publishers, 1978), p. 414.

P. 226 **President Jefferson was the visionary:** James F. Simon, *What Kind of Nation* (New York: Simon & Schuster), p. 21.

P. 226 **"We thought that if:** David Packard, *The HP Way: How Bill Hewlett and I Built Our Company* (New York: Harper Business, 1995), p. 80.

P. 229 **Delaying Gratification:** Scott Peck M.D., *The Road Less Traveled* (New York: Simon and Schuster, 1978), p.18.

P. 230 **"All 'irregularities' must cease:** David McCullough, *1776* (New York: Simon & Schuster, 2005), p.161.

P. 230 **"It will never be done:** Blaine Lee, *The Power Principle: Influence with Honor* (New York: Simon & Schuster, 1997), p.127.

P. 231 **"who have learned:** M. Scott Peck, M.D., *The Different Drum* (New York: Simon and Schuster,1987). p. 59.

P. 231 **Ms. X had:** Tom Peter, *Re-Image!* (London: Dorling Kindersley Limited, 2003), p. 333.

P. 232 **"When you ask people:** Peter Senge, *The Fifth Discipline: The Art & Practice of The Learning Organization* (New York: Doubleday, 1990), p. 13

P. 233 **Five Dysfunctions of a Team:** Patrick Lencioni, *The Five Dysfunctions of Team: A Leadership Fable* (San Francisco: Jossey-Bass, 2002), p. 174.

REMOVING BARRIERS

P. 240 **trim tab:** Peter Senge, *The Fifth Discipline* (New York: Random, 1990), p. 64.

P. 240 **murder rate of 2,000:** Rudolph W. Giuliani, *Leadership* (New York: Hyperion, 2002), p. 41.

P. 240 **"We attacked crime:** Rudolph W. Giuliani, *Leadership*, p.41.

P. 240 **"At the time crime:** Ibid. pp. 41-42.

P. 240 **Crime was reduced:** Ibid., p. 43.

P. 241 **When Lou Gerstner:** Tom Peters, *Re-imagine!* (London: Dorling Kindersley Limited, 2003), p. 331.

P. 242 **it was discovered that $1.2 trillion:** Parija B. Kavilanz, Healthcare's Six Money-Wasting Problems CNNMoney.com August 10, 2009. PricewaterhouseCoopers' Health Research Institute

P. 242 **$2.2 trillion the United States spends:** Ibid.

P. 242 **defensive medicine:** Ibid.

METRICS AND NUMERIC

P. 246 **"The "new" balanced:** Robert S. Kaplan and David P. Norton, "Using the Balanced Scorecard as a Strategic Management System," Harvard Business Review (January-February 1996), p. 76.

P. 247 **"That one must view:** Ibid., p. 76.

P. 247 **"Accountability is one:** Fred Reichheld, *The Ultimate Question: Driving Good Profits and True Growth* (Boston: Harvard Business School Press, 2006) p. 17.

P. 248 **Measurements Assumptions:** Douglas W. Hubbard, *How to Measure Anything: Finding the Value of Intangibles in Business* (New Jersey: John Wiley & Sons, 2007), p. 31.

P. 248 **Clarification Chain:** Ibid., p. 26.

P. 248 **"The first step is:** Charles Handy, *The Empty Raincoat* (United Kingdom, Arrow, 1994), p. 219.

P. 250 **"After all, facts:** Leonard Courtney, essay in *The National Review* (London, 1985).

INDEX

Apple, xiv, xv, 5, 9, 33, 45, 114, 193

Accountability, 32, 69, 96, 141, 144, 148, 153, 166, 229, 230, 233, 247

Alice in Wonderland, 27, 42, 43

Alexander The Great, 79, 80, 158

Allbritton, John L., 60

Allen, Bill, 106, 195

Anderson, Hans Christian, 125

Anderson, Maxwell, 41

Anglican Bishop, 115, 116

Arc, Joan of, 41

Attributes, 3, 4, 12, 15, 17, 26, 32, 66, 78, 80, 94, 124, 152, 217, 218, 233, 249

Attenborough, Richard, 64

Blake, William, 36

Blanchard, James, 30

Bennis, Warren G., 6, 40, 106, 226

Boeing Corporation, 8, 105, 106, 185, 194

Bradberry, Travis, 85, 98

Buffet, Warren, 19, 114

Burke, James, 55, 182

Burns, James MacGregor, 4, 6, 20, 41

Bush, Barbara, 28

Bush, George, 28

Caesar, Julius, 125, 223

Carlzon, Jan, 4, 10

Carnegie, Andrew, 13

Clarity, 188, 220, 226

Clarke, Boyd, 36

Chadwick, Florence, 52

Chaleff, Ira, 73, 89, 148

Chamberlain, Joshua L., 134

Charan, Ram, 168, 216, 218

Christ, Jesus, 23, 62, 81, 116

Churchill, Winston, 3, 9, 20, 48, 108, 142, 169, 229

Civil Rights, 17, 54, 133

Communication, 4, 14, 44, 53, 56, 89-91, 142, 151, 164, 170, 198, 210, 220, 224, 233

Competencies, 12, 17, 66, 89, 95, 98, 119, 188, 192, 216

Collins, Jim, 6, 25-27, 168, 195

Columbus, Christopher, 132

Conscious Dichotomy, 71

Copernicus, 133

Covey, Stephen, 31, 87, 88, 152

Covey, Stephen M.R., 12

Crainer, Stuart, 32

Crossland, Ron, 36

Cullman, Joe, 140

Culture, 9, 14, 23, 49, 54, 69, 78, 88, 100, 130, 153, 160, 184, 193, 212, 221, 234, 246, 251

Curie, Marie, 230

Darius, King III, 79

Decision-making, 27, 40, 55, 69, 110, 181, 186, 178, 191, 213, 241, 243

Dell Computer, 203

Deming, W. Edward, 206

Determinisms, 21, 22, 139

    Environmental, 21, 22

    Genetic, 21

    Psychic, 22

Dickey, John Sloan, 112

Discipline, 15, 20, 39, 45, 52, 62, 69, 87, 92, 100, 119, 135, 174, 195, 216, 228, 230, 240

Drucker, Peter, 31, 47, 170, 189, 200

Easwaran, Eknath, 77, 116

Ebbers, Bernard J., 60, 105

Ederle, Gertrude, 51

Eisenhower, General, 188

Emotional Intelligence, 9, 26 84, 92, 96, 98, 121, 160

    Competencies and Skills, 98

    Emotional Abilities, 98

Enron, 106, 149

Epicurus, 221

Eros, 5

Ethics, 22, 73, 103, 106, 111, 122, 130, 144, 150

Etzioni, Amitai, 108

Evans, Richard, 71

Execution, xvi, 15, 24, 27, 40, 45, 53, 97, 186, 197, 199, 203, 211, 216, 234

Followers, 4, 6, 12, 20, 26, 29, 63, 45, 50, 60, 66, 72, 80, 94, 104, 124, 155, 160

Followership, 6, 25, 29, 61, 70, 72, 74, 80, 94, 104, 124, 125, 135, 224, 228

Ford, Henry, 211, 212

Formal Authority, xv, 5, 7, 9, 66, 75, 82, 90, 104, 147, 223

Frankl, Viktor, 49, 92

Fulghum, Robert, 23

Gagarin, Yuri, 43

Gandhi, Mahatma, 17, 62, 64, 76, 81, 113, 115, 123

General Electric, 8, 41, 149, 168

Gardner, John W., 5, 141

Gerstner, Lou, 2, 187, 218, 241

Giuliani, Rudolph, 4, 48, 79, 188, 240

Global Crossing, 106

Goals, 4, 5, 9, 13, 25, 30, 36, 42, 53, 72, 99, 105, 122, 130, 148, 176, 182, 197, 216, 224, 228, 239

    Cascading, 226, 228

Goleman, Daniel, 8, 84, 94

Gonxha, Agnes, 178

Graham, Katharine, 19

Gray, EM, 228

Greaves, Jean, 85, 98

Greenberg, Maurice R., 105

Greenleaf, Robert K., 78, 81

Grewal, Daisey, 98

Hale, Nathan, 61, 96

Harding, Warren G., 182

Hawthorne, Nathaniel, 134

Helmsley, Leona, 60

Hewlett, Bill, 226, 227

Hillary, Sir Edmond, 46, 51

Hilton, Conrad, 236

Hitler, Adolph, 61, 62, 105

Hooker, Major General, 165

Huang, Chungliang A., 94

Hudson, Dayton, 217

IBM, 2, 192, 218, 241

Immelt, Jeff, 8

Industrial Age, 6, 27, 31, 114

Informal Authority, xv, 5, 9, 63, 66, 75, 82

James, William, 124

Jefferson Memorial, 124, 209

Jefferson, Thomas, 4, 232

Jobs, Steve, 9, 42, 45, 193

John Gardner, 141

Johnson & Johnson, 55, 182

Johnson, Lyndon B., 5, 54

Jordan, William George, 134

Kane, William S., 187, 191

Kelleher, Herb, 9, 114

Kellerman, Barbara, 70, 104

Kelley, Robert, 72

Kennedy, John F., 43, 44, 60, 187

Kimball, Spencer W., 51

King George, 142

King, Martin Luther, 17, 54, 62, 81, 116

Kmart, 217

Knight, Phil, 57

Knowledge, 12, 13, 16, 17, 130, 208

Knowledge Age, 6, 17, 27, 30, 31, 32, 168

Kotter, John P., 2, 6, 194

Kouzes, James M, 11

Kresge, S.S., 217

Kroc, Ray, 94

Lay, Ken, 149

Leadership Theory: 4, 6, 18, 20, 66, 78, 216

    Trait, 18, 20

    Great Event, 18, 20, 79

    Transformational, 18, 20

Lee, Blaine, 20, 60, 76, 116

Lencioni, Patrick, 233

Levels of Paradigms, 130

    Conscious Challenged, 131

    Conscious Unchallenged, 131

    No Awareness Subconscious, 131

Lewin, Kurt, 242

Lewis, C. S., 111, 127, 166

Lincoln, Abraham, 2, 4, 20, 26-27, 81, 155, 159, 165

Logos, 5

Lynch, Jerry, 94

Machiavellian, 1, 193

Mallory, George Leigh, 46

Management, 2, 6, 8, 26-27, 31, 48, 57, 98-100, 110, 171, 184, 198, 206, 226, 237, 246

Mandela, Nelson, 2, 22, 42, 62, 81, 116

Mantle, Mickey, 153

Manville Corporation, 108

Marriott, Bill, 200

Marriott Hotels and Resorts, 200, 205

Maxwell, Neil A., 167

McCullough, David, 232

McDonalds, 94, 213

McDonald, Richard & Maurice, 213

McNerney, James, 8

McKinnell, Hank, 105

Measurement, 137, 177, 245-248, 250-251

Merck Corporation, 181

Merck, George III, 109-110

Merrill, Roger, 11, 135

Michelangelo, 170

Mind-Set, 5, 29, 32, 84, 107-109, 121, 125, 128-130, 132, 137, 151

Mintzberg, Henry, 7

Model T, 211-212

Monroe, Kristen Renwick, 69-70

Mother Teresa, 67, 178

Motivating, 62

Mulcahy, Anne, 196

Muti, Riccardo, 29

Nardelli, Robert, 8

NASA, 43

Nike, 57

Nokia, 198

Nye, Joseph, 60

Obscurity, 2, 9, 17, 51

Olds, Ransom E., 211

Oldsmobile Corporation, 211

Organizational Design, 40, 137, 194, 198-203, 206-212, 217, 221, 227, 238, 247

    Elements, 198-203

Orwell, George, 74-75

Nelson, Portia, 139

Papaderos, Alexander, 23

Paradigms, 120, 128-129, 130-132, 137-139

Parcel, Bill, 186-187

Patton, General George, 231

Peary, Admiral, 72

Peck, Scott, 135, 229, 231

Peppers, Don, 190

Peters, Tom, 105

Phillips, Donald T., 159

Porter, Michael E., 110, 204

    Five Competitive Forces, 204-206

Posner, Barry Z, 11-12

Powell, Colin, 170

Power, 59, 220-224

    Coercive (Hard), 171

    Social Power (Soft), 59, 63

    Will Power, 35, 51, 87, 210

Purpose, 175-179, 220-230

Process, 10, 80, 198-210, 246-247

Raines, Franklin, 105

Ramsey, Sir Bertram Home, 25

Reichheld, Fred, 190

Results, xv, 26-28, 112, 132, 177, 198-227

Riggs Bank, 60

Rockefeller, John D., 213

Rodriquez, Alex, 183

Rogers, Martha, 190

Rogers, Will, 125

Rumsfeld, Donald, 75

Sadat, Anwar El & Madame Jehan, 151-153

Saint Crispens's Day, 38-39

Salovey, Peter, 86, 98

Sampras, Pete, 57

Schweitzer, Albert, 55

Sculley, John, 114

Sears and Roebuck, 52, 203

Senge, Peter, 232, 240

Shackleton, Sir Ernst, 56

Shakespeare, William, 19, 38, 45, 125

    Julius Caesar, 125

    King Henry V, 38-39

    Saint Crispen's Day, 38

    Twelfth Night, 19

Shaw, George Bernard, 50

Sill, Sterling W., 77

Southwest Airlines, 9, 114, 191

Stakeholder Needs, 199-200, 212, 227

Stockdale, Admiral Jim, 195-196

Stonecipher, Harry, 105

Strategy, 159, 197, 199-205, 211, 216-227

Swindol, Charles R., 92

Synovus Financial, 30

Teamwork, 153, 231-232

    The Five Dysfunctions of a Team, 233

Tichy, Noel M., 41, 208

Titanic, 127

Translation, 224-228

Trim Tab, 240-241

Useem, Michael, 37

Wal-Mart, 45, 114, 203, 218

Walton, Sam, 44-45, 154, 218

Washington, General George, 230

Welch, Jack, 8, 57, 149, 168, 208

Wolfowitz, Paul, 75

World Bank, 75

World War II, 3, 25, 69, 109, 114, 153, 210, 213, 231, 242

Wozniak, Steven, 45, 193

Vagelos, Roy, 181-182

Visibility, 50, 157-161

Vision, 8-10, 35-57

    Communicating, 45

    Vision Realization, 218-219

Von Stauffenberg, Clause Schenk Graf, 61-64

Xerox Corporation, 196

Zaleznik, Abraham, 2, 7, 9, 16

Zander, Benjamin, 45